COLONIAL ADMINISTRATION

OF

GREAT BRITAIN

COLONIAL

ADMINISTRATION

OF

GREAT BRITAIN

BY

SYDNEY SMITH BELL

[1859]

AUGUSTUS M. KELLEY · PUBLISHERS

NEW YORK 1970

First Edition 1859

(London: Longman, Brown, Green, Longmans
& Roberts, 1859)

Reprinted 1970 by
AUGUSTUS M. KELLEY · PUBLISHERS
REPRINTS OF ECONOMIC CLASSICS
New York New York 10001

·   ·   ·   ·   ·   ·   ·   ·   ·   ·

S B N   *678 00639 3*
L C N   *74 114023*

·   ·   ·   ·   ·   ·   ·   ·   ·   ·   ·

PRINTED IN THE UNITED STATES OF AMERICA
by SENTRY PRESS, NEW YORK, N. Y. 10019

COLONIAL ADMINISTRATION.

COLONIAL ADMINISTRATION

OF

GREAT BRITAIN.

BY SYDNEY SMITH BELL

OF LINCOLN'S INN, BARRISTER-AT-LAW; ONE OF THE JUDGES OF THE SUPREME
COURT OF THE COLONY OF THE CAPE OF GOOD HOPE.

LONDON

LONGMAN, BROWN, GREEN, LONGMANS, & ROBERTS.

1859

PREFACE.

——

THIS dissertation had its origin in an inquiry which, in the year 1853, I felt it my duty to make, as to the foundation of the law I was to administer under Her Majesty's Commission. The inquiry was begun without anticipation that it would lead to more than perfecting information for the discharge of a responsible duty. If any reader shall be staggered at some of the doctrines propounded, he will not be more so than I freely confess I myself was, when I first found them to be the inevitable result of reflection, as the subject gradually developed itself. Finding the inquiry to be interesting, I committed the result to paper, and completed the MS. so long ago as the year 1854.

At that time the Crimean war was in full vigor,—presently came our quarrel with China,—and immediately upon the back of it the great Indian rebellion. While these demands upon the national resources continued, it did not seem prudent to publish a dissertation of this kind; although, in a pecuniary point of view, it might have been wiser for myself to have done so, inasmuch as dissatisfaction by several of our colonies with the mode of their government was then rather lively, and public opinion a good deal directed to the subject. That state of the colonies, however, operated only as one reason the more for refraining from publication.

The Crimean and Chinese wars have ended in victory. The Indian rebellion is all but extinguished, and our vast Indian possessions have become an integral part of the British empire. These mighty objects have been achieved without any apparent national exhaustion in strength or resources. The nation seems as ready for any new demand upon its courage and energy, as if it had been engaged the while only in the pursuits of peace; and as concession to the most troublesome of the colonies has produced greater tranquillity of thinking upon colonial subjects, the season seems to have arrived when I may venture with propriety to put forth this dissertation, as a pioneer to prepare the field for wider and more effective discussion. There is nothing in the position of the empire which seems to me to make the freest handling of our colonial administration to be deprecated, nor anything, in the state of public opinion on the subject, to preclude its receiving impartial judgment from those disposed to consider so highly important and interesting a subject.

Our East Indian possessions do not come within the scope of this book. The reader will see this by referring to page ninety-five, where they are specially excepted. That passage was written long before the East Indian rebellion was dreamt of, and I see nothing in what has since passed to induce me to alter it.

The doctrine urged at page ninety-three, *et seq.*, seems likely to be sooner tested than I had supposed. On the west coast of Africa, Portugal has a vast extent of nominal territory over which she does not exercise any actual sovereignty, further than by insisting to have it recognized in anti-slavery treaties as Portuguese territory,—a claim which, in our negotiations, we have hinted a doubt of, and which France, in the matter of the *Charles-et-Georges*, seems to have done more than hint a doubt of.

I find that, in trusting to memory so long after the events, I have fallen into an error at pages twenty-nine and thirty. It was Dom Juan, who fled to Brazil during the regency there of Dom Pedro, and, after Dom Juan's return to Europe, Brazil declared itself independent, and Dom Pedro to be its emperor. This, I believe, is the correct historical account of the formation of the Brazilian empire.

I do not mean to offer here anything tending in the slightest degree to deprecate fair criticism, or even censure. I frankly confess I have read the MS. frequently, at distant intervals, with the view of testing its accuracy, so far as my judgment repeatedly applied would enable me. If it be defective or erroneous in matter or style, as nothing compelled its publication, so nothing should prevent the legitimate consequences of publication; but I do deprecate the slightest misapprehension of my political feelings. I may have meddled with questions, which some will think had better not have been mooted; or I may, in the opinion of some, have handled them with too much freedom. I confess to having had, at times, some fear upon these subjects myself,—but what I have written, I have written in the purest spirit of patriotism, and in the firmest ultimate conviction, (mistaken it may be,) that it was well for my country that it should be written, that it should be read, and that it should be well and timeously considered by those who have the greatness, glory, and happiness of Great Britain most deeply at heart; and in the equally firm conviction that, if the measure I have ventured to suggest were adopted, the power of Great Britain would remain, as, in my humble opinion, it is at present, founded entirely upon the moral, social, and political qualities of my countrymen, fostered and encouraged, as these are, by the free institutions which they enjoy; and that the position of our sovereign, with reference to the other sovereigns of the earth, will always be, as it is at present,

independent of the mere vastness of territorial possessions, and will be quite safe so long as it is known that
she reigns in the hearts and affections, as well as over
the persons, of such subjects, and so long as her power
shall be wielded by ministers, firmly and fearlessly, for
the maintenance of all that is good and right in international policy.

SYDNEY S. BELL.

Cape of Good Hope,
  February 19, 1859.

CONTENTS.

PAST AND PRESENT ADMINISTRATION

BRITISH COLONIES.

INTRODUCTION.

No sovereign, ancient or modern, ever possessed
dominions so extensive as those over which the
Queen of Great Britain reigns ; and no nation,
ancient or modern, had more just reason to be proud
of its acquisitions than the British nation has, both
as to the mode in which the acquisitions have been
gained, and as to the character in which they have
been governed.   However equivocal may have been
the motives with which Great Britain, like other
nations of that period, set out for the discovery of
the western hemisphere, or with which some of
her people, for their own individual benefit, took
the first steps, which have resulted in her vast empire
in the eastern hemisphere, it is through the active
industry and persevering activity of her inhabitants
that she has acquired by far the greater part of her
dependencies throughout the earth.

Extension of commerce, spreading the knowledge of the Holy Scriptures, and diffusing the blessings of civilized life, by just, equal, and enlightened principles of government, has been the character in which Great Britain has undoubtedly ruled her acquisitions, although, through inherent defects in her system of colonial administration, she may occasionally have miscarried in some of these respects.

Yet, with all this reason for just pride and exultation, there may be reason why we should pause in our career of glory, and reflect whether this very extent of our dominions is a source of true power, or is not rather one of positive weakness, the forerunner of decay and ultimate dissolution; whether our empire, like those which have preceded it, from Nimrod's downwards, has not attained that culminating point in its power, whence it must descend, ultimately to sink below the horizon, like the empires of antiquity; whether treating the empire as arborists do trees of excessive luxuriance, it would not be wise to lop and prune it to the very stem, in order to stop the diffusion of sap through too distant extremities, and thereby preserve its vigor and ensure the prolongation of its vitality.

Though it be true that the colonial dependencies of Great Britain have been ruled by able, virtuous, and enlightened statesmen; though it be true that the broad system of her colonial polity has been

untainted by selfishness, however individuals may
have turned the working of that system to their own
profit; though Great Britain, including her colonial
dependencies, is governed by the accumulated
wisdom of many senators, and is not, like other
countries less kindly dealt with by Providence, ruled
after the arbitrary will of an individual sovereign:
yet, if we do not go into details, but confine ourselves to a general survey of results, it would seem
as if these are little better than they would have
been had our colonial administration been dictated
by an ignorant, capricious, prejudiced, and narrow-
minded sovereign.

We recognize in the nations of Europe the dis-
tinctions of race, and we are justly proud of our
Saxon blood, and the ardent love of freedom and
independence shown by the nations in whose veins
it flows. But, in our intercourse with our colonies
—with those limited bodies of our fellow-countrymen
who have gone out from us to found for themselves
new states—we have ignored our origin, and treated
them as if we and they were sprung from eastern
races, instead of being, one and all of us, the sons
of freedom.

It is true that a change has lately shown itself in
our colonial, as in our commercial, policy, attributable,
probably, to the superior enlightenment of modern
politicians in the principles of political economy, and

especially to the magnanimity and modest propriety
of our present noble sovereign, who has not allowed
any petty, personal feeling to interfere with what her
ministers have represented to her as necessary to the
proper government of her empire, who, if she have
the lust of dominion and the love of power, vices
inherent almost universally in human nature, has
wisely and nobly subdued them, and made her own
happiness dependent on promoting the happiness of
her subjects—the true aim of a wise and virtuous
sovereign.

But it seems very doubtful whether this change
in our colonial policy is universal, reaching to all
its points ; for it does not seem to spring from
scientific and philosophic principles of government,
which, being wrought out to their legitimate
conclusions, will be certain to produce the end
apparently desired. The motley character of our
colonial government, when we consider the constitution accorded to one colony, as compared with
those which have been imposed upon others, puzzles
the mind to discover on what principle the differences
are founded, and leads it rather to the conclusion
that the force of circumstances was the true motive
for whatever has been done in each particular case.

Yet, if it be so, one cannot blame those to whom
our colonial destinies have been entrusted, from time
to time. If all the beneficial changes in our colonial

policy, which have undoubtedly been made of late years, bear the character of experiment rather than of experience—if they have more of empiricism in them than of scientific knowledge, the fault is attributable to the system of our colonial administration, rather than to the colonial minister, or those by whom he is assisted in his Herculean labor of governing fifty-four colonies, *i.e.*, of being sovereign of as many states, for such, in fact, he is.

The object of this work will be to give a bird's-eye view of our past colonial history, and thence to deduce the principles which would seem to be those that ought to guide us in our future colonial policy. The time was, and not long since, when it would have been vain to attempt such a deduction, with any expectation that it would prove acceptable to the public, or, perhaps, even to the minister. Not ten short years ago,[a] it was the almost universal doctrine, that Great Britain owed her wealth, prosperity, and grandeur to her trade, and her trade to her navigation laws and system of differential duties. So long as this delusion prevailed, it would have been hopeless to broach any doctrine which seemed to have a tendency to loosen the tight hold which, with similar delusion, we thought we should ever retain over our colonies, by the mode in which we then administered them. Now that the film has

[a] The text was written in the year 1854.

fallen from the political eye, so far as to permit it to discover that Great Britain has achieved her unprecedented position amongst the nations of the earth, not in consequence, but in spite, of her navigation laws and differential duties, an attempt to show that the liberal character — which has undoubtedly marked our colonial administration during these few years past — may be pursued to a much, greater extent without injury, but, on the contrary, with benefit to the empire, seems neither to be presumptuous nor likely to be an unthankful task. For, without doubt, notwithstanding the liberal tendency of our present colonial legislation, there are looming in the political horizon very delicate and nice questions, between Great Britain and her colonies, arising out of her sovereignty over them, which it will be well for her to consider, before the time come when they may have to be solved by the sword instead of the pen.

The extent of the sovereign power of the Crown, or of the united legislature, over the colonies has often been asserted at home, and has as often been questioned in the colonies. This subject has necessarily been much mixed up with the discussions, parliamentary and diplomatic, which have from time to time arisen in regard to our trade regulations with the colonies; and, more lately still, in those which have occurred in regard to the constitutions to be conferred upon particular colonies. But the subject does not appear to have been ever probed to its depth.　In Great Britain, the right has always been asserted, while its non-exercise has been conceded whenever the right was seriously questioned; and no one of its assertors has ever ventured to lay bare the principles upon which the right is supposed to be founded.　The right has always been assumed, but has never been demonstrated.　The time seems to have arrived when this question should be candidly, but fearlessly, discussed.

CHAPTER I.

BEFORE considering the nature or the extent of the
power of Great Britain over her colonies, it will be
profitable to take a short retrospect of the history of
colonization, ancient as well as modern, in order to
see how far the assumption of supreme power by the
mother country over colonies has been acted upon,
or been successfully maintained, by other countries
over their colonies.

The most ancient colonies we have any account of
are those which were planted on the shores of the
Mediterranean by the city of Tyre. Among these,
Utica first, and afterwards Carthage, were the chief.
We learn from the second book of Samuel, v, 11,
that Tyre was governed by a king, so early as the
time of David, king of Jerusalem. Whether the
government of this ancient city was regal, oligarchic,
or democratic, at the time at which Utica and
Carthage were founded, we have no information;
but, whatever its form of government may then
have been, there is no indication that the power of

that government extended over these colonies : the
opinion of historians seems to be that it did not so
extend. The colonies of Utica and Carthage seem
to have been, from their very foundation, altogether
independent of the mother city. At all events—
which perhaps will be found to be more to the
present purpose — they ultimately became independent. History is not so clear as to the early
history of Utica, whose foundation preceded that of
Carthage by about three hundred years, but it
certainly became independent after the fall of
Carthage; and its ruins disclose a history of former
wealth and grandeur, which seems to say that it
must have been independent originally. But we
have positive historical information as to Carthage.
That city achieved a condition of wealth, power, and
splendor, which, if it did not exceed that of the
mother city, Tyre, must, at all events, have equaled
it.[a] Carthage was founded about one hundred
years before Rome, and, so early as five hundred
years before the Christian era, she, as an independent sovereign power, entered into a treaty
with the then infant republic of Rome, and, two
hundred years afterwards, renewed this treaty at the
desire of the Romans, who were as yet without a
navy, and required protection of their trade by the
Carthaginian navy against the ravages of the Greek

[a] Polybius III, 22.

pirates. Every one in the least acquainted with
ancient history is familiar with the wars which
Carthage waged with Rome for the sovereignty of
the world, and knows how nearly she had, more than
once, overwhelmed her rival. While Carthage was
thus in the full blaze of her glory, Tyre had ceased
to be numbered among the powers of the earth—
her glory had departed. About thirty years before
Carthage renewed its ancient treaty with Rome, in
the character of a succoring ally,[a] Tyre had fallen
under the sword of Alexander the Great, and become
a tributary of that insatiable conqueror. Whatever,
therefore, may have been the original terms under
which the emigrants from Tyre settled at Carthage,
it is obvious that so much as was fettering or
restrictive in these terms had long since been worked
off, either by rebellion, of which we have no trace
in history, or by disuse. The greater probability
is, considering the vast time which it then took to
traverse the sea between the two localities—many
months—that the colonists were from the beginning
free and independent.

It has been assumed by modern writers that
Sardinia and Sicily were colonized by Carthage.
But that seems to be a misapprehension. The
original settlement of these islands is involved in the
obscurity of remote and even fabulous history. A

[a] Liv. vii, 27 ; Polyb. iii, 24.

colony from Lybia is said to have been planted in
Sardinia by Aristæus, who was one of the sons of
no less a person than Apollo. But other colonies
were also established in that island, one under Norax,
who came from Iberia, a country of Asia, and was
also of divine parentage, being a son of Mercury,
and another by Iolcas, who was the son of a king
of Thessaly, and went to Sardinia with the sons of
Hercules. The island, therefore, was colonized from
Iberia and Thessaly, as well as from Lybia. With
regard to Sicily, that island, according to very
remote tradition, was originally peopled from Spain,
and was afterwards settled in by the Siculi, a people
of Italy. In times comparatively more modern, the
Phœnicians, and, after them, the Greeks, planted
colonies in the island. That is all that we learn of
the colonization of either Sardinia or Sicily, and it
does not point to Carthage as the source of the
colonization. It is no doubt true that both of the
islands were long under the dominion of the Cartha-
ginians; but so likewise was Spain, which, so far as
appears, was never said to have been colonized from
Carthage, though, no doubt, the merchants of that
city had trading establishments in that country, as
the Phœnicians had had before them. The truth
seems rather to be, that Sardinia and Sicily, like
Spain, were conquests acquired by Carthage, and
ruled by it as such; and that Carthage, though it

had extensive and remote trading stations, had not, either in Sicily or in Sardinia, colonies properly so called. Carthage, therefore, can furnish little information on the subject of the terms on which a colony should stand with relation to the mother country,— whatever knowledge may be gained by its history in regard to the government of dependencies.

Greece, however, is a fertile source of such information, since the Greek republics planted many colonies on the shores of the Mediterranean, Ægean, and Black Seas. With regard to the Greek colonies, they were all, with few exceptions, independent from the beginning; the exceptions are neither certain nor well authenticated. These swarmings from the parent state were generally the result of political persecution, which drove the sufferers to forsake their country, and seek for peace and prosperity elsewhere. In these instances, the colonies could hardly be said to have been founded *against* the consent of the parent state; the probability is that those who ruled it for the time were well pleased to be rid of the individuals whom they had oppressed, and to see their enmity removed to a distance. On the other hand, it can as little be said that the colonies were formed *with* the consent, and still less by the direction, or under the control, of the parent state. The exiles went forth, with the wide world before them where to choose, and their settlement was oftener fixed by the accidents of wind and weather than from any preconceived selection.

In other instances, settlements of Greek colonies were the result of over population in a country naturally so poor as Greece, and incapable of sustaining the redundancy of people, which the freedom enjoyed by its inhabitants was likely to stimulate. In these instances, the new settlements were conducted under the superintendence and at the expense of the parent city, whose only object was to be relieved of such inhabitants as she could not well support. It may be supposed that these voluntary exiles would leave many behind them in whom they retained an interest. This would naturally make them continue intercourse with the parent state, as much as distance, increased by the difficulties of navigation at the time, would permit ; but, beyond this, there was no bond, except in rare instances, between the colony and the parent city. Though many of the Greek colonies in Sicily, Asia Minor, and Italy attained, by trading, a wealth and splendor unknown in Greece, yet that trading was neither the original motive to the settlement, nor was it generally, in any way, either regulated or controlled by the parent states.

In short, between Greece and its colonies there was no claim of authority on the one side, nor any feeling of dependency on the other.[a] The colonists treated visitors from the parent city on all public occasions with excess of respect; but beyond the feelings of *quasi* affection with which these honors were given and received, each state was entirely independent of the other. The colonies chose their own rulers, which, in many instances, were kings, an office whose very title was detested in Greece; regulated their trading at their own discretion; made peace and war upon other states on their own account; and gave or withheld assistance to the mother city in her wars, according to their own discretion; and even founded sub-colonies of their own.[b]

Rome, in her colonies, presents a character differing from that of any other ancient colonizing state. The lust of empire was her predominating characteristic, and she exhibited it even in her system of colonization. She did not send out swarms of her redundant population to go forth and seek for themselves countries, as yet unoccupied, in which they might pursue the arts of peace and civilization; but, by her armies, she drove out the wretched inhabitants of the cities she chose to make war upon, and replaced them with swarms of her

---

[a] Thirlwall, vol. II, p. 97.

[b] According to Seneca, Miletus founded no fewer than three hundred and eighty colonies throughout the world.

own common people.[a] After depleting the towns of their natural blood, she injected her own into them.

Colonies thus founded, were in truth, mere advanced bulwarks of the ever-encroaching republic. The colonists were not settled in a country hitherto uninhabited and uncleared, where they had everything to do for themselves, and where a question might be raised between them and the parent state whether they were to be considered as working for themselves or in subserviency to her. They were like a prize crew put into a captured ship, to retain possession for the captors. A city was taken by storm and a portion of it was allotted to a certain number of Roman citizens, that the permanent dominion of Rome might be the better ensured. As a necessary consequence, these colonists must have been dependent on the parent state, if it were only for physical protection. So long as that protection was known to be within their reach, they could live in their new abodes in quietness, and with a sense of security ; but, so soon as the protection should have been withdrawn, they must have lived in dread of the original inhabitants, by much the greater in number, rising and exterminating them. These so-called colonists, therefore, were mere *locum tenentes* of Rome ; yet, being such, it is undoubted that,

[a] Arnold's Rome, vol. III., p. 15.

with their new residence, they ceased to enjoy the
rights of Roman citizens. This fact has not been
satisfactorily accounted for by writers on Roman
history, but if the suggestion of Arnold be correct,[a]
that the colonists were taken from the poorer class
of Roman citizens, and even from the freedmen,
it may have been that the denial of the rights
of citizenship to them on their removal to the colony
arose not only, as Arnold suggests, from a desire on
the part of the Roman Government to reduce, so far,
the roll of citizens, but also from political and
prudential motives, in regard to the colonies themselves. If the Romans, who settled down among
the original inhabitants of the country colonized in
very disproportionate numbers, had retained the
rights of citizenship for themselves and their de-
scendants, they would, in this respect, have been in
an invidious position with relation to the original
inhabitants. It was only politic, therefore, to require
of the Roman settlers that they should so far
identify themselves with the inhabitants of their
adopted country as to renounce the superiority
involved in the rights of Roman citizenship, and
to concede advantages to them, as colonists, which
would make them content to descend to a lower
political position than that to which they had been
born.

[a] Arnold's Rome, vol. III, p. 17.

In short, the rule of Rome over its colonies, as well as its connection with its allies, had extent of dominion alone in view, and was regulated accordingly. It was not founded upon justice, neither had it in view an interchange of benefits. It merely contemplated extension and retention of authority, and allowed what was *not* incompatible with these objects, and denied what *was* incompatible. Its policy might be admirable, viewing it in this limited light, and be far from execrable for iniquity, inasmuch as injustice and oppression, though they might and did generally occur, were rather incidental than intentional. But the Roman colonial policy will not afford any light to another country, not actuated like Rome by the lust of universal dominion, for the course it should follow in extending the arts of peace and civilization, by colonizing parts of the earth, as yet either partially or wholly unoccupied by man.

After the fall of the Roman Empire, colonization ceased for many centuries, until the partial adoption of it by the Italian republics, in the height of their mercantile prosperity.[a]

Genoa had many mercantile factories throughout the Levant, and two settlements which, in some respects, may be said to have been colonies, namely,

a Gibbon, vol. VIII, p. 15.

Galata, on the shore opposite to Constantinople, established in 1261 ; and Kaffa in the Crimea, established a century later.[a] Galata was nominally subject to the Greek rule, but, in fact, was governed from Genoa, whence a podestà was annually sent, who ruled the settlement with the assistance of a council, pretty much as Genoa itself was governed. But the laws of Genoa had to be observed, and those enacted by the local government were liable to be negatived at Genoa.

The position of Kaffa was somewhat different, probably owing to its greater distance from Genoa. There, the local government had uncontrolled power of legislation, to the extent even of altering the laws derived from Genoa, so far as they affected the settlement.[b]

In Galata, we have the first example of the connection which England established with her colonies, not at their original foundation, but after she had resolved to make them a source of selfish advantage to herself; and, in Kaffa, founded after a century's experience of the Galata scheme, we have an example of the connection between England and her colonies, such as her recent more enlightened and generous legislation is gradually moulding it to.

Venice, likewise, had many factories, and but a

a Sismondi, vol. VI, p. 93.   b Sauli, vol. II, p. 30.

few colonies. The principal of her colonies was Candia, which she acquired by purchase. The native inhabitants were not disturbed : all that Venice did was to send some of her own citizens, nobles included, to settle in the island. The entire body of these nobles formed the grand council of the island, having a doge, elected from their own body, at their head. In short, the local government was formed upon the model of the mother republic, and consisted of officers appointed from among those who had settled down as colonists. But the island was never treated as an integral part of the Venetian state.[a] It was regarded rather as a nursery to repair the broken fortunes of the Venetian nobility, who, after having, by a residence on the island, enriched themselves in the pursuits of trade, returned to the parent republic, and were admitted to the highest orders of its nobility. These fortunes were made only by the practice of the greatest extortion upon the other inhabitants of the island, and by restraining the colonists from trading with any other than the mother state. But, the replenishment of the mother state being the true ground of the Venetian policy, and neither justice to her settlements nor, still less, consideration for their prosperity forming any part of it, the extortions of the nobility were overlooked, not only

[a] Sismondi, vol. x, p. 261.

in Candia, but in the other settlements of Venice
upon the shores of Greece, all of which were
formed after the same model.

The consequence of this unprincipled mode of
governing her colonies was, that they never formed
any support to Venice: she never increased their
strength, nor ever extended her protection to them
in any effectual degree; consequently, she never
gained their affections. Treating them neither
as parts of her own state nor yet as independent
allies, during the time of her prosperity, her
colonies were not so profitable to her as they
would have been had the rights of the commonalty
been regarded, and trade and the accumulation
of wealth been encouraged, by equal administration
of law and justice; consequently, in the time of
her adversity, the colonies were not only indisposed,
but powerless, to assist her.

The next colonies, in chronological order, were
those founded by Spain in America. The principal
original object of Spain, in establishing these
colonies, was to secure the inexhaustible mines
of precious metals with which America was
supposed to abound. The better to do this, the
feudal fiction that all land was originally in the
sovereign was transported to America, which in
this respect was theoretically treated as an integral
part of the Spanish monarchy, and, with this

fiction, the whole cumbrous, stately, and extravagant administrative forms of the Spanish government in Europe were also transported. But, inconsistently enough, the colonists were prohibited from cultivating various articles which it was advantageous to reserve for Spain, and a restriction upon social and commercial intercourse was imposed, such as had no parallel in the mother country, and had never been known to any nation, ancient or modern.

Strangers could not come within the colonies, under pain, at first, of death, and afterwards of perpetual imprisonment, and even Spaniards could not visit them without a special license from the government; and, as for commerce, the colonies could trade only with the mother country, and that only at two ports, Seville and Cadiz ; they were not permitted to trade at all, as between themselves, one colony with another. The necessary effect of these vexatious and harassing regulations was to enrich a few persons in Spain, at the expense of the colonists, and even of the great bulk of the Spanish nation itself. For though the trade was not, in form, reserved to a particular company, it was, in fact, reserved to a few houses in Seville and Cadiz ; so that, while the colonists had to buy dear and sell cheap to these monopolists, the other people of Spain did not

buy cheap and sell dear to the colonists.
The merchants of Cadiz and Seville alone derived benefit from the injury inflicted upon the
colonists. .

When the gold and other precious metals, which
had prompted this system, one of police rather
than of government, were exhausted, the restrictions
upon social and commercial intercourse were not
removed. They were continued upon the trade,
which naturally arose in countries so prolific of
every valuable natural production, as soon as the
adventurers in quest of gold were wise enough to
discover that agriculture and trade were the true
inexhaustible sources of wealth and prosperity.
The consequence was that the trade of the Spanish
American colonies never attained any great height,
notwithstanding all the prodigious natural advantages under which it was begun and carried on ;
and that the revenue derived from it to the
mother country, after the expenses of the colonial
government had been defrayed, was at all times
inconsiderable. Nay, even the precious metals,
while they lasted, never made any great show in
the metropolitan budget.

In short, the Spanish colonies, at the very best
time, were of very little direct profit to the mother
country, except, perhaps, in the way in which
Venice derived advantage from her colonies, by

their being a field for recruiting the bankrupt and broken-down courtiers, through extortions wrung from the unhappy natives and the less considerable colonists. When the day of adversity came upon Spain, so far from her colonies being of any assistance to her, they were the first part of her decaying body which fell away. She had not sufficient vital power in herself to retain her rule over them, and she had never transfused into them strength sufficient to react with advantage upon herself.

The greatest real advantage which Spain derived from her colonies was the indirect one of trading with them. This, upon the selfish and suicidal principle first introduced into colonial policy by Venice, she confined entirely to her own subjects by the enforcement of laws abhorrent to humanity, unsanctioned by any principles in the law either of nature or of nations, and alike opposed to sound sense and the most obvious dictates of self-interest. As before observed, trade between the colonists and foreigners was prohibited, under the penalty of death, and, even between the different colonies, under severe penalties; the cultivation of certain articles of commerce was absolutely proscribed, in favor of the mother country; and the manufacture of others was reserved to it as a monopoly.

To look back upon this policy, as dictated by men with sane minds, one might suppose that trade and agriculture were of the nature of fire, —though useful principles in themselves, yet having a constant tendency to spread and desolate, and therefore requiring constant control and subjection.

Naturam furcá expellas tamen usque recurret. In spite of laws so well calculated to extinguish anything like agricultural or mercantile spirit and enterprise, a certain amount of trade did arise, even between Spain and her colonies ; but that was far exceeded by the contraband trade carried on between the colonies and other countries, and even among the colonists themselves, in perfect ridicule of the restrictions of the mother country ; notwithstanding she kept a most expensive maritime force to maintain them, and even went the length of making smuggling an offence cognizable by the Inquisition.

So soon as the vast advantages of a climate and soil productive above all others had advanced the social condition of the colonists and increased their demand for those articles of commerce, which the laws of Spain were intended to compel them to buy from her alone, to an extent beyond what Spain was able to supply, all her efforts to restrain trade became gradually more and more futile. It was only the

prodigious extent to which smuggling was carried
on between her colonists and foreign nations, Britain
especially, that opened the eyes of the Spanish
government to a perception of the folly of their
system, and induced them gradually to relax it,
during the period between 1748 and 1778. Thirty
years of hard experience did it cost them to learn
what justice and honor should have suggested to
them on the instant, and, failing such a suggestion,
what as many hours of calm consideration might
have pointed out beforehand.

But the official policy of Spain, in its colonies,
was, if possible, even worse than its commercial
administration of them. The government had
sanctioned the settlement of estates in the colonies
by entail, and had thus created many families of
wealth and importance, and it had, moreover, actually
ennobled many of these families by titles of honor.
It had thus constructed a social system within the
colonies perfectly capable of self-action, and created
a society which must have been peculiarly sensitive
to interference from without. Yet all the offices of
government, from the highest to the lowest, were
given to European Spaniards alone, not with any
reference to the capability or fitness of the recipients
for the particular office or to their acceptability with
the colonists, but entirely with reference to the price
offered at Madrid, where the colonial offices were

openly bought and sold. If the social condition of
the Spanish colonies had been like that of other
colonies, this would have been bad enough, but in
their actual condition, it was as foolish as it was
wicked.

The relaxation of commercial restrictions, to have
been useful, should have been entire and immediate.
On the contrary, their relaxation was partial and
gradual. While the government was meting out just
as little of freedom as it thought the exigency of the
case compelled, the minds of the colonists were
at work to expedite the accomplishment of entire
liberty by all the contrivances of contraband traffic;
and, finding success in this, as the government
withdrew its restrictions the colonists advanced in
their demands, as is always the case where power
is so unreasonably exercised, that its right is brought
into question, and the discovery is then made that
it has been administered for the benefit of the rulers,
and not of the ruled.

The success of the colonists, by contraband trade,
in their commercial opposition to the government,
led them to inquire further into the general colonial
polity, and to take a view of their true rights and
interests, so that, in the latter end of the last century,
an attempt by the mother country to impose a new
monopoly was met by rebellion, which, even then,
threatened a dissolution of the connection. Though

that outbreak was repressed, yet the spirit, then first given vent to, grew and increased.

The colonial aristocracy, who, if their self-interests had been considered by the mother country, would have been her main support against the encroachments of the colonists, on the contrary, in the absence of this consideration, identified themselves with the other colonists, as the mother country had itself identified them, in its mode of government; for in the preference to office and power, no distinction was made between the nobles and the other colonists.

By raising up a colonial aristocracy, and then treating them in this manner, the mother country had given heads to the discontented colonists, who, in due time, led them to emancipation. Emissaries of the colonies made the tour of Europe, to gain the protection of some power while the colonists should be attempting the work of their emancipation, and they more than once during the ministry of Lord Chatham, nearly embarked Great Britain in their enterprise. Failing in this, the colonists waited their time, and so soon as the mother country became embroiled with the powers of Europe, they at once threw off her yoke, and, after a bloody struggle, achieved their independence, which they have ever since maintained.

The melancholy spectacle which the once glorious

Spain has presented to the world ever since needs not to be told. Had the government of Spain treated the South American colonies like a sister empire, how very different at this day might have been the condition of Spain herself. The wealth of these countries, as described by travelers, was fabulously great,—the revenues of the aristocracy and gentry far exceeding anything ever dreamt of in Europe. If these wealthy colonists had been allowed an interest in the government of their own country, they would have lent an irresistible support to the governors; and if the trade of countries so super-eminently productive, from the extraordinary fertility of their soil and climate, had been allowed to take its own natural channels without restriction, it is far from extravagant to say that, at this day, the South American possessions of the kings of Spain would have been infinitely more valuable to them than ever old Spain was at the period of its brightest glory.

The selfishness and near-sightedness of tyranny could not see this. South America escaped from tyranny to fall into anarchy and confusion, and old Spain has become an effete and exhausted body, scarcely able to maintain a position, however despicable, among the powers of Europe.

Portugal was the next colonizing power after Spain. Though her power and the revenue she derived from India was something miraculous, considering her own insignificance as to extent of territory and amount of population, yet Portugal never had more than commercial settlements in India. She never, at any time, had what could properly be denominated a colony.

The only Portuguese colony worth noticing was that which she founded in Brazil. If the fate of this colony has been the very reverse of that of the Spanish colonies, the accidents of war have occasioned the difference, not the superior wisdom of Portuguese statesmen. The commercial polity of Portugal, in her colony of Brazil, was very similar to that of Spain towards her colonies. It was dictated by the same selfish monopolizing spirit, and was only not quite so oppressive : and the history of the colony would probably not have been much different from that of the Spanish colonies, had not the eruption of the French into Portugal, in the beginning of this century, compelled the King of Portugal to fly from this, his ancient kingdom, and take refuge in Brazil. This involuntary visit, made at the time with the intention that it should be as short as Bonaparte would allow it to be, has proved to be a permanent one. Dom Pedro of Portugal discovered, thus against his will, that it was infinitely preferable to be Dom Pedro of Brazil,—Portugal being, though an ancient, yet a

poor and inconsiderable kingdom, and Brazil, though
a modern and oppressed colony, yet an extensive
country, fertile and rich beyond any precedent,
except perhaps in the Spanish possessions.

What the policy of the Emperor of Brazil might
have been, had he been left to himself, it is not
possible to conjecture; but fortunately for him, as
for that country, the selfishness of the British
government prevailed upon him to give to his
subjects what that government would not as yet
give to its own subjects. The British government
prevailed upon the Emperor to give freedom to
the Brazilian trade; and the consequent improvement
in the material prosperity of the country since that
time has been prodigious. If its prospects are not
now bright in other respects, the fault is easily
traceable to the vices of its government in regard
to those very respects. But, as an instance of the
substantial advantage to be gained to the government
of an ancient country by treating a colony as if it
were in fact, and not in theory merely, part of the
original dominion, Brazil is a most useful, as it is
a solitary, instance. If Dom Pedro had remained
in Portugal, it is not probable that he would have
given Brazil the same government that he bestowed
upon it, after his forced exile from Portugal had
driven him there.

The singularly beneficial effects of the freedom

given to trade soon induced the abrogation of all the ancient system of colonial restriction, and the giving of national institutions under which internal industry grew and throve, instead of languishing as it had previously done. In short, Brazil became the seat of an empire which might have been raised into a great and powerful one, but which, from causes irrelevant to the present inquiry, and therefore not necessary to be noticed, it does not at present seem likely to become.

Holland is a country which has also colonized, both in South America and in the Indian Archipelago. Berbice and Demerara were at one time valuable colonies to her, as Java is at this day. She set the example, as to her Indian colony, which was followed by England : the trade was vested entirely in one company, who made it a strict monopoly, so far as regards direct profits, though they were wise enough to leave the carrying trade open. But the destruction of the Dutch navy by Great Britain, and the consequent seizure of almost all her colonies by that power, leaves little to be said of Holland as a colonizing state, for the present purpose. This may be remarked, however, in passing, that no country has shown more wisdom than Holland, in the internal government of her colonies, and that she alone has been able to turn them to most valuable account for herself.

France at one time had very considerable colonies in America. These she ruled upon a system more liberal than had then been adopted by any other country, and such as would probably, for that reason, have long retained the colonies, unless the corrupt system by which the officials were appointed would in time have alienated the colonists, as they should grow in wealth and in a knowledge of their own strength. Every office, as in the mother country, was procurable only by court favor and influence But the French colonies never throve, as they might have done in the hands of another nation, owing apparently to the non-commercial spirit for which France has always been remarkable. Her colonies were sources neither of profit nor of strength to her. On the contrary, they were the only really vulnerable parts of her powerful body, and so soon as they were exposed to attack from this country they were cut off from her.

But this proved of little damage to France, for, having prodigious internal resources, and an enterprising, energetic people, the loss of her colonies has not, as with the other countries mentioned, been coeval with, or symptomatic of, her decay. On the contrary, it produced very little sensible effect upon her, unless, perhaps, in the opposite direction; for one immediate consequence of the termination of France's colonial sugar trade has been to create an entirely new species of agriculture and of manufacture within that country.

Until her colonies were taken from her, beet-root was cultivated in France only, like the other succulent vegetables, to a comparatively small extent, and merely for the use of the table or of the cattle-stall. But, so soon as the energy of the people, in seeking a substitute for cane sugar, discovered that the luxury could be obtained from beet, an immense breadth of land was put under its cultivation, and very large premises were erected in various localities for its manufacture. Here was a new kind of agriculture and manufacture, created within the kingdom itself, which, unless the sugar colonies had been taken by us, never, in all probability, would have existed, as it would, in all probability, never have been inquired after.

The loss of her colonies, therefore, by France, though a direct injury in the first instance, proved in the result a positive benefit, not only by this new production and manufacture, but by the consequential increase in the consumption of the products of other trades and manufactures, which this new manufacture necessarily created. The benefit to France, by this discovery, was greater than the loss of her colonial sugar trade, by how much a home trade is more profitable and less expensive than one carried on at a distance. But

France derived another indirect advantage, the full extent of which is only being daily developed. This discovery of the manufacture of sugar from beet-root may be said to have created a mercantile spirit in the French community; at all events, it gave fresh life to a spirit, which till then had only a feeble existence, but which has ever since then been daily gaining strength, and proving a source of rapid prosperity to that kingdom.

CHAPTER II.

FROM this rapid, cursory view of colonization,
ancient and modern, it would appear that, in
ancient times, colonization was seldom, if ever, used
as a means for gaining extension of territory, and
as seldom for the extension of commerce. Extension of territory has been the vice of all monarchies
from the beginning of time, and will continue to
be so till time is no more. So long as the lust of
power agitates the human breast, every monarch
will endeavor to extend his dominion, as far as his
resources will warrant the attempt, and, if he be a
despotic sovereign, there is nothing incompatible in
his so doing. His individual will is paramount
within his original dominions, and may be made
so beyond them. But conquest, by force of arms,
has been the usual mode of gratifying this appetite
of princes. Colonization presupposes distance in
the newly-acquired territory, and the benefits of
it must wait upon the successful establishment of
the colony. The ravages of war may gain at once

a neighboring and an old-established territory. We have few instances in ancient history, therefore, of colonies founded by sovereigns, unless for very special purposes.

Colonization, anciently, was peculiar to republics, by whom it was used for the purpose of relieving themselves, either from a redundancy of population, or from an inconvenient fermentation of political feeling. The exiles, whether forced or voluntary, went forth without injunction or restriction as to the place or the mode of their settlement; and if any connection, profitable or auxiliary, afterwards arose between them and the parent state, this was the result of accident operating upon old associations and recollections, rather than of original design or intention. This is neither singular nor extraordinary, but just what was to be expected, when we consider how unsuited a republic is, in the fundamental principles of its constitution, for extension of territory, distant from its own, whether acquired by colonization or by conquest; although the vices of human nature have induced many republics to attempt acquisition by conquest, always to their own ultimate destruction.

In modern times, the object of colonization has been quite different. It has been used, by republics and by monarchs alike, for the purpose of gaining, not only extension of territory, but also increase

of wealth, by the creation of new sources of
commerce. Such having been the objects of
modern colonization, modern colonies have not
been, like ancient colonies, free and independent
states, working out their success and prosperity
according to their own notions of what was for
their advantage. On the contrary, modern colonies
have been treated by the parent states as if they
had a property in them, which they might modify
and regulate according to their notions of what was
most for their own advantage, without regard to
whether benefit or injury were thereby done to
the colonies.

Notwithstanding this unreasonable principle of
administration, most of the modern colonies have
attained a very considerable degree of prosperity.
This, however, has been, not in consequence, but
in spite of the mode in which they were governed.
Their success has been the result of their own
natural advantages, which were sufficiently great
to outweigh all the burdens and restrictions which
mischievous government, for its own short-sighted
and selfish objects, had imposed upon them. But
what has been the result ?—which of the nations of
Europe, laying our own country out of the question
for the present, can at this day boast of its colonies,
as a source either of wealth in time of peace or
of strength in time of war ? Not one, with the

exception of the Dutch alone, perhaps. At no time have any of the colonies of the European nations returned to the parent state a direct revenue which was worth taking into account. In most instances, they have been a source of positive and heavy expense, and, in time of war, they have not only been a source of expense, but have invariably proved the weakest and most vulnerable points through which to attack the parent state.

If these observations, founded on the history of Venice, Genoa, Spain, Portugal, France, and Holland, be based in truth, it must be admitted that all these states have, one after the other, acted upon, if they have not openly asserted, the doctrine maintained by the elder Pitt, when speaking of the position of the British North American colonies, with reference to Great Britain, that "her sovereign authority over them extended to every point of legislation whatsoever; to bind their trade; confine their manufactures; and exercise every power whatsoever." But, on the other hand, *cui bono* have they done so? It is beyond question that colonization by all these countries has been attended with complete failure, so far as any one of them has proposed to itself direct, permanent advantage. Instead of their colonies giving them any revenue from direct taxation, every penny that has been levied in that manner has generally been spent within the colonies themselves, in defraying the expenses of their government. These expenses have invariably been very great, as might be expected where the officers who have the direction of the expenditure are at a distance from the parent government, and there is no one in the colony who has the power to control them. In many instances there has, even during peace, been a deficiency in the colonial revenue for defraying merely the colonial expenditure. In the case of war, this deficiency has been much increased. And in either case, of peace or of war, the deficiency has, of course, been supplied from the mother country. And, so far from the colonies of any country having proved an increase of strength to the mother country, when she has happened to be involved in war with other states, they have proved exactly the reverse. Being necessarily upon the sea-board, and remote from the centre of power, they are the weakest part of dominion; they have always been the point to which the first attack of an enemy was directed, and they have always fallen the earliest prey.

It is no doubt true that great and substantial benefit, in a way not yet noticed, has been derived from their colonies to all the countries which have been mentioned; but this was in an indirect manner, and one which they in few, if in any, instances, contemplated at the period of establishing their colonies. Such is the happy arrangement of the world by Providence, in this respect, as in every other, that no country can long remain independent of others. It soon requires to buy or to sell. So strong is this necessity that the most perverse and wicked ingenuity of rulers for their own selfish ends has never been able to control its mode of satisfying itself, far less to stifle and subdue it. Whatever, therefore, may have been the motive of any of the modern countries of Europe in establishing colonies, one invariable result of the establishment has been the creation of a new source of commerce, which the mother country has sooner or later discovered to be a source of great indirect as well as direct profit, and has endeavored to turn to her own account.

The colonizing countries of Europe have all, in this way, derived more or less of benefit from their colonies in proportion as their trade regulations have more or less departed from the axiom in government which, now at least, is known to be as obvious as any in Euclid, that trade, to be flourishing and prosperous, must be perfectly free from restrictions of every sort.

No nation in modern Europe, with all its pretensions to superiority in science and discovery over the nations of antiquity, ever found out this axiom, until very lately, though they had, one and all, been reading for centuries the histories of Tyre, Sidon, Carthage, Syracuse, the Greek colonies of Asia Minor and of other states, whose surpassing wealth and splendor had been founded entirely upon the freedom of trade. Each nation was quick enough in torturing its ingenuity to devise means for compelling the trade of its colonies to take that course, and that alone, which it thought would prove most beneficial to *itself*. But all were alike blinded by their selfishness from perceiving that trade, like the atmosphere, to be profitable, cannot be confined, but must be left to pervade and permeate wherever it can force itself.

Yet, to continue the simile, such are the beneficial effects of trade to all having anything to do with it, that, like the air, you cannot appropriate a portion of it by force, without deriving some benefit, however much, by so doing, you may deteriorate the qualities of what you have so appropriated. Unquestionably, all the colonizing countries of Europe derived commercial benefit from their colonies, notwithstanding they kept them in a state of pupilage and control, as to their internal government, and of positive slavery and abject submission, as to their external relations with other countries. Whether they would not have derived much greater benefits, political as well as commercial, by a course of government exactly the reverse, is at this day less than doubtful.

Having taken this cursory view of the nature of the colonies which have been founded by other countries, ancient and modern, and of the advantages which these colonizing countries have derived from their colonies, let us now turn to the consideration of how the colonies of Great Britain have been administered, with a view to ascertain how far that administration has been consistent with the principles of her own constitution, and how far her colonies have in times past contributed to her prosperity in peace and to her strength in war, and how far, in time to come, they are likely to be useful in either of these respects.

CHAPTER III.

CAUSES IN THE ADMINISTRATION OF THE BRITISH NORTH AMERICAN
COLONIES WHICH PRODUCED THEIR REBELLION AND ULTIMATE
INDEPENDENCE.

THERE can be but little doubt that events, by the
dispensation of Providence, happen to nations, as
to individuals, "for reproof, for correction, and for
instruction," would they but so receive them. Of
all the events which have happened to Great Britain,
ever since it could truly be called "Great," none
has been so grand and so awful as the rebellion
and emancipation of her North American colonies;
yet, looking at our subsequent colonial history, how
utterly dead did this event fall upon us, either by
way of reproof, of correction, or of instruction!
If we read the story of that rebellion, by the
strengthened light which persistence towards our
other colonies in the same errors that produced
the American rebellion affords, we shall see how
strongly the defects and vices of our colonial system
stand out.

Before, therefore, entering upon the subject of our
present colonial empire, let us take a short retrospect
of the circumstances under which, by the American

rebellion, we lost a greater extent of empire than we now retain, and, what is of infinitely more consequence, alienated, for a time only it is to be hoped, the affections of the inhabitants of vast regions, who otherwise might have considered themselves *of* us, though not *among* us, and have been, in our intercourse with the nations of the earth, our fastest friends and firmest allies.

Such a retrospect, though unnecessary at this time of day for any purpose of historical information, will nevertheless be useful, as it will show us that the very same causes which produced the American rebellion have been in operation in almost all our other colonies, and have been followed in some by very similar effects,—the difference being only in the magnitude of the results.

The passing of an act by the British Parliament, imposing a stamp duty upon the North American colonies, was the immediate ostensible cause of the American rebellion ; but we know now that there were many causes of heart-burning in the breasts of the colonists before that statute was even thought of — that there were many open, festering sores, which temporising measures on the part of Great Britain might have skinned over for a time, but which were sure to break out afresh at some early period, and which nothing but emancipation voluntarily conceded, or independence achieved by the colonists, could cure healthily and permanently.

The North American colonies were suffering grievously, and not silently, from the operation of our navigation laws and differential duties, which hampered their trade in the mode of conducting it and greatly enhanced the price of commodities to the colonists. It is no doubt true that these laws, which were intended to force trade through British channels for British advantage, instead of allowing it to take its natural course, were part of a system of exclusion and monopoly directed originally, not against our colonies, of which as yet we had not any, but against the other nations of Europe. The terms of the statutes, however, by which the machinery of this system was constructed, were sufficient to embrace colonies in some respects, and, when we acquired colonies, they were in due time brought under their operation, and so far as the laws were defective in their application to colonies they were from time to time adjusted to that point.

Our first settlements were upon the coast of North America. The original settlers, who went there of their own accord and at their own charge, either to escape from clerical bondage at home or as a speculation for profit, were allowed to struggle against all the hardships and difficulties which have ever to be encountered by those who, going out from a civilized community, endeavor to establish themselves in new and unopened countries. After all their difficulties had been surmounted, and the settlers had established themselves as thriving communities, having sufficient not only for their own wants, but to spare for exportation, then it was, and not before, that the government at home bethought itself of taking them within the pale of the constitution, for the purpose of making these settlements a source of profit to the mother country.

Curiously enough, the government which first adopted this notion was the Convention Parliament of 1650. In that year an act passed, prohibiting the colonial trade from being carried on in any other than British or colonial-built vessels. The colonist was no longer free to choose the cheapest freight, but must take such terms as the British ship-owner, or the colonial ship-owner, if there were any colonial ship-owners, chose to impose upon him. While James I and Charles I, so famous in our history for their extravagant notions of prerogative, and for the unscrupulous manner in which they exerted it, to raise money and support their authority, allowed the Boston merchant to select his own ship and to make his own bargain for the price of carrying away the produce of America, and bringing in return the manufactures and luxuries of Europe, it was a body of republicans, who had rebelled against and decapitated their sovereign because of his illegal interference with their purses, who, to build up their own power, first conceived the idea of putting their hands into the purses of the American settlers.

The republicans began with the ships ; Charles II was not slow to profit by the lesson. In 1660, he laid his hands upon the cargoes. The act of 12 Charles II, chap. 18, prohibited the produce of the colonies from being exported to any foreign country, and required that it must first be "laid upon the shore" of Great Britain. The effect of this act must have been to compel the colonists to sell their produce to us alone, for it could not have been sold to a foreign nation, without the ruinous charges of freight to Britain, port dues, and commission there, and a second freight to the country of sale.

Having, in effect, forced the American settlers to make us their only *purchasers*, the next step in this legislative iniquity was obviously to make ourselves their only *sellers*. In due time this happy notion was carried out. In 1663, an act was passed prohibiting "any commodity of the growth, production, or manufacture of Europe," from being imported into the British plantations, unless it was shipped in " England, Wales, or Berwick-upon-Tweed," and in " English-built " ships ! A Scotchman or an Irishman, coming from Boston to purchase Irish linen or Scotch carpeting, must have sent the goods to England or Wales, before he could ship them to his adopted home in America, and, when they had reached England or Wales, he could not have put them into a Dublin or Clyde-built ship, but must have found an English one for the purpose, however higher the charge for freight, and however less safe the conveyance might be by the one vessel than by the other.

The Americans were fully alive to the injustice and hardship to them of this selfish, and, as it has since been proved to be, short-sighted policy, even with a view to the objects it was intended to effect; and they made it the ground of constant remonstrance and complaint. Fortunately for them, the form of government, which we had given some of the states, suggested to them something beyond mere complaint, and put it in their power to attempt achieving redress.

Some of the colonies, such as Georgia, Maryland, and Pennsylvania,[a] had already, by the terms of their crown charters, the appointment of their governors; others, which had not this power, Carolina especially, had begun to question the expediency of the crown being allowed the continuance of such an exercise of the prerogative,

---

[a] Bancroft, p. 147.

because of the unfitness of the men who were
generally appointed to be governors.[a] Some of the
colonies had already the power of appointing the
subordinate government officers, civil as well as
ecclesiastical; others, New York and Virginia,[b]
which had not this power, had begun to contest
the right of appointment with the crown, either
by assuming to themselves directly the right of
nomination, or by tampering with the salaries of
the men appointed by the crown; while not directly
disputing any particular appointment, they refused
to vote a larger amount of taxes than would defray
salaries upon a reduced scale, as was done by
North Carolina and Massachusetts.[c] Some of the
colonies had the power of passing statutes, without
reference to the crown, or being subject to its
veto; others, which had not this power, had begun
to agitate a question, both as to the necessity and
the propriety of the power being conceded to them.
Some of the colonies acknowledged the right of the
crown to dispose of the unappropriated land within
their boundaries; others disregarded this right, and
preferred a title obtained from Indian chiefs, or
maintained that the right was in the colony itself.[d]

In one colony, Maryland, the proprietary governor, (Lord Baltimore), had power little short of

[a] Bancroft, p. 41.   [b] Bancroft, pp. 38 and 42.
[c] Bancroft, pp. 41 and 43.   [d] Bancroft, pp. 43 and 153.

regal, even to the granting titles of honor. He could pass laws, which were not subject to the revision of the crown, and which could not be altered by the crown, unless they were repugnant to the laws of England. In another, Pennsylvania,[a] the legislature—of which there was only one branch— met on its own adjournments, and could neither be prorogued nor dissolved. The lieutenant-governor, who was named, not by the crown, but by the proprietary governors, the Penns, had a veto upon the legislation, but one that was utterly worthless, as he was dependent on the legislature for his daily bread, and had frequently to choose between compliance with their votes and starvation. The judges were appointed by this dependent lieutenant-governor, and were, like him, dependent on the legislature for their daily bread.

In short, in Pennsylvania the people had been sovereign and independent long before the war provoked by the Stamp Act broke out; and, as to most of the provinces, that war was not one which, entered upon for another object, concluded in independence; but was one which, it seems more correct to say, had independence in view from the outset, and which nothing short of conceding independence could have avoided.

While the American people, conscious of the

[a] Bancroft, p. 158.

power which they possessed under these constitutions, were fretting and impatient at the restraints and burdens which their trade labored under, for the advantage of the mother country alone, the imperial parliament, in which the colonists were wholly unrepresented, passed an act, authorizing the levy of a stamp duty within the colonies.

Adam Smith, now known and universally recognized as one of the profoundest philosophers of modern days in the school of political economy, was, unfortunately, then an obscure student, living in an insignificant town in Scotland. This man, from his little parlor in Kirkaldy, with the light of sound sense working out plain and obvious principles to their necessary conclusions, laid bare the folly and iniquity of our system, and tried to save the empire from the gulf into which it was about to leap, in these emphatic terms, the true wisdom and philosophy of which we do not seem even yet to have fully appreciated, though we are beginning to discern them:—" To propose that Great Britain should voluntarily give up all authority over her colonies, and leave them to elect their own magistrates, to enact their own laws, and to make peace and war, as they might think proper, would be to propose such a measure as never was, and never will be, adopted by any nation in the world. The most visionary enthusiast would scarce be capable

of proposing such a measure with any hopes at
least of its being adopted.

" No nation ever gave up the dominion of any province, how troublesome soever it might be to govern,
and how small soever the revenue which it afforded
might be, in proportion to the expense which it
occasioned ; such a sacrifice, though it might
frequently be agreeable to the interest, is always
mortifying to the pride of every nation, and, what
perhaps is of still greater consequence, it is always
contrary to the private interest of the governing
part of it, which would thereby be deprived of the
disposal of many places of trust and profit, of many
opportunities of acquiring wealth and distinction,
which the possession of the most turbulent, and, to
the great body of the people, the most unprofitable
province seldom fails to afford.

" And yet, if we would do so, we might settle
with them such a treaty of commerce as would
effectually secure to us a free trade, more advantageous to the great body of the people, though
less so to the merchants, than the monopoly which
we at present enjoy. By thus parting good friends,
the natural affection of the colonies to the mother
country, which our late dissensions have perchance
well-nigh extinguished, would quickly revive. It
might dispose them, not only to respect for whole
centuries together that treaty of commerce which

they had concluded with us at parting, but to favor us in war, as well as in trade, and, instead of turbulent and factious subjects, to become our faithful, affectionate, and generous allies; and the same sort of parental affection on one side and filial respect on the other might revive between Great Britain and her colonies, which used to subsist between those of ancient Greece and the mother city, from which they descended."

Could "any good thing come out of Nazareth?" Was an obscure inhabitant of an obscure Scotch burgh to be listened to, in preference to the governors, secretaries, and custom-house collectors of America, who, we learn from the correspondence referred to in Bancroft's history, were poisoning the mind of the minister by their prejudiced and self-interested complaints? Could wisdom, crying out in the streets of Kirkaldy, expect to be heard in the lordly chambers of London, and still more in her senate-house, whence the voice of the people was then pretended to be uttered, but where, as yet, it had scarcely ever been heard? The ministers of the crown, acted upon by the misrepresentations of the local officials, as to the state of the public mind in America, and pandering to the lust of power and dominion in an arrogant sovereign, disregarded the profound reasoning of Smith and despised his warning. They passed their Stamp Act, and at once lighted up the combustibles, which were ready for explosion into universal rebellion; and were insane enough to add fuel to the conflagration, by using expressions in Parliament which could be borne only by slaves, or those who considered themselves not worthy to be better, and which could only have been uttered by tyrants insanely confident in their own security.

Lord North assured the House of Commons that the administration never meant to relax in pursuing the claims of government so long as its legislative authority was disputed. Mr. Wedderburn declared that, "till the spirit of independence is subdued, it is idle to come to any resolution or revision, as a means of conciliation;" and Mr. Rose pronounced grandiloquently, "If a clear, unequivocal acknowledgment of the legislative supremacy of the British Parliament was not to be obtained but by force of arms, he confessed he would be better pleased to see Britain dying of the wounds she might receive in this unnatural conflict, given by her rebellious, ungrateful children, than consent to one condescending step that might tend to diminish her former glory."

While this was the spirit in which the ministers of the crown announced their intention to rule a community, who, in the words of Pitt, were "the

sons, and not the bastards, of England, and equally
entitled with ourselves to all the natural rights of
mankind, and the peculiar privileges of Englishmen,"
it could only be expected that those of the colonists
who had hesitated hitherto as to resistance, would
brace their minds for it to the utmost extremity.
Accordingly, the American rebellion burst into full
strength.

After such rhodomontading on the part of our
ministers, we should have expected that the scabbard
would have been thrown away, as the sword was
drawn; but when the knocks we received proved
to be as hard as those we gave, when the issues of
war began to be doubtful, and not till then, did the
minister listen to anything savouring of conciliation.
In the year 1778, the Act of the 18 Geo. III,
cap. 12, the most " condescending step," that any
government ever took, and " tending," with a
vengeance, " to diminish Britain's former glory,"
was introduced into Parliament, and passed after a
stormy debate. That act declared that, " from and
after the passing of this act, the King and Parliament
of Great Britain will not impose any duty, tax, or
assessment whatever, payable in any of His Majesty's
plantations in North America or the West Indies,
except only such duties as it may be expedient to
impose for the regulation of commerce; the net
produce of such duties to be always paid and applied

to and for the use of the colony, province, or
plantation in which the same shall be respectively
levied."

This declaration was ushered in by a preamble
in these terms : " Whereas taxation by the Parliament of Great Britain, for the purpose of raising
a revenue in His Majesty's colonies, provinces, and
plantations in North America, has been found by
experience to create great uneasinesses and disorders
among His Majesty's faithful subjects, who may
nevertheless be disposed to acknowledge the justice
of contributing to the common defence of the empire,
provided such contribution should be raised under
the authority of the general court or general
assembly of each respective colony, province, or
plantation ; and whereas, in order as well to remove
the said uneasinesses, and to quiet the minds of
His Majesty's subjects who may be disposed
to return to their allegiance, as to restore the
peace and welfare of all His Majesty's dominions,
it is expedient to declare that the King and
Parliament of Great Britain will not impose any
duty, tax, or assessment for the purpose of raising
a revenue in any of the colonies, provinces, or
plantations."

Probably the statute-book will not furnish an
instance of such an extraordinary—it is difficult to
say what.   It is impossible to call this a statute

or act of legislation. It is directly the reverse. It is an abdication of the imperial sovereignty in the particular instance of taxation. Even if the right to tax had been the only matter of dispute with the North American colonies, this statute of 18 Geo. III, cap. 12, as it must be called for want of a better name to designate it by, would be extraordinary, not less from its matter than its manner of expression. If the minister had desired to hold out an inducement for rebellion, he could not have framed one more ingenious. The power of the imperial government to tax the colonies was not ventured to be asserted; the exercise of the power was receded from; rank rebellion against its exercise was mildly designated "uneasinesses and disorders;" and, at the same time, a begging hint was thrown out to the colonists, "to acknowledge the justice of contributing to the common defence of the empire," by granting taxes themselves.

Such an exhibition of feebleness and meanness combined could not, one would think, have expected to meet with any other reception than silent contempt. The Americans gave it no other. This matter of taxation was conceded, but their struggle was for entire emancipation from imperial legislation; and the 18 Geo. III, cap. 12, did not stop them one moment, but rather stimulated them in their efforts to achieve it. The humiliation of the

empire by such an extraordinary abdication of power
was entirely fruitless.

There can be little doubt that the government, by
the high-sounding phrases in which it asserted the
power of the imperial legislature over the colonies, and by its actual assumption of powers of
sovereignty, which, however real or nominal they
might be, had either never hitherto been enforced,
or had been allowed to fall into positive abeyance,
drew the colonies together, and forced upon them,
for mutual protection against the crown, that union,
which the natural jealousies and clashing interests
of neighboring states might have postponed for
some years; and, perhaps, as the states increased in
prosperity and power, might have rendered permanently impracticable and unattainable.   But, by
forcing this coalition, the government only hastened
an event, which would have happened with or without it, sooner or later, for there is no reason to suppose
that temporizing, however prudently managed, on the
part of Great Britain, could have prevented the ultimate independence of her American colonies, either
singly, or in one body, as it happened.   But if anything in the language of the ministers of the crown
had been wanting to induce the colonists to make
independence, and nothing short of independence, the
prize to be fought for, it was supplied by the language
of those who professed to be, and, no doubt, intended

to be, the friends and advocates of the colonists in the imperial parliament. The same Pitt, who had said that the colonists were "the sons, and not the bastards, of England, and entitled to the peculiar privileges of Englishmen," with singular inconsistency uttered the extraordinary assertion that "they had no right to manufacture even a nail for a horse-shoe" without the consent of the parliament; and Lord Sheffield said, "the only use of the American colonies is the monopoly of their consumption, and the carriage of their produce." Durst such language have been applied to the Birmingham and Sheffield smiths, or to the Lancashire or Yorkshire manufacturers? How, then, if the Americans were "entitled to the peculiar privileges of Englishmen," could it have been expected that they would submit to have it applied to them, even in the mouth of a self-constituted friend.

But, what is more extraordinary still, Pitt, while he applauded the rebellion, in the next sentence condemned it, in terms which, without anything else, must have convinced the Americans that they must either become rebels, or submit to be slaves. "The gentleman tells us," said he, "America is obstinate, America is almost in open rebellion. I rejoice that America has resisted; three millions of people so dead to all the feelings of liberty as voluntarily to submit to be slaves would have been fit instruments to make slaves of all the rest." While "the great commoner" thus boldly justified resistance to the imposition of a direct tax, he, strangely enough, closed a tempest of scorn and indignation at our oppressive rule of America in these words,—"Let the sovereign authority of this country over the colonies be asserted in as strong terms as can be devised, and be made to extend to every point of legislation whatever, that we may bind their trade, confine their manufactures, and exercise every power whatever, except that of taking money out of their pockets, without their own consent."

It is strange that a man of such acute and sensitive perceptions of political and social rights should not have seen that there was no difference, in fact, between saying to an American colonist, " You shall pay one shilling, in name of stamp duty, on every sheet of paper you use," and in saying to the same man, " You shall not employ Van Wyk of Amsterdam's vessel to carry your lumber to London, paying him only twenty shillings a ton of freight, but you shall hire Henry Soames of London's ship, and pay him thirty shillings a ton." The one shilling a sheet of stamp duty would go into the Exchequer, no doubt, and the extra ten shillings of freight into the pocket of Soames; but would the ten shillings be less than the one shilling taken " out of the colonist's pocket, without his consent ?" If he might rebel against the one, as well might he rebel against the other.

If Mr. Pitt had written to plain Jack Harris, the smith, formerly of Sheffield, who had one day acted on the notion that he could do better for his children by removing them to Boston, in the States, and plying his anvil there, than at home, and had said that he had "no right to make a single horse-shoe in Boston," might not Jack Harris have asked "Why? I am still Jack Harris. I had a right, in Sheffield, to earn my bread by the sweat of my brow; what has taken that right away? Nobody could take it away from me in Old England, not even the king, who, then, can do it in New England?" What could the answer have been, but this, "Why, the parliament in Old England could, if it would, have prevented you from working in Sheffield, but there was nobody to serve by doing so; and, if there had been any one, perhaps the other trades might have thought that their day would come next, and have combined to resist, so it is not likely that the parliament, to serve any-body, would have prevented you working in Old England; but now that you have gone to America, the matter is quite different, you and the other smiths there are but a small body as yet; you could not resist us with any effect; we wish to enrich the smiths of Sheffield and Birmingham, by making all the folks in America buy from them, and, so far from the other trades in Old England interfering to prevent this, we shall have their support, for we mean to do the same good turn by the weaver, the comb-maker, the button-maker, the needle-maker, and all the other trades. We mean to make all you colonists buy from those trades in the mother country, and from them alone." What could Jack Harris do but reply, "Well, it is true you can do it, for you are strong enough, and so my wife and children must pinch and starve, till I can learn farming or wood-cutting; but it is rank tyranny and oppression, for all that—nay, it is downright robbery —to prevent me using the hands God has given me, and commanded me to earn my bread with, and the bread of those dependent on me, that you may enrich some of the people at home. It is conduct such as I never expected to meet with from my countrymen, whom I was always proud to hear called, and to know, as honest John Bull, whose maxim was 'live and let live.' I never thought to hate Old England, and I cannot, and I will not; but my children and theirs after them, who never will have known John Bull's honest face and hearty liberal ways, will not be able to distinguish him from the ruler that speaks by his acts of parliament, the only voice they will hear; and mayhap, they may some day, when I am gone, come to think of Old England, as old recollections will never allow me to do, and to give the treatment you are putting on me a sturdy old English resistance."

This is just the language which the North American settlers at first used. But both their language and their conduct changed so soon as they discovered the length to which we carried our pretensions of sovereignty over them, and comprehended their true position, with reference to the mother country; for, although the operation of our trade and navigation laws was not perhaps made one of the substantive grounds for throwing off their allegiance, yet the injury these laws worked to the colonists, and the advantage they were supposed to produce to the mother country, at the expense of the colonists, were understood, and duly appreciated by the colonists; and, no doubt, this contributed to fill to overflowing in rebellion, the cup of their indignation against us.

The children of those men who had left England, but carried with them the sturdy independent feelings of John Bull, were not to be intimidated by the gasconading of the ministers in the debate on the stamp act, and were not disposed to take the view of "the peculiar privileges of Englishmen," drawn by Mr. Pitt, that "their trade might be bound, their manufactures confined, and every power whatever be exercised over them," without their having any voice in the matter, provided only "money was not taken out of their pockets, directly by a tax, without their consent." They became what we chose to call "rebels," and, sword in hand, determined to achieve their independence of the mother country, since she would not yield them those peculiar privileges of Englishmen, which they or their fathers had enjoyed in the mother country, and which they had never renounced; and they were no way seduced from persevering in their determination to do so by the passing of the 18 Geo. III, cap. 12.

That act was, in truth, a mere concession, by obstinacy, of that which had already been virtually gained by force. It was an impotent attempt to stop a war, the disastrous result of which was now far from problematical, by yielding the particular point which had immediately produced the war, while still maintaining, in other matters, the spirit of paramount dominion and supreme authority in which that particular point had been originally refused.

While the thankless and fruitless sacrifice of the right to tax the colonies was ungraciously yielded up by the 18 Geo. III, not to all our colonies whatsoever, but to the American and West Indian colonies alone, in the hope of propitiating them in particular, not a jot was abated of the other assertions of a right to make indirect profit of the colonies by the monopoly of their trade. Our navigation laws were untouched; we were still to compel our colonies to *bring from* our markets whatever they desired to *import*, and to *send to* our markets whatever they desired to *export*; and we were still to appoint the colonial governors and all the subordinate officers. Even, therefore, if the American provinces had accepted the boon of the 18 Geo. III, and given the return for it which was expected, by laying down their arms, the probabilities are great that the struggle for independence would have been renewed in the course of a few short years. The colonists had, in the course of the struggle, learned their own strength and capacity for walking alone, and would not, much longer, have consented to endure the state of pupilage in which they had hitherto existed. While the colonists, however, had thus acquired a knowledge of their strength, our rulers were still in the dark as to the imperial weakness. Like true empirics, they had not gained knowledge beyond what the single experiment had afforded. To insist on a right to tax directly had produced a revolution, and had all but already destroyed government; they therefore renounced this particular right, but had not gained any insight beyond, into the principles of colonial policy, and therefore left the system untouched in all other respects.

Even when conceding this power of direct taxation, the selfishness of the motive was disclosed by the manner in which the concession was made. It had been claimed upon general principles, which were applicable to all colonies generally; yet the concession was made to the American colonies alone.

As the 18 Geo. III, which gave up this right of
taxation by the imperial parliament, was a declaratory statute, it might have been left general, without
specification of any colonies in particular, had the intention been general; and it makes no difference that
we had not, at the time, other colonies; the limitation of the renunciation of the right to the American
colonies in particular reserved, by implication, the
power, and betrayed the inclination to refuse it to
any other colonies we either already had or subsequently might acquire; and it discovered to the
American colonists that although we had, on
compulsion, yielded to them in this particular, that
arose only from compulsion, not from either justice
or generosity, and that we meant, in all other
respects, to persist in our selfish government of our
dependencies.

We were silent on the subject of our trade and
navigation laws, and no concession was dreamt of or
hinted at, in regard to self-legislation and self-government, which, as before observed, the Americans had
shown unmistakable symptoms of a determination to
achieve.

CHAPTER IV.

OBSTRUCTION TO IMPROVEMENT IN THE ADMINISTRATION OF THE BRITISH COLONIES, WHICH REMAINED AFTER THE DECLARATION OF AMERICAN INDEPENDENCE, ARISING FROM THE EXISTENCE OF THE NAVIGATION LAWS AND THE SYSTEM OF DIFFERENTIAL DUTIES.

OUR rupture with the North American colonies taught a grand and awful lesson. Did we learn by it, in regard to our other colonies, or was it taught in vain? We had been found wanting, and our kingdom had been divided and given to the Americans. Did we profit by this lesson, or was it thrown away? Did we learn that man is the same, whether he live in a colony or in a mother country? that he has the same feelings, the same aspirations, the same self-reliance and self-dependence, the same love of power and independence, and the same love of political and social justice and freedom, whether he bask in the full blaze of imperial splendor, or be removed to the shade of colonial dependence?

As the maintenance and enforcement of our trade and navigation laws against our remaining colonies was chiefly dependent, in the first instance, upon the hold we retained of these colonies by our system of colonial administration, it was obviously impossible for us to liberalize our system of administration until we should first have liberalized our commercial policy. It was obviously impossible for us to concede the free exercise of popular representation to our colonies, and, at the same time, to impose such restraint upon the exercise of the sovereign and supreme legislative power of the imperial parliament, then supposed to exist, as was necessary to the enjoyment of a popular mode of government in the colonies, while we claimed, and likewise exercised, the despotic power of compelling the colonies to trade only in that way which we conceived would be most beneficial to ourselves, without regard to their interest in the matter.

Before, therefore, inquiring as to the history of our administration of those colonies which remained to us after the United States had thrown off their dependence upon us, so as to see how far we profited by the lesson which the American rebellion offered us, it will be convenient to inquire whether any change was made in our commercial policy after that event.

So soon as the Americans had achieved their independence, they fulminated against us retaliatory legislation. They copied our navigation laws, with the avowed purpose of paying us with our own coin,— of meeting restriction upon their trade by counter-restriction upon ours. Though this restrictive system had been one of the grievances which had cost us the loss of our American colonies,—though Smith, twenty-one years before this disaster, had, in his " Wealth of Nations," published an elaborate exposition of the true principles which ought to govern international trade,—yet so little impression had his doctrines, or our own loss, made upon us, that we met these efforts of the Americans to put themselves on a fair footing with us, by various devices, intended to counteract the effect of the new American law. It was not until these attempts had been discovered to be futile, that we, at length, yielded to act as justice, reason, and sound policy,—which, in this instance, obviously all pointed in the same direction,—should have dictated at the outset. Though we refused to acknowledge reason, justice, and sound policy to be our guides, like all wrong-headed persons acting unwisely, as well as unjustly, we were to yield only to compulsion, so far and no farther.

Instead of at once repealing, in favor of the world at large, those laws by which we charged a heavy duty on the tonnage of all vessels coming into our harbors, or into the harbors of our subsequently numerous colonies, and also upon the goods brought by them, we maintained a struggle of twenty-eight years, for the enforcement of them; and, only in 1815, agreed by treaty with the United States that we should not charge heavier duties upon their vessels and the goods imported in them than the States should demand upon our vessels and their cargoes. This treaty applied to the States alone. Against the rest of the world, and against our own colonies, Might was to continue struggling with Right, until the other nations, profiting by the bold example, which the infant states of North America had shown them, should have learnt their own strength, and force us to do *them* justice also.

The states of South America were the next people, after the North Americans, to try to remove the shackles which we had put upon trade. This time, our rulers were a little more adroit. Profiting by the lesson they had learned, in the twenty-eight years' struggle with North America, they anticipated the contest, when threatened by the South American states, by proposing and entering into treaties with them, which put the trade of the contracting parties on a fair footing of reciprocity.

It might have been supposed that this second instance of our yielding, now on the slightest pressure, and to states so comparatively insignificant, would at once have brought upon us a demand from universal Europe that we should renounce our unjust system, and put all trade on the same fair footing, that the highway of the ocean might be open to all alike. Nay, it might have been supposed that our own experience of the beneficial working, for ourselves, of our treaties with the North and the South American states would have opened our eyes to acknowledge the soundness of the economical principles which Smith, with prophetic clearness, had laid open to us so long before; but, such is the selfishness of human nature, that power or advantage gained or assumed over others, is hugged the more closely, the more surely its reality begins to disappear. In the plenitude of our mercantile supremacy, it was flattering to the national pride to think that we could tie down the world by our laws ; and therefore every step in the direction of the relaxation of these laws was viewed as a humiliation and a confession of growing weakness.

It is only in this way that we can account to ourselves for the pertinacity with which we clung to our navigation laws, long after the facts should, but for this, have convinced us, that whatever advantage they might originally have wrought for the nation, they had long ceased to be other than injurious, since they either prevented trade, which otherwise would have arisen, and in which we, as the most powerful naval nation, must necessarily have shared the most largely ; or they made the trade, which these laws could not repress, less profitable to ourselves, as well as to our fellow-nations, by forcing it into expensive channels.

Unfortunately for us, as our recent more

enlightened legislation now justifies being said, the
nations of Europe were as timid as we were selfish
and wrong-headed; they were as slow to discover
their true strength as we were to acknowledge it to
ourselves. They did, however, take courage by
degrees, and, singularly enough, Prussia, almost the
least naval of all the great powers of Europe, was
the first to make the move. In the year 1822,
Prussia began to increase her port dues on the
vessels of such nations as laid her vessels under
similar heavy charges. Our ship-owners began to
cry out, and our ministers were urged to represent
their grievances to the Prussian government. This
they did, whether with any real expectation of
procuring redress, or merely with the intention of
laying a ground for the measure they adopted four
years subsequently, does not of course appear; but
the attempt of our minister, at the court of Berlin,
to preserve his gravity, while making these complaints, must have cost not a little strain upon his
facial muscles, while the Prussian minister openly
admitted that the new regulations of his government
were not only directed against us, but were based
upon the model of our own port dues regulations,
and while he furthermore disclosed that these new
port regulations were but the beginning of our
sorrows, as his government meant to imitate us still
further, and intended, in the year following, to

impose discriminating duties on all goods imported in our ships. As yet, they had only pinched our ship-owners; if that lesson should not teach us, they were next to try the endurance of our merchants.

Fortunately, our minister of the day, (Mr. Huskisson), was too enlightened to attempt to meet these measures of Prussia by an increase of our restrictions; he "was not prepared to begin a system of commercial hostility, which, if followed up on both sides to its legitimate consequences, could only tend to reciprocal prohibition,"—in other words, to the stoppage of all trade between the two countries. "In this state of things, more prudently, as I contend," said Mr. Huskisson, and every one will now admit the truth of the observation, "we entered upon an amicable negotiation with the Prussian government, upon the principle of our treaty with the United States, that of abolishing on both sides all discriminating duties on the ships and goods of the respective countries in the ports of the other."

Whatever might be the ultimate result to us of these arrangements with North and South America and Prussia,—whether they might work the destruction of our trade with these powers, or only cause injury to it, or be the foundation even of its improvement,—there could not be a question as to the *justice* of the arrangements, nor as to the tyranny and injustice of our past system. Undoubtedly, then, it was "*prudent,*" as Mr. Huskisson designated it, since honesty is the best policy among nations as well as individuals, to knock under to the just assertion by Prussia of her right to tax our trade, as we had so long taxed hers. But should no higher motives than *prudence* have been consulted by a nation, holding such a position in the world as Great Britain ? We had begun our navigation laws with the view of founding a navy : we had made them more stringent, that we might destroy the naval power of Holland, then the greatest in Europe, and raise up our own power upon the ruins of hers. We had manfully fought our way to a pinnacle of mercantile grandeur and prosperity, by destroying the ships of all our opponents, during the derangements of Continental trade, produced by the long war with France ; and surely, when we had achieved all this glory and wealth, to an amount which never could have been anticipated, at the outset of the struggle,—when what began in a commendable effort for advancement, had ended in universal mercantile superiority,—we could well have afforded to act on other motives than the dry and niggardly dictates of *prudence.* Justice, honor, magnanimity, might have weighed somewhat in the scale of consideration, if self-interest was to go for nothing.

Nay, cold prudence even might have dictated a step beyond concession, simply to those who had

courage to demand it. While as yet we were a
rising power, there was not much to be said against
us for endeavoring to force trade into our own
channels out of every other. It was grasping and
unconscionable, no doubt; but other nations might
have followed the same course and entered upon the
struggle with us. The battle would have been to
that one of the nations which should prove to be
the strongest. But after Napoleon had laid the other
nations of Europe prostrate at his feet, and identified
their trade with the French trade, by subjecting it
to his Milan Decrees, thus making all the nations
of Europe our mercantile foes; and after we, by
the unparalléled success of our navy, had swept
nearly the whole mercantile navy of Europe off
the seas, and engrossed to ourselves the trade of
the world,—to continue the maintenance of those
restrictions upon the trade of other nations which
we had used as the means of attaining this super-
eminence, was to persist in that which, whatever
it might originally have been designated, had now
become tyranny and oppression, and would soon
be received in that light by other nations, and be
resisted by them accordingly, so soon as peace
should give them the means and the opportunity
of offering that resistance. It would have been only
prudent, then, to have anticipated this spirit of
justifiable opposition; to have abandoned those

restrictive regulations which our naval superiority had enabled us to maintain, and to have proclaimed, voluntarily, that trade was in future to be a race in which all might join freely and fairly. *Dat bis qui dat cito.* We should thus have disarmed the jealousy of the nations, and have gained for ourselves a character for generosity, instead of earning, as we did, that of a covetous, grasping "nation of shopkeepers."

If our ministers took this view of what our conduct, even in a prudential view, ought to have been, they were before their countrymen, for the nation was evidently not yet prepared to renounce an iota more than it could help of the advantages, real or imaginary, righteous or iniquitous, of our navigation laws. The arrangements made with Prussia, though just and honorable, had to be communicated to Parliament in an apologetic tone, as if the minister had done something which he could hardly justify ; and, instead of bringing in an act to sweep away our mercantile restrictions, once and for ever, and as to all nations, the statute of 6 Geo. IV, cap. 1, was passed, whereby power was given to His Majesty in council to admit foreign vessels into British ports, upon payment of the same dues as should be payable by British vessels, in the ports of the countries to which these foreign vessels might belong. In other words, instead of openly and manfully foregoing, for the future, all our restrictions, whether against weak or against powerful nations, or against nations bold or timid, we were to recede, inch by inch, and step by step, just so far and no farther than each and every nation should feel bold enough or powerful enough to force us.

We had not long to wait. If Denmark and Sweden had not found out the illiberality and oppression of our system until Prussia resented it, they were not long in profiting by the lesson which she had shown them. They very soon threatened the adoption of the same course by which Prussia had succeeded, and they soon had the same success. Instead of giving spontaneously, we yielded upon compulsion and upon its first pressure, to nations, too, of such comparative weakness as Sweden and Denmark.

At length another step in advance in the right direction was made by the passing of the act of the 6 Geo. IV, cap. 109, whereby goods were allowed to be imported into the United Kingdom and its possessions in ships of the countries of which the goods were the production. But still, if a French ship in the harbor of Stockholm had been ready to take in a cargo of Swedish iron for London, this statute would not have enabled her to do it. She must have refused the cargo, and, if no other cargo offered, she must have returned home in ballast; and the merchant—he may have been a Swede, or he may have been a citizen of London—instead of having the benefit of the competition of this French ship with English or Swedish vessels, must have submitted to such terms of freight as the Swedish vessels, or any English vessels accidentally in the harbor, chose to exact.

All this petty system of restriction and counter-restriction, of reciprocal and differential duties, is now happily at an end, as to every nation which chooses to trade with us on the footing of fair and open competition. An Englishman may now hold up an honest face of pride, when industry, activity, and enterprise in foreign trade produce to him their usual fruits—success and prosperity. It is no longer necessary for him, against inward conviction, to justify his nation from the imputations of its wealth being acquired by grasping from others and by excluding them from the enjoyment of those advantages of soil or climate which nature has given in differing degrees and qualities in order to promote intercourse between the nations of the earth, and, with it, civilization in all its forms.

It is now not far from a century since the American colonies complained of the hardships inflicted upon them by our restrictive system of trade, and since, though the justice of that complaint had been demonstrated, they were called by

one of the ministers of the time "rebellious and
ungrateful children" for resenting it, yet it was
only the other day, so to speak, that these restrictions were expunged from the statute-book, notwithstanding their impolicy had, a century ago, been
exposed in the works of Smith, as clearly as it has
ever been since in the parliamentary effusions of any
minister, however popular or powerful, or however
fervent he may have been in advocating the doctrines
of reform or of free trade. Every "interest," "West
India," "landed," and "manufacturing," pertina-
ciously held to the advantages which restriction
professed to give long after it had ceased to be
doubtful that the advantages were more nominal
than real. It was only when the house was tumbling
about their ears that each "interest" began to yield
its chamber, and allow this rotten part to be pulled
down.

But how did it fare with our colonies, during all
this tardy, reluctant progress towards freedom of
trade with foreign nations? The fetters upon our
trade, of which the Americans had complained
while they were yet dependent upon us, equally
galled the trade of all our other colonies, then
existing or subsequently acquired. While we kept
the commercial world in bondage, did we relax
as to our own children? While we refused to
concede to other nations the advantages, which

our navigation laws and differential duties were
supposed to withhold from them, in fear lest they
should not follow our example in liberality,—while
we opened our trade only to such nations as should,
by treaty, declare their willingness to pursue a system
of reciprocity,—did we throw open our harbors to our
colonies, resolved to do them justice, and to forego all
the advantages which our restrictive system was supposed to have earned for us? By no means. We held
our colonies firm in the vice in which our assumption
of power over them had, at the outset, enabled us to fix
them; nor did we in the least relax, even in regard
to them, until the rising commercial prosperity of the
world, through the long continuance of peace, began
to put us in fear for our manufacturing and commercial supremacy, and opened our eyes to the conviction
that, while we were injuring other countries by our
restrictive system, we were damaging ourselves more
seriously by how much our commercial interests far
exceeded those of any other nation. Then, and not
till then, did we concede free trade to our colonies.

While this system prevailed, "the most visionary
enthusiasist," as Smith said, "would scarce be
capable of proposing such a measure as that Great
Britain should voluntarily give up all authority over
her colonies, and leave them to elect their own
magistrates, to enact their own laws, and to make
peace and war as they might think proper, with

any hopes at least of its ever being adopted." But, now that we have thrown open the trade of the empire to all the world,—now that our colonies can employ their own ships, or hire foreign ships in preference to ours, if so minded, for the conveyance of their exports and imports,—now that they may buy in whatsoever market they consider to be the cheapest, and sell in the market they consider to be the dearest, without reference to whether these markets are British or foreign,—the field is cleared, so far as exclusive trade is concerned, for considering what inducements there are for retaining the colonies in dependence upon us, and whether it would not be more wise and more prudent for us, " voluntarily to give up our authority over them," and " to settle with them," altering the words of Smith according to the change of circumstances, " such treaties of commerce as will effectually secure to us a trade more advantageous to the great body of the people, though less so to the merchants, than the monopoly which we have parted with." At all events, an attempt may be made to show that this would be our most prudent course, without incurring the imputation of attempting to do that which only " a visionary enthusiast" would be capable of proposing, as Smith sarcastically observed of any one who, in his time, should have risked such a proposal.

CHAPTER V.

BUT before entertaining questions of policy it will be
well first to ascertain rights, and especially how far
Great Britain possesses a sovereign authority over
her colonies, "extending," as Mr. Pitt said, "to
every point of legislation, to bind their trade, confine their manufactures, and exercise every power
whatsoever, short of taking their money out of their
pockets;" and, in connection with that, it will be
useful to consider the constitutional power of Great
Britain to acquire extension of territory.

The ground will then be cleared for a more
perspicuous view of the soundness or unsoundness
of our past colonial policy, and for consideration of
the principles upon which our connection with our
colonies should be maintained in time to come.

The course of Great Britain in her colonial policy
has, in some respects, been different from that of
the other countries of Europe. But, in fundamental
principles, she has shown very little if any difference.

Her policy has been based upon the doctrine of Mr. Pitt, that the imperial parliament has a supreme legislative power over the colonies ; and her practical application of that doctrine has been to assert the other doctrine of Lord Sheffield, applied to the North American and West Indian colonies, that " the only use of them was the monopoly of their consumption and of the carriage of their produce."

This notion of supreme power over colonies, and its practical application of ruling them merely with a view to the extent of pecuniary profit to be derived from them, give the clue to the colonial policy of all the modern nations, Great Britain included. But there is this great distinction between the mode in which Great Britain and the other monarchical states of Europe have worked out this colonial policy, that, whereas each of those countries,—France, Spain, and Portugal,—has done this according to the spirit of its own domestic government, Great Britain has done so, as it would seem, in direct violation of the spirit of her constitution.

France, Spain, and Portugal were each and all of them despotic monarchies at the time they founded their colonies, as, with the exception of Portugal, they are at this day. Their monarchs could kill and imprison the subjects of their original dominion at their capricious will and pleasure. It was far short of such an exercise of despotic power to say to these subjects, when they removed to newly-settled countries, that they should not cultivate or trade but in a prescribed mode, at the peril of their lives, their liberties, or their fortunes.

But Great Britain, praise be to the Almighty, was a free country, where, neither in theory nor in practice, could the will of any individual, or body of individuals, control the free exercise of natural rights by any other individual or body of individuals, where the law alone is paramount, or has any control over the life, or the liberty, or the property of the subject, or the mode of exercising his natural faculties ; and where every subject in reality, or virtually, has power over that law to enact, repeal, or modify it ; and where no law can be made, without his voice being heard in dissent or approval, either by representation or actual appearance.

The whole government of the British colonies has been at every step, as it seems, a denial of this and an exercise of power which had for its foundation despotic will, and nothing else. If that will, like the despotic power of Spain, had pronounced to its colonies, that a stranger entering a British colony should suffer death, an exercise of power so utterly unknown in Great Britain itself, and therefore, necessarily so violently and abhorrently repugnant to the feelings of Britons, would have provoked inquiry among them into the foundation on which this power was rested; and no doubt this inquiry would have exposed its true character and have terminated its existence. It is only because the exercise of the power has been limited to passing regulations under the innocuously sounding names of "customs" and "navigation" laws, that the true nature of the power which has been exercised by Great Britain towards her colonies has escaped inquiry. But, however much it might have startled Mr. Pitt, or those who echoed his sentiments in his day, to be told so, the truth will probably appear to be that the rule of British colonies has been as despotic in its character as ever was that of the Spanish rule, and that the difference has been, not in the character of the rule, but in the extent to which it has been exercised.

If it were necessary, it would not be difficult to prove, from the internal history of the colonies, especially the ceded or conquered ones, that governors, without the knowledge of the government at home, or of parliament, did, in former days not very remote, exercise a power which was neither more nor less than despotic in its character, and to an extent which would be incredible with those who have never left the shores of Britain to live under the shadow of a great little man's power. But to go into any inquiry of that sort is foreign to the present object, which has to do, not with the abuse by individuals of the powers that were entrusted to them, but with the character of the power which the government at home, with the sanction of parliament, asserted to itself over the British colonies, not for the purpose of showing that the power so asserted has been exercised by the government with cruelty;—far from it. If we except the war with the North American colonies, and the mode in which that war was carried on, and if we make a further exception, (but a large one, no doubt,) of our customs and navigation laws, it is beyond a question that the British colonial rule has been milder and more beneficent than that of any other modern European country, without exception.

But the colonies have been indebted for this, not to the limited character of the power asserted to be within the capacity of the crown, or of the imperial parliament, to exercise over them, but to the character of the British ministers in whose hands that power has been deposited, and to the political and social atmosphere in which those ministers have been born and brought up. The colonists, so far as the government has been concerned, have hitherto been safe as to life, limb, and liberty. But it was within the competency of the power alleged to exist in the crown as to conquered colonies, and in the imperial parliament as to original and ceded colonies, to have made this otherwise. Further, the colonists, in questions between individuals, have been safe as to their property, and as to the power of increasing it. The laws of the colonies, such as they have existed for the regulation of private rights, have been duly administered to the colonists, and, so far, their condition has been the same as that of the inhabitants of Great Britain itself. But, in questions between the colonists collectively and the imperial government, in regard to their property and the means of improving it, the colonists have not enjoyed the same rights as the inhabitants of Great Britain. In our customs and navigation laws, and, in many respects, in the internal administration of the colonies, there has been an actual exercise of that despotic power which has been theoretically alleged to exist in the crown, as to conquered colonies, and in the imperial parliament, as to original and ceded colonies.

The existence of such a despotic power would be consistent with the sovereignty of France, or of Spain, and its exercise only to be expected of their sovereigns so long as power of every kind is sweet to mortal man; but its existence is incompatible with the British constitution, and its past exercise has been in violation of that constitution, and would have been repugnant to and repudiated by every Briton, had the power been exposed in its nakedness, stripped of all those conventional phrases under which it has been disguised, even to those by whom they were used.

It has been said that the power of the British Parliament, of King, Lords, and Commons united, is omnipotent.   So it is in one sense, beyond all question, for every form of government requires the existence of such a power in some quarter.   But so *is it not*, in another sense, and equally beyond all question.   If the parliament be omnipotent, may it not be despotic?   *Major continet minus?*   It may not, beyond all dispute.   The parliament of Great Britain is omnipotent, that is, it has power to alter the law, as it exists, and to make such new laws as may, in effect, deal with particular men's lives, liberties, or properties, in a manner different from what the law had sanctioned, as the law existed previously to this change; but it *may* do so, only on the ground that this particular departure from the general law has been rendered necessary for the security or advantage of the rest of the community. It *may not* do it, for the gratification of any one passion known to the human breast.   The parliament, no doubt, if such a case can be supposable, *can*, for the gratification of spite, malignity, or hatred, order, by act duly passed, a man's head to be cut off, or his estates to be sold, and the proceeds to be paid into the treasury; or it *can*

order him to sell his goods at a certain price, while
the rest of the community are selling at a higher
price, as it has done to the colonies. But what it
can do is beside the question, which is what it
may do, according to the written constitution of
the country, which has ascertained the rights of
every individual in it, from the highest to the
lowest.

A despotic, that is, an irresponsible sovereign, for
the gratification of any passion, or even of any whim
or caprice, may order a man's life, or his property,
to be taken away. The despot both *may* and *can*
do this, without violating any defined or ascertained
rule of government, under which he is bound to act,
there being none such in the case supposed. Whether
he does not, as between him .and his Maker, violate
the implied rule under which all kings govern,
namely, that what they do shall be for the good
of their subjects, is another question, which he
must answer to Him with whom there is no respect
of persons, whose laws of justice and equity are
laid upon all alike, kings as well as beggars.

But no member of the British parliament, be he
king, peer, or commoner, can vote for the passing
of any act by which an individual, or any number
of individuals, short of the whole community, can
be capriciously dealt with, as to life, limb, or
estate, without violating those principles of the

constitution distinctly defined and ascertained by
Magna Charta and the Bill of Rights ; the observance and protection of which form an implied
condition upon the inheritance of each monarch,
and of every peer, and upon the election of every
commoner.

The parliament of Britain, then, is omnipotent
for good, for everything that shall tend to promote
the welfare and safety of the empire and its inhabitants ; but powerless for evil, or for the doing of any
thing which shall have for its avowed object injury
to the welfare or safety of the empire, or of any of
its inhabitants.

When any act of the legislature is passed,
whereby an individual, or any number of individuals,
is injured for the benefit of the community at large,
this is done upon the principle which regulates all
bodies of men associated together, under whatever
denomination of compact, that the rights or interests
of the minority must yield to the interests of the
majority ; which involves the implication, if there
be no express stipulation to that effect, that each
member of the community has, at the outset, given
his consent to this mode of action.   But such an act
is never passed without the matter being fully
discussed and investigated, both by the majority and
by the minority, nor without an equivalent being
given to the minority for that which has been taken

away. A park is required in the neighborhood of
a large city, for the health of its inhabitants; a
railroad is required through a certain tract of country,
for expediting the commerce of the kingdom. In
these and many other similar instances which might
be cited, the land required is, by act of parliament,
authorized to be taken from the owners, whether
they will or not; but how? Without paying them
the value? On the contrary, the full value is to be
paid. In short, all that is done is just saying, in effect,
"If we were all of us reasonable persons, disposed
to act for the benefit of our common society, those
of us who are proprietors of the land required would
cheerfully sell it for the common good; but, since
they are so selfish and narrow-sighted as to refuse to
sell the land, and will consider their own individual
pleasure alone, without regard to the wants of the
community, which if each of us were to do there
would soon be an end of the social compact, we
must compel them to be reasonable, and to part
with their land on a fair valuation." This is the
extent to which the omnipotence of parliament can
be carried—not further—without inflicting a wound
upon its own body, which, in its consequences,
might prove fatal.

There is nothing new in these doctrines. They
are trite enough. But the repetition of them here
may be a useful introduction to what is about to

follow, in regard to the extent of our power over our colonies, in the course of which it will be seen how far those doctrines are applicable to them. But before entering upon that subject, it may be as well to consider the right to acquire territory by colonization, with special reference to the power of Great Britain in particular to hold and govern territory so acquired.

CHAPTER VI.

THERE are three modes by which extension of
territory may be gained by a state :—1. By taking
possession, through its subjects, of countries which
have either not been peopled at all, or have been
peopled very partially, or which have been peopled
by men living under separate chiefs, and not under
any united form of government, and possessing
habits and manners which the nations of the earth
who call themselves civilized have been pleased to
designate as savage; 2. By conquering territory by
force of arms from another state; and 3. By
voluntary cession from one state to another.

With regard to the two last of these modes of
acquiring territory, namely, by conquest and by
cession, they give a title which is definite and
precise, and well acknowledged by the nations of
the earth. In this respect they do not call for any
observation. How far acquisition of territory by
either of these modes, however, is consonant to the

spirit of a constitution such as that of Great Britain is worthy of observation. This shall be delayed until we come to speak, in this respect also, of these three modes of acquiring territory by Britain.

In the meanwhile, the first mode of acquiring territory which has been mentioned, technically known as title by occupation, suggests observations well worthy of consideration, with reference to our colonial empire and the mode of its administration.

This title by occupation is founded upon the natural right, which every human being has, to the enjoyment of so much of the earth's surface as is necessary to his existence; and also upon the express gift of the Almighty, in these words, " Be fruitful and multiply and replenish the earth, and subdue it, and have dominion over the fish of the sea, and over the fowl of the air, and over every living thing that moveth upon the earth. Behold I have given you every herb bearing seed, which is upon the face of all the earth, and every tree, in which is the fruit of a tree yielding seed; to you it shall be for meat."

There is no title which is so simply defensible, upon first principles as occupancy, where it is strictly built upon the natural right which is its foundation, as it was in the case of Lot and Abraham, and probably in the establishment of all colonies in the ancient times of the world. But there is no title more vague, indefinite, and indefensible than the title by occupancy, as it has been used in the practice of modern nations when establishing colonies. There has not been a pretence, even, of the necessity on which the title is founded, namely, the sustenance of those who have seized the occupation ; but resort has been had to arbitrary, capricious, and undefinable rules. In truth, the title has not had any other foundation than that of covetousness and ambition, supported by physical power.

The title of Great Britain to her East Indian possessions, though the one which has been most assailed, is probably that one of all her colonial titles which was the most defensible, in its inception at least, however much it may have been open to reproach subsequently, as to the modes by which, or the pretences under which, her territory in those regions has been extended. Commercial intercourse between nations being apparently as much an ordination of Providence as agriculture, if, after the peaceful establishment of a mercantile settlement in a country, the inhabitants, either by fraud or by violence, provoke the settlers to defence, which, by the unavoidable course of circumstances, merges into conquest, the inhabitants have themselves to blame if the settlers become eventually their masters instead of their neighbors. Having acquired these Eastern possessions in that way, the principle on which we hold them, of treating them, not as parts

of the empire, the inhabitants of which are entitled
to the rights of Englishmen, but as conquests to be
ruled under such laws as parliament shall from
time to time enact, is simple, intelligible, and
practicable.

But what shall be said of the title which Spain set
up to the whole of South America, by virtue of a bull
from the Pope of Rome, though the country was
already thickly inhabited by nations advanced in
the arts of civilization greatly beyond that point
which ascertains a right of property in individuals
to the soil cultivated by them ? Or, what shall be
said of our title to the whole of Australia, a country
which, though thinly populated, is larger than all
Europe, and therefore, of necessity, much larger
than would be requisite for all the inhabitants of
Great Britain put together, should any necessity have
driven them out of their own island, but which only
a few of them, without being impelled by any such
necessity, have visited, and none of whom has yet
been able to take even a cursory survey of, in its
full extent.

The truth is that the title by occupancy, as that
title has been practically understood in modern
times, will not bear examination,—neither France,
Great Britain, nor Portugal paid much attention to
it, when set up by Spain, in order to exclude them
from South America ; and, so soon as that shall be

worth the while of any nation, it will have as little attention paid to it, should we set up this title in order to secure our monopoly of Australia.

The community of nations will, for the general peace, not permit any one nation to inquire too curiously how far another nation has put the soil within its own territory to that profitable use, which, as before observed, constitutes the very foundation of the title by occupancy. But when a nation, as in the instance of Australia, leaves its territory for any purpose, political or social, and affects to appropriate to itself a much larger portion of the surface of the earth than even the wildest suggestions of necessity can justify, there is nothing which can prevent any other nation from stepping in to claim a share, nor which should induce the other nations of the earth, the only supreme tribunal in such cases, to interfere and prevent it so doing. Vatel, lib. I, cap. 18, sec. 207, speaking of the possession taken by navigators, says, "Communement ce titre a été respecté pourvû qu'une possession réelle l'ait suivi de près."

"Mais c'est une question de savoir si une nation peut s'approprier ainsi, par une simple prise de possession, des païs qu'elle n'occupe pas réellement, et s'en réserver de cette manière, beaucoup plus qu'elle n'est capable de peupler et de cultiver. Il n'est pas difficile de décider, qu'une pareille prétention serait absolument contraire au droit naturel, et opposée aux vuës de la nature, qui destinant toute la terre aux besoins des hommes en général, ne donne à chaque peuple le droit de s'approprier un païs, que pour les usages qu'il en tire, et non pour empêcher que d'autres n'en profitent."

If the proportion of the people to the acres of territory in any nation become excessive, with reference to the maintenance of the people of the nation, it is according to the primary laws of nature, that the surplus population should swarm off to some other part of the earth, either entirely uninhabited or, if there be none such, to some part less densely inhabited than that which they have left. Or, if large tracts of the earth's surface are uninhabited, it is not opposed either to the primary laws of nature, or to any of the conventional laws of nations, that, without the urgency of any necessity, but purely for the purposes of increased commerce, the government of a nation, or any voluntary association of a part of the inhabitants of a nation, should establish a settlement in this uninhabited country by actual possession.

Neither any one man, nor any nation of men, is tied down to the occupation of that particular part of the earth's surface on which they may happen to have been born, so long as there are other parts of its surface as yet unappropriated. Vatel lib. I,

cap. 19, sec. 220, says: "Tout homme nait libre;
le fils d'un citoyen, parvenu à l'âge de raison, peut
examiner s'il lui convient de se joindre à la société
que sa naissance lui destine. S'il ne trouve point
qu'il lui est avantageux d'y rester, il est le maître
de la quitter, en la dédommageant de ce qu'elle
pourroit avoir fait en sa faveur, et en conservant
pour elle, autant que ses nouveaux engagemens
le lui permettront, les sentimens d'amour et de
reconnoissance qu'il lui doit." The earth has never
yet been so densely inhabited as to render necessary,
or to justify an inquiry, as to the exact extent of
its surface, which any nation was entitled to appropriate for the exclusive use of its inhabitants.
Should it ever become so, there can be little doubt
that, according to natural laws, no nation could
appropriate more than was strictly necessary for
the support of its inhabitants, to the exclusion of
those of another country, which had become so
densely inhabited as to be incapable of supporting
its inhabitants.[a]

While so great a portion of the earth continues
uninhabited, as has been the case since its creation,
the law of title by occupancy will probably continue
to receive the same liberal interpretation which has
hitherto been given to it, and no nation, or other
community of men, will be justified in inquiring

[a] Puffendorf iv, 4, 5.

too closely as to the extent of surface appropriated by a new settlement.

It is obvious that when a new settlement is formed, as the number of settlers will naturally increase from day to day, provision for this must be made beforehand, by appropriating more land than will be necessary for the support of the original settlers, but the excess must be limited, within the bounds of probability, as to the numerical increase of the settlers within a reasonable period of time; otherwise any other body of settlers, with whose projects this excess of appropriation interferes, may step in to prevent it.

If, therefore, a certain district of the earth's surface be appropriated for a colony, either by a national government, or by a voluntary association of emigrants, the appropriation need not necessarily be confined to what is strictly required for the support of the first settlers. It may allow a broad margin, as the merchants say, for the natural increase of the population by births and new arrivals. But an arbitrary, capricious appropriation of an extent of the earth's surface, without reference to any natural necessity as its cause, or to the probable increase of the settlement, either by births or by continued immigration, is an appropriation which no nation or individual is bound to recognise, not even the other inhabitants of the very nation by whom the appropriation may have been made.

This subject is not one of mere speculative inquiry; it is one of serious practical importance. It involves a question which has already been raised between Great Britain and her subjects in two of her colonies. In one instance, without any injurious consequences, but in the other with most disastrous results—the shedding of much blood, and the production of angry, revengeful feelings, which it will take generations to obliterate; and a third instance of an opposite kind is now occurring, while these lines are being written.

The first instance to which allusion has been made, occurred in Australia. Certain of the British colonists of Van Diemen's Land wished to establish a settlement at Port Phillip, a part of the continent of Australia which had not as yet been actually occupied. Lord Aberdeen first, and afterwards Lord Glenelg, the then Secretaries for the Colonies, answered this application to the effect that *no settlement could be allowed* at the point proposed, as the policy of the government was rather to concentrate than to disperse the population of the colonies. The government was quite entitled to refrain from making a new settlement on its own responsibility and at its own expense, but to say that it would " not allow " any settlement to be made was quite beyond the sphere of its action; unless the whole continent of Australia, whether

occupied or unoccupied, formed part of the British
dominions, an assertion which no government would
be bold enough to maintain against France, Russia, or
any other country powerful enough to assert and maintain the contrary. Fortunately, no foreign country was
interested. British subjects only were forbidden—
and they paid as much obedience to the prohibition
as if they had been foreigners ; they utterly disregarded Lord Glenelg's attempt to restrain their
enterprise,—they founded the colony *nolens volens*
the minister.

In ten years afterwards, the population of this
originally prohibited settlement, but now recognised
and wearing the happy name of Victoria, amounted
to 28,000 ; its exports to £464,000, and its imports
to £248,000 ; and in 1851, or in sixteen years, the
population had grown to 82,000, its imports to
£1,056,000, and its exports to £1,423,000. In
1852 the population amounted to 120,000, and the
exports and imports had increased in the same
extraordinary progression.[a]

The second instance in which a question as to
title by occupancy occurred was in Africa.

An extensive district of country, between the
Orange and the Vaal rivers, which had originally

---

[a] The text was written in 1854. The *Standard* of 21st September,
1858, says the inhabitants were 500,000, and the exports
£15,000,000 in 1857.

been occupied, more or less, by Hottentots and Bosjesmen, was afterwards overrun by the Basutus, a tribe of Kafirs, over whom there were several chiefs. The country was also occupied by a tribe called the Griquas, who were in fact an assemblage of all the bastard issue of intercourse between Dutch settlers within the colony of the Cape of Good Hope and women of color. These bastards, being neither black nor white, had, under the assumed name of Griquas, gone out of the colony and settled in this country, for the sake of greater independence, and were by common consent governed by two persons as chiefs, viz., Adam Kok and Waterboer.

One part of this country, viz.; that bordering on the Quathlamba or Drakensberg mountains, was cultivated, and produced every variety of grain—the remainder, consisting mostly of plain country, having the richest pasturage, was admirably suited for the rearing of cattle. The agricultural portion was mostly in the possession of three chiefs—Moshesh, Sikonyella, and Molitsani. The pastoral portion, on the other hand, was roamed over by the cattle of the Griquas, and occasionally, in dry seasons, by those of boers, who crossed the Orange River from the Cape colony, for the sake of the superior pasturage to be found in these plains.

To this district of country there were native " titles, which covered every inch of the entire country—nay, in many cases, the same tract of land was loudly claimed by several chiefs at once."[a]

Such was the state of that portion of the earth, which subsequently got the name of " the Orange River Sovereignty," while, as yet, it had not been interfered with by any British authority. Presently, the boers began to convert their occasional visits into permanent settlements, which were made partly on the land occupied by Moshesh, and partly on that occupied by the Griquas. In this they were encouraged by Moshesh, as to his portion of the country, in the hope of thereby securing protection against the Griquas, who, having come originally from the Cape colony, had brought with them fire-arms and a knowledge of the use of them, luxuries as yet unknown out of the colony. What these boers did in this respect was without the permission or sanction of the colonial authorities having been obtained, or even asked.

In the years 1835 and 1836 a great exodus from the colony took place. There has always been a tendency in the Dutch boer, dating long prior to the British possession of the colony of the Cape of Good Hope, to escape into the unsettled open country beyond the limits of the colony for the time. To this they have been stimulated by two feelings—a

[a] Attorney - General's opinion in correspondence presented to Parliament, on 19th May, 1851.—p. 8.

desire for emancipation from the restraints of settled government, and a longing for the possession of unlimited range of pasturage for cattle, as a means of provision for their children. This erratic feeling was much increased in the years which have been mentioned by other accidental causes. The boers were exasperated against the government on several accounts. It had itself issued paper rix-dollars at the value of 4s. 6d., and had then made sterling money a legal tender, and declared the value of the rix-dollar to be only 1s. 6d. It had next emancipated the slaves of the colonists, and told the colonists that they should be compensated in money, which would be paid in London, where the boer, who could not even speak the English language, had neither acquaintances nor connections. Many of the boers, in their simple ignorance, looked upon the whole affair as a fraud, and refused to take, and never have to this day taken, the documents which would entitle them to the compensation; of which £5,000 is in this way still unclaimed—others were glad to take what they could get, and, in many cases they received prices little better than nominal for their compensation certificates; and in all cases they were subjected to a heavy deduction, in name of agency, commission, and correspondence. While the boers suffered in this way from the ill-considered arrangements for payment of the compensation money, the colony suffered more seriously from the equally ill-considered arrangements for effecting the slave emancipation.

On the 1st of December, 1834, the middle of the Cape summer, while the crops were yet on the ground, slave emancipation was proclaimed at Graham's Town, the eastern capital of the colony, and throughout the colony. The slaves vanished to enjoy the first moments of their freedom, leaving the crops to perish on the ground ; and, before the month of December had ended, the Kafirs burst into the colony, and, there being no precautionary provision by the government for resisting them, they carried off 111,418 head of cattle, 156,878 sheep and goats, 5,438 horses, and 58 wagons ; burnt 456 farm-houses, and pillaged 300 houses ; thus commiting ravages of the lowly estimated value of £288,625 4s. 9d., besides murdering, in some instances with circumstances of great atrocity, hundreds of individuals. Emancipation of slaves at an injudicious season destroyed the cereal crops, the Kafirs swept off the live-stock,—and now the ruin of the farmer was complete.

As this was by 'no means the first inroad from which the colonists had suffered, and as it followed so immediately their other grievances against the government, it maddened many of them into a determination to sell their farms and such effects as remained to them, at whatever prices they could obtain, to abandon the colony altogether, and seek beyond its boundaries, a country, where they could be free from the oppression of the government, and safe from the forays of the Kafirs.

Actuated, partly by these feelings, and partly by the desire for freedom from the restraints of government, and the inconvenience of neighborhood to which reference has before been made, a very large body of Dutch colonists sold their farms, at prices, which would be ludicrous were they not melancholy,[a] and emigrated with their wives and children into the country beyond the Orange River, which has been already described as subsequently becoming the Orange River Sovereignty. There they separated themselves into three bodies. One of these passed over the Quathlamba or Drakensberg mountains, and founded the colony of Natal; the two others took lands from the Griqua chiefs of the country upon long leases, and there settled down. The fate of the party which went on to Natal was a melancholy one. The Secretary of State, Lord Glenelg, "disclaimed in the most distinct terms any intention on the part of His Majesty's government to assert any authority over any part of this territory" of Natal.

But the Governor of the Cape colony, without any authority from home, took possession, by military force, of the country in which these boers

[a] Many a farm was given away for the price of a wagon; and some for much less value.

had settled down. The boers now saw it was useless to contend longer against the British power, which seemed resolved to put forth its strength against them, and submitted in form. This is the history of the foundation of the colony of Natal, which, from the geniality of its climate, and the fertility of its soil, promises to be one of our most valuable possessions, though made, like Victoria, despite the expressed determination of Her Majesty's government.

Soon afterwards, a large body of the boers resolved to seek, once more, some quarter of the earth, where they might enjoy their loved independence and self-government. They recrossed the Quathlamba mountains, and rejoined their fellow-countrymen in the Sovereignty, who, as before mentioned, had settled down partly on the lands of the Kafir chief Moshesh, and partly on those of the Griqua chief Adam Kok. Moshesh had been content with the protection the boers had afforded him against the Griquas, and had not exacted any payment from the boers for their possession of his land. On the other hand, the Griquas retained the knowledge of the arts of life, which they had brought from the colony, and along with it the indolent habits of the colored race. They therefore had leased their lands to the boers for long terms, upon money payments. With this hold upon the land, the boers established judges and magistrates, under the same names, and with similar powers as had been enjoyed by these officers in the Cape colony while it was still under the Dutch dominion.

Presently, the Griquas began to perceive the good account to which the industry of the boers had turned the fertility of the soil. They then became anxious to get the soil again within their own power, and to be rid of their tenants, and a pretext for a quarrel was not long of being found. The Governor of the Cape colony, on the assumption that the emigration of the Cape colonists to this country did not free them from his authority, sent a body of troops across the Orange River, to assist the Griquas; and the result, as might be expected, was the defeat of the boers in an engagement fought at Boomplaats in the year 1845.

Shortly afterwards, the Governor of the Cape colony, under his commission and instructions for the government of that colony alone, without mention of any part of the earth's surface beyond it, who, therefore, as to all beyond the colony, was, it would seem, as powerless as the meanest of Her Majesty's subjects, on the 3rd of February, 1848, proclaimed to the world " the sovereignty of Her Majesty the Queen of England over the territories north of the Great Orange River, *including the countries of Moshesh, Moroko, Molitsani, Sikonyella, Adam Koh, Gert Taaybosch, and other minor chiefs,* so far north as to the Vaal River, and east to the Drakensberg or

Quathlamba mountains, with no desire or inclination whatever, on the part of Her Majesty, to extend or increase her dominions, or to deprive the chiefs and their people of the hereditary rights, acknowledged and recognized by all civilized nations of the world, as appertaining to the nomadic races of the earth; but, on the contrary, with the sole view of establishing an amicable relationship with these chiefs, *of upholding them in their hereditary rights,* and protecting them from any future aggression or location of Her Majesty's subjects, *as well as of providing for their rule, and the maintenance of good order and obedience to Her Majesty's laws and commands, on the part of the Queen's subjects, who, having abandoned the land of their fathers, have located themselves within the territories aforesaid ;* and I hereby proclaim that *all the chiefs of the territories aforesaid are under the sovereignty of Her Majesty, as the paramount and exclusive authority in all international (?) disputes as to territory, or in any cause whatever tending to interrupt the general peace and harmony of South Africa ;* but *that their authority over their own tribes shall be maintained,* as well as their own laws, according to their customs and usages.

"And I hereby proclaim that all Her Majesty's subjects within the territories aforesaid shall be governed by the laws, ordinances, and proclamations,

framed, and *to be framed*, for *Her Majesty's colony of the Cape of Good Hope*, and that they shall henceforth be *in full possession of the rights of citizens of the said colony.*

"And I hereby proclaim all the missionary stations, with the territories aforesaid, to be under the special protection of Her Majesty the Queen of England.

"And I hereby proclaim and declare that this sovereignty and paramount authority is for the sole protection and preservation of the just and hereditary rights of all native chiefs, as aforesaid, and for the rule and government of Her Majesty's subjects, their interest, and welfare. That no benefit whatever accrues, *or is desired* by Her Majesty, *beyond the satisfaction Her Majesty the Queen will ever feel,* in the maintenance of a just peace and the improvement of the condition of her people, and in their advancement in the blessings of Christianity, civilization, and those habits of industry and honesty which will elevate and civilize the barbarian, and support and uphold the Christian community, and thus will that peace be established which Her Majesty desires to effect, and has the power and *determination* to maintain."

The Secretary of State expressed his willingness to believe that what the Governor had done was called for in the circumstances, and justified by the motives, to which it professed to be attributed, and informed the Governor that " Her Majesty's government will be prepared to sanction the extension of British sovereignty in the manner which you have detailed, when we shall be enabled to determine what are the steps which are necessary to give legal force and validity to the measures in question." With this view, Earl Grey required from the Governor further information as to facts, and a report from the law officers of the colony as to the legal validity of his measures.

The Attorney-General, on the statement submitted to him by the Governor, expressed himself as " disposed to view the colony created by the declaration of British sovereignty as a colony by *occupancy*, instead of by conquest or by cession."

This opinion was submitted to the Privy Council, who, by a minute, repeated a summary of the history of the Sovereignty, and stated that, having weighed with attention the Attorney-General's opinion, they were " unable to concur in his conclusion. We are of opinion that the Orange River Sovereignty is to be considered *as a conquest*, effected by your Majesty's arms."

Before the minute of the Privy Council had reached the Governor of the Cape colony, " some doubt having arisen in his mind as to the nature of Her Majesty's authority in the territory beyond the

Orange River,"[a] he asked the Attorney-General to reconsider the opinion, by which he considered "the colony created by the declaration of British sovereignty as a colony by occupancy," and, by his Military Secretary, laid before the Attorney a new case, "being apprehensive that you had not a full statement of the facts of the case before you when you pronounced that opinion."

"Before the emigration of British subjects into the country north of the Orange River commenced, that country *must be held to have* belonged to the native chiefs; nor was *the occupation of British subjects* in any way recognized, so as to make the Sovereignty. a British possession, *until the date of His Excellency's proclamation of 3rd February,* 1848.

"Previously to the issue of that proclamation, His Excellency had *conferred with all the native chiefs, who agreed to cede the sovereignty* of the country to him, as Her Majesty's representative, as the means of securing British protection.[b]

The Attorney-General, being set right "upon a question of fact," answers the Military Secretary,— "His Excellency's statement of what took place beyond the Orange River, previous to the issue of his proclamation of the 3rd February, 1848, *establishes*

[a] P. 73 of Parliamentary Papers, presented 19th May, 1851.
[b] Ibid.

that the native chiefs then made a *cession of the country*, now called the Sovereignty."

" The Orange River Sovereignty must therefore be deemed to be a *colony by cession*, and not, as I was disposed to think, when ignorant that the chiefs had agreed with His Excellency to cede the Sovereignty of the country to Her Majesty, *a colony by occupancy*."

" *The title by conquest* His Excellency appears, with myself, to view as one which *is inconsistent with the facts of the case, since we never, at any time, were engaged in hostilities with any native chief in that country;* and since we *could not, of course, make title by conquest*, under those rapid and successsful *military movements against rebel British subjects*, which *did not go before, but, on the contrary, followed* the proclamation of *the 3rd February*, 1848, *establishing Her Majesty's authority*."

" Title by cession, however, is quite another thing, and being of opinion that no particular form is necessary to such a cession, nor *anything but an intention to cede the sovereignty* and the country, *sufficiently expressed by chiefs, competent to make the cession*, I think it quite clear, from *His Excellency's statement*, that the Orange River Sovereignty *is a colony by cession, and subject to the legislation of the crown*."[a]

[a] P. 74 of Parliamentary Papers, presented 19th May, 1851.

This title by cession must have been rested upon one or other of three documents. The *first* of these is a paper, dated 10th March, 1846, signed with the mark of *eight chiefs*—Kok, Moshesh, Sikonyella, Moroko, Molitsani, Pieter Davids, Carolus Batje, and Thomas Taaybosch, in which, "for the purpose of endeavoring to come to a mutual and amicable settlement of certain disputes *existing between us, relative to our* land boundaries, *we hereby solicit the intercession and assistance of the British Government.*"[a]

The *second* document is an agreement, dated 25th January, 1848, between the Governor and *Adam Kok* of the Griquas alone, "*in order amicably to settle on a permanent basis the relationship between Captain Adam Kok and the emigrant British subjects,*" whereby the Governor "proposes to Captain Kok that, in lieu of the quitrents he now receives, in virtue of the treaty of the 5th February, 1846, he shall receive £200 a year, in half-yearly payments of £100, and that his people, for the lands they have let, shall receive £100 per annum, in two payments of £50 each."[b]

The third document is a paper which sets out with saying, "His Excellency the High Commissioner

[a] Application from Native Chiefs, p. 23 of Parliamentary Papers, 19th May, 1851.

[b] P. 62 of Parliamentary Papers, presented July, 1848.

and the great chief Moshesh, having met this day for the purpose of discussing the matter of the territory occupied by the British emigrants, part of the possessions of the great chief aforesaid, as well as for the purpose of considering *the affairs of Southern Africa*, north of the Orange River, generally, the great chief fully concurred in the proposition of His Excellency, that peace, harmony, and tranquillity could neither be established nor maintained without the existence of some great and paramount authority. For the purpose, therefore, of effecting this object, and, *at the same time, maintaining inviolate the hereditary rights of the chiefs, and of effectually restraining the boers within the limits* and *upon the locations they now possess*, and that magistrates might be appointed and surveyors employed to ensure the same, His Excellency proposed the proclamation of the sovereignty of the Queen of England *throughout all the territory over which Her Majesty's subjects have spread themselves*, partly by purchase, partly on toleration, partly without either. Of the expediency of this measure, in which the chiefs *previously conferred with*, namely, Moroko, Adam Kok, and various other minor chiefs, *had fully concurred*, the chief Moshesh most fully approved, and strongly expresses himself that such paramount authority was absolutely necessary, for the purpose of maintaining in strict alliance with Her Majesty of England that harmony and unanimity" (? *sic in orig.*) "which it had been his wish to preserve and his desire to effect."

If "cession" is not to be found in one of these documents, or in all three put together,—and there can be little hesitation in saying that it is to be found neither in any one of them, nor in all three together,—there is no other which has been presented to Parliament as evidence of such a title.

For the purpose of creating the relation of subject and sovereign between any of the inhabitants of this Orange River Sovereignty, (a country 50,000 square miles in extent,) and the British monarch, to whom neither by birth, nor by any of the other known modes by which allegiance is created, the natives, at least, (who are by far the greater number of the inhabitants,) owed any allegiance whatever—the proclamation of the 3rd February, 1848, of Her Majesty's sovereignty was not worth the paper it was written upon. Yet, singularly enough, the Governor who had taken upon himself to make the proclamation, felt that he had not power to govern this territory of his own creation, without an express commission to that effect. He had power in himself *to do the greater act,* but *not the lesser.*

Of the chiefs who occupied the Sovereignty,

Moshesh had become the most powerful, having no less than 80,000 men under his dominion, and had, in consequence, been able to compel other chiefs to recognize him as such ; but so soon as these chiefs were told that the Queen of Britain, whom they knew to be still more powerful than Moshesh, meant her authority to be paramount, they set Moshesh at defiance.   Not only so, but identifying the boers with the British Government, and resenting upon them the iniquity of making their territories part of Her Majesty's dominions, they no longer permitted them peacefully to occupy the lands which they had obtained by their permission.   Accordingly, a game of confusion and turmoil soon opened under this proclamation of Her Majesty's sovereignty.[a]

In September, 1849, some of Sikonyella's tribe came across the boundary of one of the magisterial districts fixed by the Governor, and carried off a

[a] Sir George Clerk says: "With regard to the native tribes, I find it most difficult to persuade myself that it was either *just* or expedient for a governor of the Cape colony, by a proclamation extending Her Majesty's sovereignty over settlers who had emigrated into these wilds from that colony, and had occupied this territory in parts, *to bring also under dominion a powerful and friendly chief*, with his numerous tribe, *who up to this day had, in formal documents, been recognized as an independent ally*, as well as other minor chiefs and tribes, who had not less abstained from every act that could have properly led to their being treated, *or even regarded*, as our vassals."—p. 25, Papers presented to Parliament, 10th April, 1854.

number of cattle. Thereupon, instead of prosecuting
these people for a trespass before the courts, which
the Governor had constituted, which would have
been the right course, if the country had really
become a British settlement, the British Resident
marched an armed force into Sikonyella's territory,
and exacted of him an *arbitrary* fine of two
hundred and fifty head of cattle, which that chief
agreed to pay. While the British Resident was
waiting for this payment, he received intelligence
that another chief, Molitsani, had made an attack
upon the missionary station of Umpakani. All missionary stations being, by the proclamation, under
the " special protection " of Her Majesty, the
Resident, without waiting to get payment from
Sikonyella of the fine imposed on him for his own
trespass,—which, by the way, has never been paid to
this day,—called upon Sikonyella *to accompany him*
and the troops on a punitory visit to Molitsani;
and he made a similar call upon Moroko, another
chief.

Molitsani was required, like Sikonyella, to pay a
fine of cattle, but, unlike Sikonyella, he refused to
pay it, and forthwith he was attacked, and three
thousand head of his cattle were seized, together with
eleven wagons of another chief, Gert Lynx, who
either was, or was supposed to be, a participator
with Molitsani in his depredations.

The British Resident returned to his residence at Bloemfontein, but he had hardly arrived there when intelligence came that Molitsani had got Moshesh to join him, and, in order to punish Moroko, for his obedience to the Resident's call upon him, and to recompense himself for the cattle which the Resident had taken from him, had fallen on Moroko's people and had carried off four thousand five hundred head of their cattle, besides a number of horses !

Moroko immediately called upon the Resident to avenge him on Moshesh and Molitsani. The Resident acknowledged the justice of this call, and required from these chiefs restitution of the cattle and horses. After some time, spent in demands on the one side, and delay on the other, Moshesh returned two thousand head of cattle, and promised the remainder, so soon as he could collect them.

Towards the end of 1850 this promise had not as yet been performed. This being represented to the Governor of the Cape colony, (Sir H. Smith,) he resolved to compel performance, and was collecting a military force with that view, when he found himself, all of a sudden, cooped up in Fort Cox, in British Kaffraria, by an irruption of the Gaika Kafirs into that district, which had its origin, probably, if the truth were known, in the suggestion of some of the chiefs whose names have been mentioned. The Governor's hands being thus too full with other matters more attractive, the Resident in the Sovereignty was left to work out the assertion of Her Majesty's "paramount authority" there in the best way he could.

Throughout the early part of 1851, the Resident received continual reports of robberies, and appeals to him for redress, without his feeling himself in a position to avenge past disorders, far less to redress these accruing ones. At length, in May, 1851, a representation by Moroko of a threatened attack from Moshesh came with such an urgent request for assistance, that the Resident marched his whole available military force to the point whence it was represented that the attack was to come. The troops remained there for a fortnight without seeing an enemy. The Resident then thought this a favorable opportunity for enforcing against Molitsani and Moshesh performance of their promise to restore the remainder of the cattle which they had taken from Moroko. With this view, he called upon the boers, the Griquas, Moroko, and Taaybosch to come to his assistance. The boers sent him 100 men, the Griquas 200, Moroko 800, and Taaybosch 70. With these forces, added to the regular troops, a march was made into Molitsani's country, and, on the 30th June, his place at Vierfoot was attacked, and there the combined forces—Her Majesty's troops and her allies—sustained a signal *defeat*, with the loss of 200 men ! !

The troops were withdrawn without an attempt to retrieve matters, as an attack on Bloemfontein, the Resident's own head-quarters, was threatened. A call was made on the boers for further assistance; but they did not respond to the call, and there not being, without them, a sufficient available force for the resumption of offensive operations, after the alarm as to Bloemfontein had proved to be unfounded, *the assertion of "the paramount authority" of the Queen of Great Britain against a petty African chief had again to slumber for a time,* until the Governor should have got the Cape colony rid of the Kafirs.

During these proceedings, the war with the Kafirs, which had begun so inauspiciously in the government of Sir H. Smith, was taken up by his successor, Sir George Cathcart, who, in the month of August, 1852, made an expedition into Kafirland, which was so successful as to allow him to withdraw his troops within the colony, and direct his attention to the Orange River Sovereignty.

It was before remarked as somewhat singular that though the Governor of the Cape colony thought himself competent of his own authority, and in the face of positive instructions to the contrary from Her Majesty's government, to make a new territory of this Orange River Sovereignty, yet he did not feel himself competent to govern the new territory, without a commission from Her Majesty. On the 3rd of February, 1848, Her Majesty's sovereignty over the Orange River territories was proclaimed by the Governor, as already observed, and forthwith the same authority established courts, for the trial of civil causes and *criminal offences*. Under this authority there have been many trials, convictions, and punishments. But it was not until the 22nd of March, 1851![a] three years afterwards, that letters patent actually passed the great seal, annexing this territory to the empire, and empowering Sir Harry Smith to administer it as Governor. On the 15th of March, 1853, Sir George Cathcart writes the minister, that the existence of these letters patent, "only recently and *accidentally* became known" to him. They had never been gazetted nor publicly proclaimed, "and till," says Sir George Cathcart, "some definite instructions be received, it is impossible to say whether that portion of Her Majesty's dominions is, at present, to be considered under the government of a high commissioner, according to the proclamation of my predecessor or under the letters patent." Three years this territory had been under the dominion of

[a] P. 80 of Parliamentary Papers, presented the 10th of April, 1854.

the Lord Harry, and now it is under the dominion of the Lord knows whom ! !

The *private* despatches of Governor Cathcart recommended the *abandonment* of the Sovereignty, and pointed out the non-publication of the letters patent as a fortunate circumstance in case that course should be adopted, and expressed his wish, that a special commissioner should be sent out to adjust the matter, so as to leave him free to devote his undivided attention to his proper government, the Cape colony; and it is due to the high honor of Sir George Cathcart to state that it was he who pointed out to the Home Government the iniquity of our presence in the Sovereignty, and recommended its abandonment.

In compliance with this wish, Sir George Clerk was sent from England in April, 1853, as a special commissioner, for effecting the abandonment of the Sovereignty, and on the 13th of February, 1854, six years after the sovereignty had been proclamed, the Secretary of State transmitted to Governor Cathcart letters patent, revoking those of the 22nd of March, 1851, whereby the Orange River Sovereignty had, on paper, been made part of Her Majesty's dominions, together with a proclamation, to be promulgated by Sir George Clerk, declaring that "upon, and from, and after such promulgation, all dominion and sovereignty of Her Majesty over the said territory, and the inhabitants thereof, shall cease and determine." As the Sovereignty, whether it be considered a settlement by occupation, by cession, or by conquest, was never, owing to the non-proclamation of the letters patent of 1851, formally annexed to the empire, it is not worth while inquiring whether it has been formally dissevered from any virtual annexation by these letters patent of 1854.

Upon a review of the whole subject, Sir George Clerk says: "The Orange River Sovereignty is a vast territory, possessing nothing that can sanction its being permanently added to a frontier already inconveniently extended. It secures no genuine interests, — it is recommended by no *prudent* or justifiable motive,—it answers no really beneficial purpose,—it imparts no strength to the British government, no credit to its character, no lustre to the crown. To remain here, therefore, to superintend or to countenance this extension of British dominion, or take part in any administrative measures for the furtherance of so unessential an object, would, I conceive, be tantamount to my encouraging a serious evil, and *participating in one of the most signal fallacies* which has ever come under my notice, in the course of nearly thirty years devoted to the public service."

This expression of a determination to have nothing further to do with our proclamation of sovereignty over the Orange River territory, and its consequences, was approved by the government, which, acting on Sir G. Clerk's information, carried out the abandonment, by publishing the proclamation before mentioned, and by handing over, through Sir George Clerk, the government of the boers to representatives appointed by themselves provisionally.[a]

This ends the account of the second instance, (in

---

[a] The text was written in 1854. Since the abandonment of Her Majesty's sovereignty, Moshesh has complained of land encroachments by the boers of the Free State, and these boers have complained of constant cattle depredations by Kafirs, either of Moshesh's tribe or of tribes in alliance with or in dependence upon him. No adjustment of these mutual complaints having been effected, the boers resolved to punish the alleged depredations by waging war on Moshesh. That wise and wily chief allowed them to come to the mountain on which he resides, without opposition, while he either allowed or sent predatory parties into the Free State, who fired the houses and carried off the cattle of the boers. When the boers got a view of Moshesh's defences, they felt themselves powerless to attack it, and on this account, and by reason of the condition which they learnt their own country had fallen into, in their absence, were only too glad to disband and each to hasten to his own homestead. The result has been that the Free State, terrified by the conviction of the power of Moshesh which they have now gained, and at the consequences of having provoked his wrath, have entreated the mediation of the Governor of the Cape colony (Sir G. Grey), and Moshesh, having always been wise enough to see the prudence of keeping well with the representative of our government, has agreed to the mediation ; and while these lines are being written, Sir G. Grey is engaged in endeavoring to adjust matters amicably between the Free State and Moshesh.

the course of which a third instance, that of Natal, has also been given,) of our making title to a settlement by occupation; and few will be of opinion that our connection with the Orange River territory (now called the "Free State") was ever, from its inception to its conclusion, honorable to such a nation as Great Britain, or, otherwise than disreputable, in every sense of the term. By our misrule of the colony of the Cape of Good Hope, an exodus of substantial, respectable farmers took place, which—for extent of numbers, respectability of individuals, and amount of self-imposed suffering, whatever difference there may be in the causes of either step—has no better analogy than what occurred when the Church of Scotland was rent in twain some years ago. The present Recorder of Natal,[a] in a published history of this exodus from the colony, laments it in these terms: "No one will deny that any causes which could have led to the expatriation, not of single individuals merely, but of entire clans, at the head of which such names appear as those of Retief, Uys, and Maritz, Potgieter, Landeman, Du Plessis, Zeitsman, Boshof, and Otto, must ever be viewed as producing a serious national calamity; although, in the course of years, some such

[a] This was written in 1854; the Recorder, (Mr. Cloete,) is now one of the Judges of the Supreme Court of the Cape of Good Hope.

families may be replaced, yet the words of the sweet descriptive poet will, in this case, be found fully verified :

> ' Princes and lords may flourish and may fade,
> A breath may make them, as a breath has made;
> But a bold peasantry, their country's pride,
> When once destroyed, can never be supplied.'

" I was myself personally known to many of these earliest emigrants from the colony, and counted among them *some of my oldest and best clients.*"[a]

These persons go forth in sorrow to seek a resting-place free from real or imaginary harassment of governors. They are pursued to Natal and forced back into the Orange River territory, and there they are overtaken, under the false pretence of protecting the natives from their oppression ; the true one being to prevent any more emigrants escaping from the colony,[b] to its great detriment, in the loss of men and money ; and in order, against all law, or justice, or humanity, to be able to rivet more closely the fetters of British government on these escaped colonists, the independence of the natives is filched from them by Her Majesty's representative.

It would be monstrous to accuse our ministers of having seen these matters as they are now presented

---

[a] Lecture by the Hon. Henry Cloete, Recorder of Natal, who had been a barrister at the Cape bar before being raised to the bench.

[b] Vide p. 65, of Parliamentary Papers, presented February, 1848.

to view, stripped of all the false glosses with which they were presented to them at the time. No one can suppose that any minister, looking at each step in these transactions as they occurred, with reference to its antecedents, his mind undistracted by the affairs of all our other numerous colonies, would have sanctioned such illegality, such folly, and such iniquity.

These instances of what has, within comparatively few years, been done, under the title of possession by occupancy, must produce very grave reflections in the mind of every thinking man. In the case of Port Phillip, British subjects pressed the government to take actual possession of a district which lay within what, as yet, the government had only imaginary possession of; the government refused to do so, and prohibited individuals from doing it on their own account. But, so soon as the settlement had been effected and had proved itself to be valuable, then the government stepped in, and made that actual which had hitherto been merely nominal, by covering the settlement with the aegis of its administration. The settlers made no objection to this, but if they had been so minded, there is nothing in the law of nature, or of nations, which could have prevented them from asserting against the British government the same right of self-government, which the British government has, by its commissioner, recognised to be in the settlers within "the Sovereignty" in Africa. Vattel says, Lib. I, cap. 18, "Si plusieurs familles libres repandues dans un païs indépendant viennent a s'unir pour former une nation un état elles occupent ensemble l'empire sur tout le païs qu'elles habitent;" and in the same place, "Tous les hommes ont un droit égal aux choses qui ne sont point encore tombées dans la propriété de quelqu'un et ces choses là appartiennent au premier occupant."

In the case of Natal and of "the Sovereignty," British governors—of their own authority, and in the very teeth of express instructions to the contrary —took the initiative. They seized actual possession of a country, which had hitherto been possessed by natives and by emigrant boers, by declaring upon paper that it was in future to be considered part of the British territory, and by marching troops forward in order to maintain this declaration against such as should presume to dispute it. But it is difficult to conceive what right these governors had to do so or on what ground the attack of these boers by military can be justified.

The only imaginable ground on which the pursuit and slaughter of British subjects in Natal and at Boomplaats, in the Sovereignty, can be justified, is that they were found doing that which the government had winked at at Port Phillip and afterwards taken advantage of, viz., in the pursuit of establishing themselves beyond the colony, in a district over which the government assumed to itself the power of preventing them from settling, by virtue of some title by imaginary occupation. But if what has been before observed, in regard to the title of possession by fictitious occupation, be correct, there is nothing in the law of nature or of nations, which could have prevented these much-injured boers from settling in the place in which they were overtaken, or from resisting to the death the attempt to prevent them.

In fact, the title of possession by virtue of any occupation,[a] short of actual occupation, not of what is strictly sufficient for the support of the original settlers, but of what is sufficient for the support of them and of such as may reasonably be expected, within a reasonable time, to be added to their numbers, by birth and new arrivals, is not founded upon law, human or divine, however much it may have the sanction of example in the conduct of modern nations. It is a title open every day to be questioned by other nations, strong enough and sufficiently interested to do so.

Neither does the notion that a government may prevent such of its subjects as, through their own private motives, may have taken actual, not symbolical, possession of an unoccupied country, from retaining

---

[a] Puffendorf iv, cap. 6, sects. 3 and 8.

that possession, or may adject to the retention of possession the condition that the possession shall be held only under its authority, seem to be rested on any sounder foundation.

Lord Mansfield, in Campbell v. Hall, said *obiter*, that " all colonies have been established by grants from the crown," and that " he wished it to be understood no colony can be settled without authority from the crown." Lord Mansfield must have meant to use here the words, " All *British* colonies," and " no *British* colony," and to intimate that, before British subjects, who have settled in any foreign country, can claim for that country the administration of English laws, for the protection of life and property against civil broils within it, or the assistance of the British army or navy for protection against outward invasion, the settlement must either have been formed under the authority of the crown, originally, or have had that authority accorded to it, subsequently. In this sense, it may justly be said that no colony can be settled without authority from the crown ; and it is possible to conceive cases in which settlers, who had not procured the ægis of their own government, or of some other recognized government, to be thrown around them, might be treated as pirates by the nations of the earth. In this view, it is but prudent for a body of settlers to obtain the authority of their original government ;

and history shows that settlers have generally followed that course.

It is also true that there is no means by which the authority of the crown can be made to extend over a settlement without holding the soil of the settlement to be in the crown, so as to lay the foundation of individual titles to land, and, in this sense, it may be true, that " all colonies have been established by grants from the crown," *i. e.*, the lands in all the colonies have been granted out by the crown.

But, if the language of Lord Mansfield was intended to assert, *as a fact*, that all colonies have been established by actual prior grants from the crown, or to lay down *as law* that no body of Englishmen can go and establish themselves in an undiscovered country, without having previously obtained the authority of the crown, the passage seems to be open to very great question. For, first, as to the assertion of fact, it is undoubted, whatever may have been the case in regard to some of the North American colonies, that all our modern colonies have been formed by bodies of British subjects going to new and uninhabited countries and establishing themselves there, for the purposes of trade and agriculture, without any previous authority. In that sense, colonies have been established without any grant from the crown. Of this,

Newfoundland is one instance,[a] and Port Phillip, now Victoria, is another, and not the least memorable, instance.[b] But it is equally true that, after individuals had, for their own purposes, and at their own expense, established themselves in a new country, and had begun to prosper in it, then the government of Great Britain, either of its own accord, or at the solicitation of the settlers, has stepped in to give them a form of government, and the obvious advantage of this boon has induced the settlers, either to invite the government's interference, or to refrain from opposing that interference when spontaneously offered; and, with the exception of Pitcairn's Island, there is perhaps no place where a body of settlers has located itself for any length of time, without the government having, in one of those ways, thrown its protection over them. After it has done so, the government, in regulating the internal economy of the colony, has acted on the fiction and principle of law, that all land was originally in the crown, and must be held mediately or immediately of it.

With regard to the assertion in law, on the other hand, that "no colony can be settled without authority from the crown," if the words are used to express that a body of individuals cannot settle down for their own advantage, and upon their own

[a] Vide infra.   [b] Vide supra, p. 101.

risk and responsibility, in a new country, without having the previous authority of the crown, there does not seem to be ground, either on principle or on authority, for such a proposition. A British subject may, without leave of the crown, go to Japan and establish himself there, for the purpose of trade or agriculture, or for any purpose whatsoever. There is no law, international or municipal, which says that the same individual may not, from the same motives, establish himself on the shores of Australia or New Zealand. It is said in a case in *Peer Williams*, that "the natural-born subject of one prince cannot, by any act of his own,—no, not by swearing to another,—put off or discharge his natural allegiance to the former; for this natural allegiance was intrinsic and primitive, and antecedent to the other, and cannot be divested, without the concurrent act of that prince to whom it was first due." And, in *Foster*, p. 184, it is said, "The well-known maxim, which the writers upon our law have adopted and applied to this case, *nemo potest exuere patriam*, comprehendeth the whole doctrine of natural allegiance." In another passage, the same learned judge carries the doctrine of allegiance so far as to say that, "if an alien, seeking the protection of the crown, and having a family and effects here, should, during a war with his native country, go thither and adhere to the king's enemies, for purposes of hostility, he may be dealt with as a traitor."

These doctrines were uttered in the case of M'Donald, a native of Great Britain, who had been educated from early infancy in France, had spent his manhood there in the enjoyment of a profitable office, had latterly accepted a commission in the French army; and had ultimately been taken in arms, acting under that commission against the king of Great Britain. In these circumstances, M'Donald was convicted of high treason, and righteously,—for, whatever doubt may suggest itself in regard to the soundness of the second doctrine, which has just been quoted, there cannot be any as to the accuracy of the first assertion, that a natural-born subject " *non potest exuere patriam*," for, if he might, there would soon be an end of nationality, and, with it, of all civilized society.

But, if the second dictum be also sound, then M'Donald owed allegiance to the French monarch, as well as to the English monarch. Under his English allegiance, he was bound to obey the call of the English monarch, in case of a French invasion, and to fight against the French; and, under his French allegiance, he was bound to refrain from so fighting. He might thus be in a position in which he could not escape from high treason to the one sovereign or to the other. Nevertheless, the one doctrine may be as sound as the other. It may be as true, in international law, that an alien, having a family and effects in a foreign country, and enjoying the protection of the constituted authorities of its government, cannot take up arms against that country, even in the cause of his own natural sovereign, as it undoubtedly is, that a natural-born subject cannot throw off his natural allegiance. The apparently unreasonable position in which the alien is found is the fruit of his own act, and his individual interests must yield to those of society at large.

But in neither of these dicta is it said, or hinted, that the native-born subject of any country may not, at his pleasure, remove to a newly-established country, not having as yet any form of government, doing so for the purposes of trade or of agriculture, or even of pleasure, and may not there remain, until the day of his death, without doing thereby anything which his sovereign can either complain of or punish. The second dictum of *Foster*, on the contrary, sanctions the assertion that a natural-born subject of one country may remove to and settle in another country, having already an established government, and there raise a family and purchase and hold effects, so much so that he will contract a new and limited allegiance to the sovereign of this his adopted country, to the extent that he may not, even in the service of his natural sovereign, bear arms against his adopted sovereign; so that, if the question hinged upon this alone, there would be the authority of M'Donald's case for saying that a subject may, without question, remove to a new country, and there remain till his death.

Does the maxim in the other dictum, " *nemo potest exuere patriam,*" then, imply a restraint upon a subject against his living where he chooses. " Patria" is not used here to signify the soil or geographical limits of a country, but to signify the society inhabiting these limits, with all its degrees of constituted authority, from the sovereign downwards; and the sense of the maxim, which Sir Michael Foster says " comprehendeth the whole doctrine of natural allegiance," is that no one can disown the social community in which he was born; revert to his natural rights, as an independent man; and assert these rights in defiance of, or in hostility to, that community. However far he may remove from his native country, he remains a subject of its government, bound to recognize its authorities, and to obey its laws. Now, neither the authority nor the laws of a government have force *extra territorium,* even over its own subjects, except in this matter of allegiance, and then only to the effect of restraining the subject from doing anything *extra territorium,* which may have for its end the overturning of the government.

Allegiance varies, therefore, according to the locality of the individual by whom it is due. The allegiance due by a natural-born subject to the sovereign of the country in which he was born, while living within the local limits of that country, is not the same, either in kind or in degree, as is the allegiance due by the same individual, while residing in a foreign country, having either a government of its own, or being as yet without any such authority. In the country of his birth, allegiance is due by the subject, in the utmost extent to which that term can be used; but, beyond the boundaries of that country, the allegiance due is different, both in kind and in degree. While, as to personal locality, within the kingdom of his birth, a subject is bound to obey all its laws, that is, to submit to all those restraints which these laws have put upon his enjoyment of life, after that fashion which may be most congenial to his temperament, and which, if he were free and independent of any society, there would be nothing to restrain but his inward sense of responsibility to his Maker. He may not do anything to alter or annul these laws, except he proceed, in attempting to do so, according to the mode allowed by the constitution of his country, however much and however oppressively these laws may act in restraint of his natural rights. He is, by the accident, no doubt, of his birth, and without the exercise of any act of volition on his part, a member of a society called a monarchy or a republic, as it may happen, and he must, as a condition necessary to the very existence of that society, conform and submit to all the artificial rules it may have established.

When the subject of any kingdom lawfully goes without the boundary of that kingdom, he cannot, as a condition equally necessary to the existence of the kingdom, do anything which, though in its inception begun beyond the territory, will, in its perfection, take effect within the territory to overturn its laws or its authority. In this respect, and in this respect alone, is a native-born subject, being beyond the territory of his native government, bound by the laws of that government, be it monarchical or republican, for in this respect, and in this respect alone, are the laws of any kingdom binding *extra territorium,* and in this sense only can it be said, *"nemo potest exuere patriam."* As a right correlative to this obligation, the subject is entitled, wherever he may happen to be, to claim the protection of the authorities of his native government against all other external authorities, whensoever that protection can be efficiently extended to him ; but he may forego this right if he choose.

With this qualification, a natural-born subject of any government, regal or republican, so soon as he goes without the territory of that government,

assumes all the rights which a man born upon the
earth, ere any governments had been established,
would naturally have, so long as he does not go
within the territory of any other government, and so
bring himself into the condition of obedience, which
every individual, whether native or stranger, must
pay to the authorities of the country in which he
may happen to be for the time. If the natural-born
subject of any government, after leaving the territory
of that government, can find a country which, as
yet, has been unoccupied by man, he may establish himself, as free for the enjoyment of all its
advantages of soil or climate as Adam was on
the first morning he found himself in Eden. But,
if other individuals come after him to this newly-
occupied country, whether from the same territory
that he left, or from other territories, they are,
equally with him, entitled to the enjoyment of
its advantages, so long as these advantages are
equal to the maintenance of all; the first-comers
having the prior right, whenever the sufficiency is
in doubt.

If a new country may be thus occupied by
individual settlers, it may, equally well, be occupied
by settlers coming in *collective bodies*. The rights
of each individual settler, coming as a member of
a collective body of settlers, are as great and as
free and independent as are the rights of one

individual coming by himself, while as yet the collective body of settlers has not adopted any body of laws, or imposed upon its community those restrictions upon natural right, which have always been found necessary for the enjoyment of peace and comfort, where men have come together in any number.

It is very true that men have generally gone in collective bodies, in order to form new settlements, and that these bodies have generally been composed, in great part, of the subjects of one and the same existing government. Generally, bodies of Spaniards, or of Portuguese, or of Englishmen, or of Dutchmen, have gone to form settlements in new countries; and it is equally true that where these settlements have not been made by the orders, and at the expense and risk, of an already existing government, but by private subjects of their own accord, and at their own risk and expense, these individuals have, for obvious reasons, found it more convenient to take advantage of the already constituted authority of the existing home government, and either voluntarily to invite its protection or to submit to its authority when asserted.

It is no doubt true, also, that any government may, like any individual, seize upon an unoccupied portion of the earth as its own, against every other government and against all mankind, whether its own subjects or subjects of other governments. But it cannot, like an individual, do so *as a matter of right.* If the earth should ever become so densely inhabited as that the produce of its whole surface would be necessary for the maintenance of its inhabitants, each individual would, as a matter of right and without respect to nationality, be entitled to that aliquot portion of the earth's surface, the product of which was necessary for his own individual maintenance. It is beyond the range of probability that such a state of things will ever occur, but, if it should occur, the necessities of existence would make it necessary to resort to this resolution of rights into their primitive element. Every individual man is a grantee under that original gift, " Be fruitful and multiply and replenish the earth, and subdue it. Behold, I have given you every herb, bearing seed, which is upon the face of all the earth, and every tree in the which is the fruit of a tree yielding seed ; to you it shall be for meat."

While necessity has not yet compelled the allotment to each individual of any particular portion of the surface of the earth, as that which is to raise " the meat " necessary for his existence, an individual may take possession of that portion which he, for any reason, affects; provided no other individual have previously exercised the same right of election. His right is as good as that of any other who may come after him. But this cannot be said of the *government* of any community, inhabiting a fixed portion of the earth's surface. It cannot be said that those who wield the government of any portion of the earth's surface can, *as a natural right*, seize any other portion of the earth's surface, and extend their authority over it, while the community over which they preside retains the ancient portion. A government has no *natural* right, nor even a natural existence; it is the mere creature of artificial life, and has no rights but what are purely conventional and fluctuating according to the artificial and arbitrary necessities of social life.

If the inhabitants of any portion of the earth, living under a particular form of government, emigrate from that territory, either through necessity created by its over-population, or from the gratuitous and innocent love of change, they may do so, if they please, under the authority and protection of their native government: that is, conscious of the necessity for constituted authority, in order to ensure peace and safety, when many men are living together, they may choose, while leaving their native country, to transport its authority with themselves to their new place of abode, instead of waiting till they get there, and then going through all the turmoil and difficulty of constructing a society with constituted authorities *ab ovo;* provided, always, the government of their native country will consent to follow them. But, if they do so, it is entirely of their own free will and accord ; as their exodus is voluntary, so is their subjection to this authority, which they carry with them—as their government has no right to thrust them forth from its territory, so has it no right to thrust upon them its authority, when they are voluntarily beyond that territory. The authority of any government, whatever form it may have assumed, is, in short, purely territorial.

If, therefore, any of the subjects of a government, emigrating from its territory to a country as yet unsettled, choose to repudiate the authority of that government over the new country, and to set up one for themselves, there seems to be nothing in principle which can prevent them from so doing. They do not thereby " divest " themselves of their natural allegiance, any more than did M'Donald[a] divest himself of his natural allegiance to the king of England by going within the country of France, and there incurring a new allegiance to the king of that country. All that they do is to create for themselves, as he did for himself, a new allegiance, which is subordinate to that which they owe to their native country. All the allegiance which continues to be due by the natives of a territory to the government of that territory, after they have gone

[a] Supra, p. 136.

without the territory, will continue to be due by these settlers. But it is no part of that allegiance that, after going without the territory, they should not live where they please and under such form of government as they prefer.

Richard II required the authority of a statute to prevent lords, great men, and notable merchants going out of the kingdom ;[a] and Henry VIII, despot as he was, had to resort to the same authority, in order to restrain persons from trading to certain countries.[b] No doubt the crown might, by the great or the privy seal, recall British subjects from abroad ;[c] but that seems to have been a feudal procedure, founded on the services due by the crown vassals to the sovereign, for there is no instance, it is believed, of the issue of writs under either seal, directed to any but landholders, and the only penalty for disobedience to the writ was forfeiture of the recusant's land until his return. As to the writ *ne exeat regno*, whatever may have been its original use, it is now merely a judicial writ to prevent the escape of a debtor from his creditors ; and, without questioning the power of the crown to protect the kingdom by an embargo, when it is threatened from without, it seems certain that, now-a-days at least, at common law every man is free to leave the kingdom, for purposes of trade or

[a] Vide 5 Rich. II, cap. 5—*repealed.*

[b] Vide 26 Henry VIII, cap. 10.   [c] 3 Coke inst., 180.

travel, and to remain abroad so long as he may choose.

Some of the powers of the earth have taken upon themselves to go beyond the boundaries of their jurisdiction, and to seize upon other portions of the earth, and place them within their jurisdiction. But it is equally indisputable that the other powers of the earth have not sanctioned this proceeding by their acquiescence, unless when there was *actual occupation* to justify it. Whenever it has suited their convenience, they have treated symbolical occupation, by planting a flagstaff and the like contrivances, as mere empty ceremonies; and where there has been a dispute, it has always been settled by the powers of Might, and not by the rules of any supposed right.

It is equally true that many governments have asserted their right to rule settlements, which have been formed by their own subjects, as if the territory of these settlements became, *ex necessitate* of the transport to them of the natural bodies of these subjects, a part of, or an adjunct to, their original territory. This, as before observed, has sometimes been invited, and in other instances has been merely acquiesced in, by the settlers; but, where not invited, it seems to have been an assertion of a right which, for the reasons before given, had no existence.

It is equally true that some governments, our own in particular, have selected parts of the earth on which they have established settlements for the purpose of transporting thither the criminal convicts of their own population. So far as the portions thus selected have had any proportion to the probable increase of the settlers, there was nothing of which any other government, or any individuals, could complain. The government has, for its own municipal reasons, compelled these convicts to leave their native country, and abide, for a time at least, upon another portion of the earth selected for them. In exercising this social power, it has not trespassed upon the natural rights of any, except of those subject to this power, and whom it might have punished in any other way. And the exercise of this power being more or less necessary to the healthy existence of the ancient societies of settled countries, the case is within the category of circumstances which the comity of nations has recognized as deserving of acquiescence and non-interference. These penal settlements, as they have been called, though in some respects an anomaly, so far as they are claimed to be the territory of the governments by whom they have been formed, have hitherto been respected as such by other governments. They are part of the police of the general world, whether the word police be used in its original or in its modern signification; and as such they have hitherto been untouched and unquestioned, and upon this ground they seem as unquestionable as most of the other acts resulting from the artificial rules of international law.

It has been assumed, whether correctly or erroneously matters little at present, that if the criminal portion of the inhabitants of a densely-inhabited country were to be kept pent up within the country, this would occasion, or at least threaten, the dissolution of society in such a country; and that deportation of the criminals is the proper remedy for this. As no existing society could be dissolved without violently affecting and endangering the existence of others, it is the common interest of all nations to prevent such a catastrophe. In this view, probably, these penal settlements have hitherto been respected as part of the territory of the governments by whom they have been formed, pretty much as acquisitions of old-settled portions of the earth by conquest have, for reasons of international police, and against all natural right, been recognized as part of the territory of the conquering power.

If, then, no government, whatever be its form, whether monarchical or republican, has any right to extend its authority over another portion of the earth than that over which its authority has been constituted, when the persons inhabiting that new portion have gone there and settled themselves, of their own free will and accord, it is still more unquestionable that the sovereign of Great Britain, of all sovereigns of the earth, cannot do so, possessing as he does only a limited accountable authority, even over the British dominions.

With these observations upon the general right of any nation, or body of individuals, to take possession of an unoccupied portion of the earth's surface, or to establish colonies, and upon the inconsistency of our conduct, in the way in which we have sanctioned or prohibited new settlements by British subjects, let us consider, next, the constitutional power of Britain to administer foreign settlements, however acquired.

CHAPTER VII.

PASSING from the mode in which settlements or
colonies may be acquired, let us consider how they
are to be held or governed, in consistency with those
ruling principles of the British constitution which
distinguish the British monarchy from all others.
In doing this, let us first consider if, in this respect,
the sovereign alone can legislate for British colonies,
whether they be acquired by conquest, or by cession,
or by voluntary settlement.

SECTION I.—POWER TO RULE POSSESSIONS ACQUIRED BY CONQUEST.

With regard to colonies acquired by conquest or
by cession, if a district of country or an island
have been either taken by force of arms from the
possessors, or have been voluntarily ceded, the
monarch for the time, in exercise of the rights of
sovereignty which are in theory recognized to be,
as fully and with as little limitation, in the King
of Great Britain as they are in the Autocrat of all
the Russias, may, in the case of forcible conquest,

impose such terms upon the conquered inhabitants as he pleases, and in the case of cession, he may make such terms with the ceding power as he pleases. In neither instance is there, either in the theory or in the practice of the British constitution, any check, at this stage of the proceeding, upon the exercise of the most despotic and tyrannical power, which the terror of the sovereign's arms may compel submission to.

The sovereign of Great Britain, as the depositary of the executive power of the empire, must necessarily, for the discharge of that power with efficiency and with the dignity due to the empire, be unlimited as to the mode of its exercise in all external relations. It would be both inconvenient and impracticable if the sovereign, before he could accept a capitulation or a cession of territory, were obliged to refer the terms to the parliament of Great Britain, however near the place about to capitulate or to be ceded might be geographically to London. Nay, even if time and space, which railway and electricity have gone far to annihilate, did not present any difficulty, it would still be impracticable as well as inconvenient if the sovereign were obliged, from time to time, to make public beforehand the advantages he meant to ask and the concessions he meant to make, while conducting, through his officers, the terms of a capitulation or a cession of territory.

In these instances, therefore, of capitulation and cession, as in the instance of treaties, and for the same reasons, the sovereign is unfettered and uncontrolled in the exercise of the executive power, except in so far as the sovereign and the officers through whom he acts have before their eyes the fear of parliament, to which they must render an account afterwards of the most minute article of every capitulation or cession, and of the reasons which induced it.

The parliament may not repudiate the terms of a capitulation or cession, any more than it may repudiate the terms of a treaty made by the sovereign. It cannot, like the Roman senate in the second Samnite war and in other instances, repudiate what the executive has concluded, when that is considered to be disadvantageous or dishonorable to the empire ; neither can the parliament punish the monarch in his person for the injury done to the state, but it may punish, with death even, the officers of the monarch who, by yielding to him, have put in force orders which, without their concurrence, could not have been executed; and it may punish even the sovereign himself, in an indirect manner, by withholding from him the supplies of money, necessary for the continuance of his government, until the matter of complaint shall have been repaired, so far as that is possible to be done in the circumstances.

In effect, therefore, it is only in theory that the monarch of Britain is absolute as to the terms upon which he may permit a capitulation to his troops, or accept a cession of territory from an enemy. Practically, the conditions—both those that are to take effect immediately, and those which are to continue in operation for a period of time—are always made with reference to those principles alone which are recognized by the British constitution, and which are sure to be appealed to in the scrutiny which each and every member of the legislature is entitled to make of them.

Vattel, speaking of conquests, says: "It is asked to whom the conquest belongs, to the prince who made it, or to the state? This question ought never to have been heard of. Can the sovereign act, as such, for any other end than the good of the state? Whose are the forces employed in the war? Even if he had made the conquest at his own expense, out of his own revenue, or his patrimonial estates, does not he make use of his subjects' arms? Is it not their blood that is shed? Is it not for the cause of the state and of the nation that he takes arms? Therefore, all the rights proceeding from it appertain to the nation."

In Calvin's case, in Coke's reports, it was resolved that, "If a king come to a kingdom by conquest, he may, at his pleasure, alter and change the laws of that kingdom, but, until he doth make an alteration, the ancient laws of that kingdom remain ;" and, " also, If a king hath a kingdom by conquest, as King Henry II had Ireland after King John had given to them, being under his obedience and subjection, the laws of England for the government of their native country, no succeeding king could alter the same without parliament."

As the power of the sovereign over a conquest was not the question before the court in Calvin's case, these resolutions are mere *obiter dicta*, which have no weight, further than they are justified by reason and principle. Testing them in this way, however, they are of great value. The first affirms the doctrine, which has been contended for in these pages, that the sovereign, *in the first settlement of a conquest*, is absolute in his exercise, for that purpose, of the executive power of the state. And the second resolution affirms the other doctrine, which will presently be ventilated, that, for regulating *the permanent* laws of a conquest, or directing its legislation, parliament is the sole authority.

It never could have been the meaning of the judges in Calvin's case to affirm, by the first resolution, that the king might, by his own authority, rule a conquest to all eternity, by either continuing its ancient laws, or by altering or changing them, so long as that alteration or that change did not import the giving of the laws of England, in which case alone the parliament would have a right to interfere. Such a construction would amount to this, that a conquest, though made for the cause of the state, at the expense of the state, and with the blood of the subjects, does, nevertheless, in contradiction of Vattel, belong, not to the state, but to the sovereign individually. If that were the true construction of the first resolution, it would make the second a mere puerility—it would then amount only to this, that the sovereign cannot alter the laws of England without the assent of parliament, a position which is too trite in itself to have required any judicial resolution for its establishment.

The second resolution cannot be used to show that, by the gift of the laws of England, and by that gift alone, and not until that gift, a conquest becomes part of the empire. There is nothing in the mere gift of a body of laws, which infers any transfer of sovereignty. If the king, prior to the gift of the laws of England, might rule a conquest "at his pleasure," there is nothing in the nature of such a gift which should give the parliament of Great Britain any right to prevent the king altering the laws of England in this new territory, so far as they affect it, whensoever it should be his "pleasure," or which should give the parliament of Britain any power to control him in this respect.

If the nature of the constitution of England be, that the king cannot, in conformity with it, legislate "at his pleasure" and *per se*, but must share his authority with *a* parliament, his gift of the laws of England to a conquered country may oblige him, at the instance of the inhabitants of that country, to form a parliament within the conquest, and restrain him from changing these laws, or revoking the gift of them, without the consent of that parliament. But what is there in the gift of the laws of England to a conquered country—say France as it was conquered by Henry V—which should give the parliament of England any right to interfere with a change of the laws of England as applied to France? None whatever, unless France became, by the fact of the conquest, part of the realm of England, without regard to what laws might have been given to it at the moment of the completion of its conquest.

There can be no doubt—upon the authority of reason and common sense, as these are reduced into terms by the passage which has been quoted from Vattel—that a country conquered by the power of Great Britain, under the direction of its sovereign, cannot belong to the sovereign *personally*, but ought to become, *ipso facto* of the conquest, part of the empire, if the constitution of the empire will admit of this, *quod est adhuc demonstrandum;* and what the laws are, under which it is to be governed, as such part of the empire, should be a question to be determined in subserviency to and in harmony with those rules and principles, which regulate the government of the empire at large.

If a conquered country become then, *ipso facto* of the conquest, part of the empire, is it consonant to the principles of the British constitution that the sovereign should make laws for *any part* of the empire "at his pleasure," as would be the case, if the true meaning of the first resolution in Calvin's case be that the king may, to all eternity, and "at his pleasure alter and change the laws" of a conquered country, so long as he does not give it the laws of England? The consequence of such a doctrine might be very perilous to the liberties of Britain. For some centuries past the acquisitions of Britain have been at a distance from the island, but suppose that, in the dispensations of Providence, the sovereign of Britain should again conquer France with British blood and treasure, and, after having done so, should rule France, "at his pleasure," by laws of his own framing, which in their operation should be so mild and equitable as to reconcile the French to his sway, though a foreigner ; and suppose, further, that all this should be done by a designing sovereign, as a means to the end of overturning the constitution of Great Britain, in what a predicament would the liberties of Britain be, under the sovereign conspiring against them, with all the power and wealth of France at his command!

This is an extravagant case to suppose, but it is within the range of possibility, and therefore may well be used as a test of the doctrine of absolute power in the sovereign of Britain to legislate for a conquest "at his pleasure." But, if a conquered country become part of the British empire, what act of parliament or other authority is there for saying that the life, or liberty, or property of any subject of that empire is at the arbitrary disposition of the sovereign? There is none whatever, except this first extrajudicial and *obiter* resolution in Calvin's case, that the king may " alter and change " the laws of a conquered country " at his pleasure," and except that resolution be read to mean that he may do so, not only when *first* putting the conquest under a form of government, *but for ever after;* and yet, if this doctrine be sound, the life, liberty, and estate of any British-born subject, be he the highest peer of the realm or the lowest commoner, may be at the arbitrary disposition of the sovereign, should the individual allow himself to wander into any British colony, originally acquired by conquest, so long as, according to the second resolution in Calvin's case, the sovereign shall not have made the colony a gift of the laws of England.

In the case of Campbell *v.* Hall, it was laid

down, and incontrovertibly too, that "the law and legislation of every dominion equally affects all persons and property within the limits thereof, and is the true rule for the decision of all questions which arise. Whoever purchases, sues, or lives there, puts himself under the laws of the place and in the situation of its inhabitants. An Englishman, in Minorca,[a] or the Isle of Man, or the Plantations, has no right distinct from the natives, while he continues there."

This is sound doctrine, without the necessity of any argument to prove it so, as we have not yet adopted the distinction of Rome between her own citizens and the rest of the world. If, then, the sovereign might, "at his pleasure, alter and change" the law of Minorca, or of any other colony acquired by conquest, not only at the first arrangement of the colony after its conquest, but in all time to come, as the first resolution in Calvin's case is suggested to mean, and if an Englishman in Minorca "has no right distinct from the natives while he continues there," as Campbell v. Hall establishes, then any British-born Englishman, from the moment he puts his foot within the conquered territory, would be living under laws which might be "altered and changed" from time to time by the sovereign, "at his pleasure," and which, of course, might be so

---

[a] Minorca was at that time an English settlement.

" altered and changed " as to bring this Englishman's
life, liberty, or property within the arbitrary disposition of the sovereign !. Rather a startling doctrine,
certainly, though it be an inevitable conclusion from
the resolution in Calvin's case, if that resolution must
be read in the way suggested.

So startling a consequence is sufficient to show
that the true reading of that resolution is, that as
every territory cannot, for a day, be without some law
or other, unless, at the risk of anarchy and confusion,
the monarch, at the time of completing the conquest,
but not after, as the depositary of the executive
power of Great Britain, who, in all transactions
external to the existing empire, is absolute and
uncontrolled in the discharge of his functions, may
either continue the previously existing laws of the
conquered territory, or give it such new ones as in
his wisdom may seem to be required. But that,
whether he continue the old laws or give new ones,
the arrangement is, in either case, subject to the
control of the imperial parliament, either to be
sanctioned by it, or to be altered by it, in whole
or in part.

Nay, more, although the sovereign may give new
laws to a conquered territory, at the first settlement
of it after the conquest, yet even this he must do
upon principles, recognizing the supremacy of the
imperial legislature. In Campbell v. Hall, Lord

Mansfield said, " If the king has power," (and when I say the king, I mean in this case to be understood without concurrence of parliament,) " to make new laws for a conquered country, *this being a power subordinate to his own, as part of the supreme legislature in parliament, he can make none which are contrary to fundamental principles;* none excepting from the laws of trade, or authority of parliament, or giving privileges exclusive of his other subjects."

In Fabrigas *v.* Mostyn,[a] this doctrine had been acted upon the year before it was thus laid down. Campbell *v.* Hall was decided in 1774, in the Queen's Bench, and Fabrigas *v.* Mostyn in 1773, in the Common Pleas.

In Fabrigas *v.* Mostyn, which arose out of a transaction that occurred in the island of Minorca, (the recollection of which, no doubt, suggested to Lord Mansfield the illustration of Minorca which he gave in Campbell *v.* Hall,) the governor of that island was sued, in the Queen's Bench, in London, for damages by reason of his having first imprisoned and then banished from the island a native, who had been born after its acquisition by conquest, without having given him the benefit of any form of trial. The defendant formally justified what he had done, by alleging that the plaintiff had endeavored to create

[a] Howell's St. Trials, vol. xx, p. 82.

a mutiny among the inhabitants of Minorca, where-
upon he, as governor, was obliged to seize the
plaintiff, to confine him six days in prison, and then
to banish him to Carthagena, "*as it was lawful for
him to do.*" No lawyer would have been silly
enough to allege that such outrageous treatment
was "lawful," according to the law or constitution
of England; any London juryman could have de-
tected such an attempt at imposition.

If, then, what the governor of Minorca had done
was "lawful for him to do," it must have been lawful
after another fashion of law than the jurymen of
London knew themselves to have been living under.
Accordingly, Serjeant Davy, this defendant's counsel,
explained how it was lawful, by laying down to the
jury that the Minorquins, being a conquered people,
"the king was to appoint the governor of the island
to govern them by such laws as he thought proper
to direct,—*an arbitrary government* or a qualified
government,—under whatever sort of magistrates, or
whatever order the crown of England should think
proper." This was taking the bull by the horns,
and giving such a reading of the first resolution in
Calvin's case as the boldest stickler for the despotic
authority of the crown could well desire.

The answer of Serjeant Glynn, as counsel for the
plaintiff, was that, if such were the true construction
of the powers conferred by the royal patent to the

defendant, as governor, " if a patent passes the great
seal containing such words, there is not so feeble
a jurisdiction in this kingdom as will not dare to
pronounce it void, and every act done under it
illegal; and I will venture to say, too, it is impossible
but the great man that should dare to put the great
seal and prostitute public authority to a patent of
that kind, would have to answer to public justice
with his head."

These are but the indignant words of a counsel,
which might, no doubt, be in direct opposition to
his own real opinions; but which of the two doctrines
received the sanction of the court? Mr. Justice
Gould, before whom the cause was tried, charged
the jury so tenderly upon the constitutional question,
that he left it pretty much as he found it, allowing
the jury to act either upon the assertion of the
defendant, or upon the answer of the plaintiff. The
jury showed their notion of the despotic power of
a governor by giving a verdict for £3,000 damages,
" an immense sum for a Minorquin to recover," as
Chief Justice De Grey said, in the subsequent proceedings. The defendant moved the court for a new
trial. On the hearing of that motion, the chief
justice, after adverting to the article of the treaty
of Utrecht, (the treaty under which the island of
Minorca had been ceded by Spain to Great Britain,)
whereby the inhabitants were to enjoy their honors,

estates, and religion, and to an assurance merely, made by the British plenipotentiaries, that they should likewise enjoy their own rights and privileges, continued. " Those rights and privileges which they were to enjoy, were the established municipal laws of the island, under such regulations *as the legislature of this country* should impose upon them;" and afterwards, when commenting upon the imprisonment which he said the defendant had inflicted upon the plaintiff without trial, " as I do believe, under the old practice of the island," the chief justice continued ; " but the governor knew that he could no more imprison him for a twelvemonth, *than he could inflict the torture ;* yet the torture, as well as banishment, was the old law of Minorca, which fell, of course, when it came into our possession."

The judgment of the chief justice was a refusal to disturb the verdict, either upon grounds of law or as to the amount of damages, and this was warmly concurred in by the other judges. Upon a writ of error, the judgment of the court was confirmed.

This case of Fabrigas *v.* Mostyn, besides negativing the notion that the sovereign is despotic within a conquered colony, so as to have power to alter, by his governor or his deputy, the laws of the colony at his pleasure, goes somewhat further, for it likewise negatives the power of the crown to authorize the administration even of the ancient laws of the colony, so as to authorize the infliction of a punishment which the British constitution repudiates. Though the old law of Minorca sanctioned imprisonment without trial, (the act complained of,) and even putting to torture, yet the court would not listen to a justification founded upon this, holding that the old law " fell, of course, when the colony came into our possession,"—meaning, that from the moment of the capture or cession, the ancient laws became dead, until resuscitated by the conquering sovereign ; and that thus taking their new life from him, he must qualify this resuscitation, so as to strip the laws of everything repugnant to the British principles of constitutional liberty.

Were this otherwise, the singular and dangerous anomaly would arise, which has before been adverted to, that a British subject, born to the enjoyment, and having enjoyed in all his past life, the protection of his life, liberty, and property from all attempt upon any of them, until tried by a legally constituted court, acting under fixed constitutional laws, might find himself suddenly, on his landing in Minorca, transformed into the slave of a despotic governor, abusing, in his brief authority, the power given him by his sovereign. For, according to the doctrine which has been quoted from Campbell *v.* Hall, that the law of a place applies equally to all persons that are found within it, if the governor of Minorca might imprison and banish without trial, or might torture even after trial, a Minorquin-born subject of the empire, because the old Minorca law authorized this, he might equally imprison, banish, or torture a British-born subject, high or low, who, either for the purposes of pleasure or of business, had come within the island.

But there is still another view, which shows that the power of the sovereign to give laws to a conquered colony must be subject to the control of the imperial parliament, whether that gift be of the laws of England, of the ancient laws of the conquered country, or of laws of the conqueror's own framing. If the revenues of the conquest should prove insufficient for the discharge of the expenses of its internal government, as has proved to be the case with nearly all the colonies of Great Britain, at one time or other of their existence, the deficiency must be supplied from the revenues of Great Britain, under the authority of a parliamentary vote. If parliament were to refuse this vote, and the sovereign were to tax the conquered colony in consequence, and the inhabitants were to rise and rebel against any increase of their burdens, the soldiers to reduce them to submission must be found in the armies raised and paid by Great Britain, under the authority of a parliamentary vote.

In either of these cases, the crown must, in its

necessity, come to the parliament, and in this way cannot avoid the interference of parliament in the administration of the colony, to whatever extent it may consider to be proper in the circumstances. The houses of parliament may not constitutionally refuse the supplies to the sovereign, with the view of compelling him to do an illegal act, such as to hang before trial an inhabitant, either of the county of York or of the island of Minorca. But it may most constitutionally refuse the supplies to a sovereign who, for the gratification of the lust of power, should attempt to tyrannize over an inhabitant of the county of York or of the island of Minorca, by authorizing the administration of laws, which would sanction such an act of tyranny as has been suggested.

What, then, becomes of the doctrine that, until the crown gives a conquered colony the laws of England the colony is not subject to the control of parliament, or that parliament cannot interfere with the sovereign's "change and alteration" of the laws of the colony "at his pleasure," so long as he had not given it "the laws of England," which alone the king "could not alter without parliament." Would the parliament open their purse-strings to supply the deficiency in the revenue of a colony in such a state?

If, on the other hand, the revenue of the

conquered country should be superabundant and increasing, might not the king, through this means, become too strong for the parliament, and, in the end, worst them in an attempt to protect against him the liberties of Great Britain itself, if he might rule the conquered country " at his pleasure."

In every view, therefore, it seems to be incontestible that the power of the British sovereign over a conquered country, to give it laws for its government, has its origin in the necessity of the case, and extends no further than that necessity requires, and is, therefore, limited to the period of *first acquisition*. As the supreme executive officer, acting independently and uncontrollably in all matters affecting the external relations of the empire, the sovereign, *at the time of subduing a territory*, may—nay, is bound to—give it such laws, either temporary or permanent in their nature, as may be necessary to prevent that anarchy and confusion, which are sure to arise in any society of men living without law. But this *once done*, the power of the sovereign, in this respect, is at an end. It is the parliament, with the sovereign as a constituent part of it, which alone, *in time to come*, can legislate for this newly-acquired portion of the empire, as it is the parliament alone which can legislate for its most ancient portions.

To the parliament should be referred, for its sanction, whatever laws the sovereign may have deemed it prudent to give the colonists. It is by the parliament that all changes upon these laws should in all time thereafter be authorized. No doubt it is by the sovereign that the laws of the new acquisition, whether they be those which have been given by him, sanctioned by parliament, or whether they be others, imposed originally by parliament, must be executed; and this the sovereign must do by governors appointed by commission with relative instructions. But beyond giving authority to execute the existing laws, it would seem that the royal commission and instructions to any governor have no warrant or sanction, either in law or constitutional principle. ·

It is, no doubt, true that in all the British colonies the governor has been appointed by the crown, under the great seal, and that if, in any of them, as indeed it has been the case in most of them, there have been councils, or assemblies, or courts of justice, these have all been called, or held, under the sole authority of the crown, signified by patent under the great seal; and it is equally true that in all of these patents, since the first settlements in North America, there has been a reservation of an appeal from the decisions of the courts in the settlements, not to the House of Lords, but to the King in Council. This gives an appearance as if all that had been done had been done by the crown, in exercise of some right vested in the sovereign, as a person or an individual, and not as a sovereign and in right of the crown. But if that notion were correct, it would go to make the colonists, not subjects of the British empire and subjects of the sovereign of Great Britain, as head of the general constitution of that empire, but subjects of that sovereign in some other relation analogous to that subsisting between the Autocrat of all the Russias and his subjects. The reservation of an appeal to the king in council seems to be a confirmation of the argument which will be used in these pages, in regard to the want of legislative power in the House of Peers over colonists, for if such power did exist, there would also exist the correlative right of judicial jurisdiction. The exercise of such right, however, has never been attempted, the remedy having been acknowledged to be an appeal to the crown alone; and the right of appeal to the crown must be rested on the inherent right of the crown, as the fountain of justice, to administer justice to the subjects, of whom colonists form a part.

SECTION II.—POWER OF BRITISH SOVEREIGN, CONSTITUTIONALLY, TO RULE BY HIMSELF POSSESSIONS BEYOND THE LIMITS OF THE UNITED KINGDOM, SETTLED BY THE VOLUNTARY EMIGRATION OF BRITISH SUBJECTS.

If the sovereign of Great Britain cannot, *per se*, legislate for colonies acquired by *conquest*, or by cession, *multo minus* can he do so for colonies acquired by the *voluntary settlement* of British subjects.

There is no adjudicated case upon this question. All that is to be found in the books, in the nature of direct authority, is extrajudicial opinions of judges and lawyers of eminence.

In the year 1629, Charles II wished to recruit his exhausted treasury by levying taxes, of his own authority, from the colonists in the island of Jamaica, which, by the departure of the Spanish residents, had become a British colony. With this view, His Majesty consulted his attorney-general, Sir W. Jones, an eminent lawyer of that day, but he received for answer that the sovereign could no more grant a commission to levy money on his subjects in the plantations, *without their consent by an assembly*, than *they* could discharge themselves of their allegiance.[a] Again, in the year 1717, the ministers of George I consulted Mr. Lechmere, the attorney-general of that day, in regard to the same power of the crown to levy a tax on the island of Jamaica, by the authority of the crown alone, and the answer he gave them was, that " the person who should advise His Majesty to take such a step *would be guilty of high treason !*"

Five years afterwards, namely, in the year 1772,

a Smith's History of New York ; Phipps's Memoirs.

the assembly of Jamaica refused to vote the supplies
necessary for defraying the expense of the government of the island.   In consequence, the minister
of that day consulted Sir Philip Yorke, attorney-
general, and Sir Clement Wearg, whether the crown
could raise the necessary taxes by its own authority.
The answer of these eminent lawyers was, that if
Jamaica was to be considered in the same light as
the other "colonies," that is, as having ceased to be
a conquest, and having become a British settlement,
as Lord Mansfield, in Campbell v. Hall, held that
it had become, then "*no tax could be imposed upon
the inhabitants but by an assembly of the islands, or
by an act of parliament.*"

Undoubtedly, these authorities, such as they are,
go no further than to show that the crown has no
power, *per se*, to tax a voluntary settlement, or a
settlement by occupation; and Mr. Pitt, in the
passage before quoted, while contesting the justice
of taxing the colonies, and almost justifying their
rebellion against the attempt to tax them, drew a
distinction between "taxation" and "the governing
or legislative power," but he did not show how he
proved this; and, in a subsequent part of the same
speech, he asserted that the "sovereign authority of
Britain over the colonies extended to every point of
legislation whatsoever. We may bind their trade,
confine their manufactures, and exercise every power

whatsoever, *except that of taking their money out of their pocket, without their consent.*"

If " taxation," by which must have been meant "the right to tax," really be no part " of the governing or legislative power," there is not much of inconsistency in what was said by this great statesman. But, if the right to tax *be*, in fact, a part of the " governing or legislative power," then, as Mr. Pitt denied the right of Britain to tax her colonies, or take their money out of their pockets, without their consent, as he called taxing them, he has himself denied, to that extent at least, " the sovereign power to every extent," which he subsequently asserted to be in the mother country, and his authority upon the subject of that sovereign power must be unsatisfactory and inconclusive, though his authority is that which has always been referred to upon the subject.

It is, no doubt, true that " the taxes are," in form as well as in fact, " a voluntary gift and grant of the commons," but not of the commons " alone," as Mr. Pitt said, and subsequently himself disproved, by showing that the peers, spiritual as well as temporal, had a share, though not an equal share with the commons, in the gift. It is equally true that there is a material difference, in form, between an act of parliament, regulating the distribution of bankrupt estates among the relatives of bankrupts and their creditors, and an act of parliament by which the

crown is empowered to levy a tax upon the subject.
But is there any difference in substance? If a man
were to get goods from another, on a promise to pay
for them, and he should not pay according to his
promise, if the two lived in a state of nature, the one
would try to compel the other, and, according to his
strength or agility, he would fail or prevail. But
since the two live in the society of other men, who
cannot, for their own sakes, allow such contests to
occur, a law is made, which the crown, holding the
executive power of government, is, by its officers, to
enforce, whereby the disputes between creditor and
debtor, and the power of the one over the other, are
to be regulated. But the crown cannot discharge
this one among its other functions, without being
impressed with money wherewith to pay its officers:
a law is therefore passed giving the crown power to
levy so much money for this purpose from each of
the people. Without the united authority of king,
lords, and commons, the crown could not, by its
officers, compel distribution of a bankrupt estate,
according to a particular mode; and, without the
united authority of king, lords, and commons, the
crown could not, by its officers, levy any money from
the subject. The single authority of the commons
would no more justify the levy of one shilling of
tax than would the single authority of that branch of
the legislature, or of either of the other two branches,

authorize the enforcement of any act of administrative power, however foreign to, or unconnected with, taxation that act of administrative power might be.

Though, therefore, an act for the levying of a tax may, in its initiative, take the form of a grant or gift from the people to the crown; yet, in its working out and in its perfection, and also in its enforcement, it is for all purposes, as well practical as speculative, an act " of governing and legislative power." Probably, on another occasion than that on which Mr. Pitt declared the reverse, he would have concurred in this view, but it then suited his purpose to take taxation out of the category of governing or legislative power. To have retained it, and, at the same time, to have justified rebellion against the exercise of this power, would have exposed himself to a charge of the same crime which was being imputed to the American colonists. Mr. Pitt, therefore, drew a distinction where there seems not to have been any difference, and, while he asserted "the sovereign authority of Great Britain over the colonies" as extending "to every point of legislation whatsoever," he denied that "taxation was" part of "the governing or legislative power." If there were overstatement in this, it seems to have been intended as a cover for what was to follow—" America is almost in open rebellion. I rejoice that America has resisted." If that " rebellion " or " resistance " was not offered to

" an act of governing or legislative power," Mr. Pitt
did not show, nor does it seem possible for any one
else to show, to what else it was offered. But even
Mr. Pitt was forced to say that the concurrence of
the peers and the crown to a tax is only necessary to
" close (clothe ?) it with the form of a law."

Assuming this *dictum* of Mr. Pitt, that taxation
is no part of the legislative power, not to have any
foundation in truth or in principle, but to have been
merely introduced by him, in order to prepare his
audience for the fulmination of one of those bursts of
eloquence, bordering in this instance on comforting
treason, wherewith he overwhelmed all opposition,
and compelled the virtual repeal of the American
stamp act, and that, on the contrary, a right to
tax is not only a part, but an inherent " part of the
governing or legislative power,"[a] then, on the
authority of the law officers of Charles II and
George I, that the crown could not, *per se*, exercise
that right over a voluntary settlement of British
subjects, it would seem · to follow that the crown
cannot, *per se*, exercise any other branch of the
governing or legislative power over such a settlement.

But, setting aside authority, how will the supposed
power of the crown to legislate, *per se*, for voluntary

[a] Burke says, vol. III, p. 74 : " A right of taxation is necessarily
involved in the general principle of legislation, and inseparable from
the ordinary supreme power."

settlements stand upon constitutional principles. Sovereigns, who have emancipated themselves from all human control, and exercise a power for which, as they say, they are accountable to God alone, and which, therefore, they may exercise in such way as they themselves choose to think acceptable to God, if they do employ the blood and treasure of their subjects, beyond the limits of their proper territories, in conquering new territory, may as lawfully and much more innocently acquire increase of territory, by compulsory but bloodless settlement of their subjects, in new and unsettled countries, or by asserting a right to rule over their subjects in settlements which their subjects have themselves made of their own accord in such countries. Their rule at home is as variable as are the tempers and dispositions of the rulers who succeed to each other, and is as liable to be wicked, as the rule of man over his fellows has almost invariably been wicked, when that rule has been exercised without any moral or physical check upon the passions of the ruler.

There is, therefore, no reason, in principle, why this state of things should not be extended by such a despot, beyond his original territory, into any other part of the earth over which he can force it. Principle has no part in his original government. He violates nothing, therefore, when he tries to extend that government : he acts but consistently.

Not so the British sovereign. It is the peculiar boast of the monarch of Great Britain, above all the monarchs of the earth, that he rules not for his own personal gratification, but for the happiness of the millions under him. It is the peculiar consolation of the monarch of the present day, that the various checks upon the sovereign power, which the contests between her ancestors and their subjects have evolved, are self-acting to restrain the working of the evil passions, and the thirst for absolute power in particular, wherewith kings are cursed in common with their fellow-mortals.

The very rudimental principle of the government of the king of Great Britain is, that he rules not only for his subjects, but in and by his subjects,—that he is but the hand, as it were, to execute their volition. Though, in appearance and in mode of action, as uncontrolled as the most absolute despot, the checks of the constitution free him from the fearful responsibility of governing millions " at his pleasure," with a consciousness of those infirmities of temper and disposition which he has in common with all his species. A British sovereign, acting strictly in the line of the duty which the constitution has imposed upon him, need no longer cry out with his ancestor, " Oh, thou dull god, why lyest thou with the vile in loathsome beds, and leav'st the kingly couch a watch-case or a common 'larum bell. Uneasy lies the head that wears a crown."

Possessing to fullness everything that heart can desire for the gratification either of sense or of intellect, short of the power to dispose arbitrarily of the lives, liberty, or estates of his subjects, the sovereign of Great Britain has no burden imposed upon him, in return for all this, but to consent to those acts which shall be conducive to the prosperity and happiness of his people. He can have no personal motive to desire extension of territory, and the principles of the constitution have denied him the power to make it, as a personal acquisition.

Within the bounds of Great Britain and Ireland, a personal act of the sovereign, for which he is *irresponsible*, is unknown to the British constitution, if we make the ever-to-be-remembered and ever-glorious exception of an act of mercy towards a condemned criminal. How is it, then, or by what means, or from what source, is it, that the sovereign of Great Britain can derive power to legislate, " at his pleasure," over any part of the earth, whether it be a conquered, or a ceded, or a settled colony. Such an entity as a sovereign of Great Britain per-forming any act of government for which he is irresponsible is unknown to the British constitution. Legislation forms no exception. On the contrary, while many acts of the governing power of the

sovereign may be begun and finished, under the
responsibility only of having to justify the act, in
case it should be called in question, legislation is
that act of all others in regard to which the sovereign
power is limited. The sovereign cannot take even
the initiative step in legislation of proposing an act.
It is his subjects who frame and who perfect the law.
His ministers introduce acts, not in that character,
but as members of parliament, and his power is
limited to consenting to, or rejecting, what the two
houses of parliament present to him, as the result of
their united deliberations.

On what principle, or on what authority, in the
constitution is it, that this can be set aside in the
colonies, whether they be conquered, ceded, or
settled—that the crown, which in Great Britain has
only the *executive* power of the state, shall, in the
colonies, have both the legislative and executive
power? Can the nature of the act change with the
locality? Can that be executive in Australia which
is legislative in Great Britain? Can the power
change with the locality? Can the sovereign be
despotic in Australia and responsible in Britain?

No, it may be answered, nor has this been said;
for all the authorities constantly assert the supremacy
of the *imperial parliament*. Lord Mansfield speaks,
in Campbell *v.* Hall, of the power of the king,
without concurrence of parliament, to make new laws

for a conquered country, "as subordinate *to his own authority*, as a part of the supreme legislature in parliament;" and, in another passage, he says, "Taking these propositions to be granted, he," the king, "has a legislative power over a conquered country, limited to him by the constitution, and subordinate to the constitution and parliament."

Supremacy of the parliament is no doubt recognized in these passages, while the legislative power of the crown, or "the subordinate" legislative power of the crown, as Lord Mansfield calls it, is asserted. But it is not shown by that learned judge how this subordinate legislative power has been "limited to the crown by the constitution." None of the six propositions, upon the granting of which he rests that assertion, in any way support it. On the contrary, only two of them, in any degree, bear upon the subject, namely, the first and the sixth. The first, which is thus expressed, "A country conquered by the British arms becomes a dominion of the king, in right of his crown, and *therefore necessarily subject to the legislative power of the parliament of Great Britain*," directly negatives the idea of a legislative power resting in the sovereign alone, for, in right of his crown, the sovereign has no such power, and the concluding terms of the proposition assert the power to be "necessarily in the parliament of Great Britain."

The sixth proposition says: "*If* the king has power, without the concurrence of parliament, to make new laws for a conquered country, this being a power subordinate to his own authority, as a part of the supreme legislature in parliament, he can make none which are contrary to fundamental principles, none excepting from the laws of trade or authority of parliament." These expressions do not assert a legislative power to be in the sovereign. On the contrary, being merely a caution that, "*if*" he has such power, it is "subordinate to the supreme legislature in parliament," they rather suggest a doubt as to the existence of the power at all.

But the expressions of this sixth proposition suggest a doubt, even beyond that which they were intended to convey. Lord Mansfield felt the danger of countenancing the notion that the sovereign had an irresponsible legislative power, and, therefore, he was anxious to assert the supremacy of the parliament, but the very terms used, and necessarily used, to express this seem to negative the existence of the power, even in this subordinate degree, by showing its impossibility. If the king have a legislative power, he says, "it is subordinate to *his own* authority, as a part of the supreme legislature in parliament." It is difficult to understand how power, in an individual, can be subordinate to power in the same individual, or, at least, how it can be so to any practical effect, unless volition through which the power is to be exercised can be supreme and subordinate in one and the same individual.

Let it be assumed that what is put only hypothetically exists in reality. Let it be assumed that the crown has an individual legislative power, independent of the other two estates of the realm. In exercise of this power the crown appoints a governor by patent, with power to make laws for a colony, subject to the crown's approbation. The governor enacts and the sovereign approves. The law is made and must be obeyed, however ill-advised, however injudicious, nay, however despotic or tyrannical it may be in its terms, however inconsistent it may be with the British constitution, or however repugnant it may be to all notions of British liberty. This may have been done by a sovereign, either willfully wicked, or ignorantly so, or it may have been done by a sovereign, imposed upon by a secretary of state in abuse of his sovereign's confidence, and for the gratification of some appetite of his own.

This is very bad, but, says the caution of Lord Mansfield's sixth proposition, what the sovereign has thus done of himself, or what his secretary may have done for him, but for the benefit of himself, was in the exercise of a power " subordinate to the sovereign's own authority, as a part of the supreme legislature in parliament." This *sounds* very well. It is constitutional that all power in the sovereign, or in any one else, is subordinate to the power of parliament. But how will this suggestion, that the individual legislative power of the crown is subordinate to the collective legislative power of the parliament, of which the sovereign is an *independent* member, work? To continue the case supposed : The law made by the crown for the colony is a binding law, till altered by the supreme legislature in parliament, and must be obeyed. The colonists bring the matter to the knowledge of individual members of parliament, and succeed in finding one who will take up their case. The member proposes a bill to amend, or perhaps to annul, the colonial law. The bill passes through the houses of lords and commons, and is sent to the crown, from whom the answer is given, " Le roi s'avisera." There the bill drops, and the colonial law must, as before, and for all time to come, be obeyed, unless a bill, introduced in a subsequent session, should be more fortunate.

So far, then, from the power of the crown, individually, being subordinate to the power of the crown, as a member of the legislature, if such a thing be intelligible, it turns out that the power of the crown individually is *paramount*, and that the only *subordinate* power is that of the other two branches of the legislature. They may ratify and approve what the crown has already done, but they are powerless to condemn or annul it.

If this were a true representation of the power of the crown, the British colonies have all this time been in the same condition, with reference to the crown, that England was in two hundred years ago, when the crown issued proclamations as law, which it could enforce in the Star Chamber. But it would be a libel on the British constitution to say so. There is no power in the crown to legislate independently. Lord Mansfield has not said so, nor has any other authority, nor is it probable that that eminent judge would have entertained the suggestion that the crown *might* have such a power, even over a conquered country, fenced with the caution that if it had the power it must be subordinate to the supreme power of the legislature, which is all that he did suggest, had he probed the matter further, and seen how inoperative the fence must be.

If a country be conquered or ceded, the crown, as the depositary of that executive power, which is necessary not only for taking actual civil possession, either of a conquest or of a cession, and setting the machinery of a government in motion within it, and which must exist somewhere in every government, whatever be its form, may either, as before observed,

continue the old laws of the place, or give a body
of new laws. It is only in this sense that Lord
Mansfield could have put the case hypothetically of
the crown having power to legislate over a conquered
country. Undoubtedly, in this case, there will be
all the difficulty, which has already been pointed
out, of altering this act of the sovereign, through
the legislature, of which he is an independent part.
But this is unavoidable, and a necessary result of the
circumstances. It is one of the misfortunes of war,
which time and a change of views in the sovereign,
or the accession of a new sovereign to the throne,
can alone remedy.

There is nothing in the British constitution which
can remedy it; but no violence has been done to
that constitution by the act complained of. If the
inhabitants have been unjustly or unkindly treated
by the laws which the sovereign has given them,
they were foreigners when this was done, at least,
they had not yet become Britons; they were in a
transition state. But there is this consolation for
them,—the crown cannot *again* legislate for them.
Ever after they have the same rights as British
subjects. No, not the same rights, but a moiety of
the rights of British subjects. They can for the
future be legislated for only by a popular body.
Instead of having laws framed for them by nominees
of the crown, in the silence and privacy of the

official chamber, this can only, on the supposition
of the supremacy of the imperial parliament, be done
by the parliament of England,—a popular body,
whose proceedings are open, and before whom they
may succeed in getting themselves heard before any
law is passed.

But where a country is settled by the voluntary
emigration of British subjects, at their own risk and
expense, it is at least doubtful whether the British
government of king, lords, and commons has any
power over them whatever, unless with their own
consent. At all events, the crown, *by itself*, has no
legislative power over them. If a government have
a right to follow its subjects out of its own territory,
and to lay its authority upon them in the new place
of their abode, the British government, meaning in
this instance by that term the British parliament,
may have that power; but assuredly the power of the
crown individually cannot there be greater than it
was at home—it must be purely executive.   It
cannot be legislative, for no such power can exist
independently in a British sovereign.   Neither is
any such power asserted for it, either by judges or
by crown lawyers.   Even the hypothetical legislative
power, suggested by Lord Mansfield in Campbell *v.*
Hall, is confined to " a conquered country;" not the
slightest hint is given of such a power over a British
settlement.   Sir W. Jones, Charles II's attorney-

general, said the crown had no more right to exercise such a power than the settlers would have to discharge themselves of their allegiance. Mr. Lechmere, George I's attorney, said that any minister who would advise the crown to exercise such a power "would be guilty of high treason." And Sir Philip Yorke and Sir Clement Wearg, George I's lawyers, said the settlers could be legislated for only by an assembly, or by an act of parliament.

CHAPTER VIII.

IF the sovereign of Great Britain may not legislate,
per se, for a colony, it seems very questionable
whether the imperial parliament of king, lords, and
commons united may do so. It is true that the
authorities which have been referred to, while denying
such a power to exist in the crown *alone,* assert it to
exist in parliament; but it must be observed that the
question put was only whether the power existed in
the crown—whether it existed in the parliament was
not asked. Not being able to discover it in the
crown, and assuming, unnecessarily it would seem,
that it must exist somewhere in the mother country,
they referred it to parliament, the only other body
where, by possibility, it could exist. Had they been
asked their authority for saying that it existed in
parliament, probably they would have found it
difficult to assign any, and might have found it easier
to say that it existed in the crown than to assert that
it was in the parliament.

However fondly we may cherish the idea that the

people have always, from remote antiquity, had a voice in the government of the country, it seems to be but a fond delusion, after all.   If the terms used in ancient charters and acts of parliament, on which this idea has been founded, be read by the light which the history of Europe generally, as well as of England individually, affords, the result will probably be found to be, that the monarchs, in times when they were not much above the great land-owners, either in power or in wealth, summoned the land-owners to their councils, by whatever titles or designations they could be generically designated, or omitted to summon some of them and summoned others, just as the monarchs saw the necessity of the one or of the other course, in order to accomplish the object they had in view for the time.   But it would be preposterous to imagine that the British monarchy had then the same limited form that it has now, or that all ranks of society, as at present constituted, had each their representation in the parliament.   In truth, the present ranks of society had not then any existence whatever.   Betwixt the land-owners, whether inheriting British, Saxon, or Danish titles with their lands, or possessing the lands without any titles of honor whatsoever, and the abject serfs or villeins, there were no intermediate ranks whatever, worth designating as such.

These land owners being sturdy and independent,

and the monarch being without any standing army, he was obliged to ask their assistance with arms, whensoever he desired either to attack one of the more powerful members of the body, or to defend the kingdom against foreign invasion, or to go out of the kingdom to make foreign conquest. Money contributions, by the subject to the monarch, were not known to the feudal system which then prevailed. The levying of taxes in money was a later contrivance, suggested by the increasing wealth of a portion of the community, which, in the times of the early Norman monarchy, had no consideration; indeed, had hardly yet a distinctive existence. Traders in goods and wares were few in number and insignificant in condition, until the places, where, for mutual protection against the feudal tyrants, these individuals congregated together, had risen into the importance of towns and burghs.

The monarch, in early Norman times, was as despotic and absolute as these terms can express, so far as his command of physical power would allow him to be. His power was not fettered by any constitutional rule or principle. What he *could* do, that he *might* do. What he could not do without the assistance of his people in men and money, that he was obliged to defer doing until he could secure that assistance. The extent of his necessities, in short, was the sole limit of the sovereign's power.

In the other countries of Europe—France, for example—this same state of things took its natural course. In proportion as the monarchs became powerful, as they did more or less in every kingdom, from a combination of circumstances, they were able to subdue the great land-owners, and to *compel* from them that assistance which hitherto they had been obliged to ask. From being elective they gradually established themselves as hereditary, and in time they became, *in fact*, absolute and despotic over all the land-owners, as they had always been in theory. Power, concentrated in *one*, became an overmatch for power diffused through a number. Then it was that the monarchs amalgamated, as it were, the two notions, one derived from the barbarian heathen nations, that their chiefs were descended from gods, and the other from imperial Rome, that the sovereign was the personation of all the powers of the state. From the combination of these two notions, after actual supremacy of physical power had been established, sprang the maxim of the divine hereditary right of kings, which has pervaded all the states of Europe, and forged the chains of their slavery.

In England, the growth of kingly power was entirely different. While, in other countries, this was accomplished by gradual encroachment on the power of the land-owners, and by the gradual forfeiture of their lands, in England the power of the sovereign started into existence at once full-blown. This fact seems to have been the cause of its subsequent limitation, by compelling the higher orders to combine with the middle classes, as the only means of resisting the inordinate power of the crown, and thus reacting by inducing the sovereign to countenance and encourage the middle classes, as the best means of restraining the encroachments of the nobility on the kingly power.

William of Normandy came as rightful sovereign of a dynasty whose rights relatively to the subject are hidden in obscurity, but his claim as rightful sovereign was a mere cloak to cover his designs. The character of hereditary sovereign he soon laid aside for that of conqueror, having despotic power over the lives and estates of the inhabitants. He accordingly redistributed the lands of the kingdom, taking them from the Saxons and bestowing them upon his Norman followers. This he did upon conditions, framed according to the strictest rules of the feudal system, that all lands were holden of the crown, and he reserved to himself and his successors such an extent of demesnes, as created a great disproportion between his power and that of his barons, and, under ordinary circumstances, made him independent of assistance from his people for supplying the necessary expenses of his government and household.

The monarch was thus, at the outset, placed immeasurably above his subjects, even the highest of them, and several monarchs before the accession of John to the throne, particularly Henry II, increased this distance very much, " so that the nation," in the words of Hume, "during the course of one hundred and fifty years, had groaned under a tyranny unknown to all the kingdoms founded by the Norman conquerors." And yet the first Henry and King Stephen had granted the barons charters favorable to their liberties. But these, though confirmed by Henry II, " had," according to the same authority, "remained without effect, and the same unlimited, at least irregular, authority continued to be exercised, both by them and their successors."

In order to overcome this regal tyranny, and enable themselves to keep any head against the crown, the barons were forced to league with the commonalty. In that view, the barons who extorted Magna Charta from King John did not confine its terms to special clauses, benefiting their own order alone. They comprehended in them the rights of the inferior orders of society, by clauses expressed in general and comprehensive terms, asserting the supremacy of the law, and providing for its just and equal administration. This charter, Hume says, "involved all the chief outlines of a legal government, and provided for the equal distribution of justice and the free

enjoyment of property, the great objects for which
political society was at first founded by men, which
the people have a perpetual and inalienable right to
recall, and which no time, nor precedent, nor statute,
nor positive institution, ought to deter them from
ever keeping uppermost in their thoughts."

In thus obtaining from the sovereign a concession
by Magna Charta of clauses, the necessary effect of
which must have been to confer the enjoyment of
liberty and the administration of justice on the lower
orders, the barons were unwittingly playing a game
which the sovereign apparently had already begun.
Henry I had been the first monarch who had levied
taxes on the personal estates of the people, nobles
as well as commoners. His predecessors had confined themselves to the exactions on the crown
tenants, which were sanctioned by the feudal tenure.
This monarch and his successors took advantage of
the increasing wealth of that small part of the
people, which consisted neither of land-owners nor
of villeins, but of persons, being either foreigners or
natives, who, in one or other of the few ways then
open for such a result, had obtained their freedom
and established themselves in trade or manufactures.
Discovering a source of revenue in their industry,
Henry and his immediate successors levied taxes
upon them of the most arbitrary nature and amount,
and by their own authority, and enforced them,

when that was necessary, by all the contrivances of despotic tyranny.

One of the clauses of Magna Charta declared that no tax should, for the future, be levied on the subject but with the consent of the Great Council. Hitherto the Great Council had been called when assistance with men and arms, the contribution due by the feudal tenant to his lord, was required. Henceforth, the Council was to aid the monarch in levying money taxes upon those of his subjects, who had been hitherto without the pale of the constitution, as it were, but who, from their increasing wealth and the substantial power which wealth gives, it was found convenient to bring within it.

As yet, those from whom these money taxes were to be levied were not admitted to the Great Council. But Edward I, being much pressed for money for his war projects against France and Scotland, perceived that it would be for his own advantage to have the tax-payers represented in that council. He therefore commanded the towns and burghs to send two representatives each to the Great Council. They did so unwillingly, not then witting the power that was thus unconsciously, by the sovereign, about to be thrown into their hands ; for out of the clause of Magna Charta, which prevented the levying of taxes without the consent of parliament, which, at the time, must have been confined in its application to a very small portion of the community beyond the land-owners, since the great bulk of the people were mere villeins, has arisen the great shield for the protection of British liberty.

The right under this clause to refuse money to the crown is the great lever wherewith the power of the people is worked, and by which alone they can constitutionally resist the encroachments of monarchical power. It is the Alpha and Omega of their power. It is what alone they can begin their opposition with, and it is what alone they must end it with. Beyond, all is rebellion and treason.

The commons, properly so called, since their first introduction into parliament in the reign of Henry III, and their final and permanent establishment there in the reign of Edward I, have worked so well the engine of power contained in this clause of the great charter, perfected as it was by the statute *De Tallagio non concedendo* of Edward I, and have done this so infinitely beyond what the nobles who originally framed these instruments, and the sovereigns who conceded or confirmed them, could have contemplated, that they have in time engrossed all the active power of legislation, and have left to the sovereign nothing but a negative, and to the barons practically little else.

The rights expressly conceded by the great charter, and those which have since been achieved through the bold working of the power of the commons in regard to taxation, have been, in truth, conquests upon kingly power, which, from the time of William I, had by right of conquest been purely despotic, as much almost in theory as it certainly had been in practice.

But the Great Charter, the statute *De Tallagio non concedendo*, the Bill of Rights, and the Act of Settlement, on which, at the present day, the liberties of Englishmen are founded, have no application beyond the territory of Britain and Ireland. Scotland and Ireland have derived the benefit of them, by virtue of their acts of union, which made these ancient kingdoms part of the consolidated empire; but these acts have no application, either by their terms or in principle, beyond the limits of the United Kingdom. If, therefore, such an entity can constitutionally be supposed to exist, as a king of Great Britain having, as such king, territory lying beyond the limits of the three kingdoms, acquired either by conquest or by cession, that territory may be under the same despotic rule which the kings of England possessed previously to Magna Charta, and the instruments and acts which followed it, and which alone have fettered that despotic rule; but it is very difficult to conceive how that territory can, upon constitutional principles, be under the active rule of the British parliament.

The whole power of the two branches of the legislature, as opposed to that of the sovereign, is purely negative; there is nothing active either in its history or in its character. The beginning and the end of its operation is to restrain the power of the sovereign, and prevent its encroachment on the liberty of the subject. History will be ransacked in vain for any authority to show that, by the constitution, there is a right in either house, but least of all in the commons, to exercise any *active* power of government within the United Kingdom, and still less beyond it.

The sovereign of Great Britain may declare war and make conquests of other countries, at his pleasure, and for the gratification of his pride, envy, ambition, or whimsical caprice, and he may make peace as arbitrarily. What he gains to-day he may give away to-morrow, without there being a right in any part of the community actively to stay his hand. If the sovereign had pecuniary means wherewith to do this, and could thus avoid having to meet his parliament, there is no power which could prevent its continuance for any given length of time. But, not having pecuniary means for independence, the sovereign cannot avoid meeting the parliament without violating the law; he must summon it within stated times. When so summoned and assembled, all that the body can do is to frame

resolutions, expressing approbation or disapprobation
of what the sovereign has done; and, if these resolutions are not given effect to, to withhold the grant
of taxes, when the sovereign comes to ask for them,
and, it may be, to impeach, try, and punish the officers
of the sovereign through whom the act disapproved
of has been done, if in the nature of the act, or in
the mode in which it has been done, there have
been anything done contrary to the law, or injurious
to the realm.

But in all this there is no active power of
government. It is all negative and *ex post facto*.
It would be not only indecent, but highly unconstitutional, to resolve, beforehand, that the sovereign
should not do this or that act, and to refuse the
taxes until the sovereign would undertake to conform
to the resolution. Parliament may, in anticipation of
any course of action by the sovereign, express its
opinion upon the subject, but it cannot so frame
that expression as to involve the requisition of
obedience; neither can it, beforehand, practically
compel obedience by refusal of taxes. It must,
even after its opinion has been expressed, wait till
some act has been done by the sovereign, in defiance
or disregard of the opinion, before it can begin to
exercise even its negative power.

But it may be said, if the sovereign conquer a
territory, or acquire one by cession, and the

parliament afterwards confirm the act, what is there wanting to the entire power of governing the newly-acquired territory, both legislatively and executively ? *Ex concessis*, the sovereign has *the right*, as much as any other sovereign, and, if the other branches of the legislature give him also the *power*, what is wanting ?

It is unnecessary to repeat here the arguments against the *constitutional* legality of the sovereign's share in such a transaction.[a] But let us see how far the other branches of "*the legislature*" may lawfully bear *their* part in it. In the first place, the very term by which alone the English language can designate them would seem to negative such a supposition. "Legislature" is a term which expresses a body having power to make laws for a community inhabiting an existing territory. If it be meant to express an individual or a body, having power by himself or itself, or by his or its officers, to acquire a new territory, make laws for its inhabitants, and enforce their obedience, the word "*government*" must be used, as it will embrace both legislative and executive powers. But executive powers are unknown to a "legislature," and yet that is the only word by which the two houses of parliament can be designated. No doubt a legislative power is necessarily part of a governing power, and, in so far as

---

[a] Vide supra, p. 151.

this part of the governing power resides in the two houses of parliament in conjunction with the sovereign, these houses may be said to be part of the government; but still the power of these houses is purely legislative, that is, they have no power but to make laws for an existing territory. This argument may be *vox et preterea nihil.* Let us go into the matter, then, a little more closely.

It is beyond all question that, if the sovereign of Britain make a conquest of any territory, and the parliament afterwards confirm the act, the conquest may, *as a question of fact,* be retained and governed by the sovereign alone, or by the sovereign in some way subordinate to the parliament, or in any way that these two powers choose to regulate; for, in them both united, there is all that goes to make up sovereign power, whose acts, just or unjust, there is none under heaven to judge or control. But the question is whether, as a matter of *constitutional principle,* the king of Great Britain, having conquered a territory, the parliament can legislate for it.

SECTION I.—POWER, CONSTITUTIONALLY, OF THE HOUSE OF PEERS
    TO LEGISLATE FOR POSSESSIONS BEYOND THE LIMITS OF THE
    UNITED KINGDOM.

With regard to the House of Lords, the question is not so difficult to solve, perhaps. That house, which consisted originally of all the crown vassals, including both the earls and barons and the lesser vassals, who subsequently merged into the House of Commons as knights of the shire, formed, in truth, the Great Council mentioned in Magna Charta and the other early instruments of the liberties of England. Under the feudal system each member was bound to furnish his quota of the sinews of war, and the sovereign might have exacted it by summons upon each vassal to appear, at a given place, at a given time, with his men-at-arms. But the monarch, when he wished to enter upon any great warlike undertaking, and there were then few great undertakings which were not warlike, found it more prudent to summon the crown vassals to attend him in a Great Council, that he might enlist their will to give voluntarily those contributions of men, armed, horsed, and provisioned, which, by the terms of the feudal tenure of their lands, they were bound to supply only for a limited number of days.

All those persons, therefore, who held their lands directly of the sovereign, as their fedual lord, were propitiated by being summoned to *consult* as to the expediency of what was about to be undertaken, and what was finally resolved upon bore to have been resolved on " by and with their advice and consent." Hence the Great Council; and in that council, when so summoned, matters of civil and internal government were also discussed and resolved on.

The present House of Lords is the true representative of the Great Council. Each member of the council in ancient times was summoned " *de arduis negotiis regni tractaturi et concilium impensuri*," and he appeared in answer to that summons, in his own right and for the protection of his own individual interest. The summons to the members of the House of Lords, in modern days, and the personal right to appear continue ; the interests to be protected only have varied. If, therefore, in such an assembly as the House of Lords, it should be resolved, in answer to the monarch's summons to treat and consult as to the affairs of the realm, that a foreign conquest should be made, and that, being made, it should be retained under any given form of administration, however foreign in its nature to the British form of government and repugnant to the British constitution, there would not in this be anything very inconsistent with the ancient mode of proceeding : the only difficulty would be as to the means of accomplishing what had been resolved on. The feudal services have fallen into disuse, and in their place have come the taxes levied upon peers as well as commoners by the original authority of parliament. Under the ancient system, the peers had to protect themselves against the excessive demands of the sovereign, by virtue of his feudal rights. In modern times they may have to protect themselves against the excessive imposition of taxes upon them by the vote of the commons. But, in other respects, the peers retain their original feudal position as councilors of the sovereign, and, as such, they may, if they choose and if they can bring themselves to do so, vote what will be agreeable to the sovereign's love of power and aggrandisement, as their predecessors the crown vassals, sitting in the Great Council, did, when supporting the monarch in his aggressions upon France; and they may, if they choose, do as their predecessors did in many instances, make their own interests their sole consideration, in contempt and disregard of the other orders of the state.

It is not very likely that, in these days, the nobility of England would pursue such a selfish line of conduct. Whatever may have been the case formerly, it is not such fruit that, in modern days, has been yielded by this branch of the legislature. Still the peers have the power, historically, theoretically, and practically, of voting each according to his own view of his own individual interest, if they choose to exercise it, to isolate themselves, and to throw out of view what they owe to their country.

The peers of Great Britain then may, if they choose, vote in parliament for the making of a foreign conquest, and for the retention of it under the dominion of the sovereign. But how can they, from time to time, legislate for the conquered territory? Leaving the practical objections to a subsequent stage, how, theoretically, can a peer of Great Britain legislate for a district of Australia or for a province of France? The interest of each peer is in his own barony, and the collective interest of the whole body of peers in the House of Peers is just the aggregate of these individual interests, which, upon feudal theory, is supposed to include the whole interests in the soil of the kingdom, all its land being supposed to have been portioned out among the crown vassals, and all these vassals being supposed to be assembled in the House of Peers.

As a baron of Great Britain, what interest can any individual peer have in the government or legislation of any portion of Australia, a country the most remote from Great Britain, or of France, immediately adjacent to it? The very ground and origin of his summons to parliament is the protection of his enjoyment of his barony against the encroachments of kingly or of a foreign power, and he and his order have wisely, as well as generously, extended their deliberations in this assembly to protecting the sovereign against the encroachments of the commons, and the commons against the encroachments of the sovereign. But, out of Great Britain, what political existence can a peer of Great Britain have?

It will never be said that, within the United

Kingdom, there is a plurality of sovereigns, consisting of the king and the peers,—the king being only the highest among them, the *dignior persona*. In the United Kingdom there is but one sovereign, who engrosses to himself all the attributes of royalty, not excepting even the attribute of legislation, for though the two houses of parliament originate and must concur in the making of laws, it is the sovereign who enacts ; all that they do is, to give their "advice and consent." The constitution has compelled the monarch to this restraint on his kingly power, in order, as regards the peers, that each peer may be enabled to protect his own individual life, estates, and liberties against the sovereign, in his mode of administering the kingdom. But, if the sovereign conquer, through some means or other, the whole or a portion of France, how can he, in legislating for this conquest, affect the life, estates, or liberties of any peer of Great Britain ? If he cannot, then by what right can such a peer interfere in the legislation with his advice, or at least with his *consent ?* What right has he to advise, and to what can his consent be necessary ? If he do interfere, it cannot be as a baron of Great Britain, it must be as co-sovereign with his king.

That the conquest has been made with the blood, sinews, and treasure of British subjects can make but little difference. The circumstance may give each peer an interest as a British subject, and, in common with his fellow-subjects, to revenge or recover the expenditure; but it cannot give him any *right* to legislate for the territory or inhabitants of the conquered country. His individual right is confined to his barony, and the right of the whole house of peers is merely an aggregation of such individual rights. A barony in Yorkshire gives a baron a right to meet in the House of Peers with the other barons of the kingdom, and to consult what laws should be passed for the administration of the baronies of the kingdom, his own included, and to tender the sovereign, supposed in theory to be present in the House of Peers, his "advice" and his "consent" upon the subject. But how can a barony in Yorkshire give the baron a right to tender either his advice or his consent for the administration of the baronies of France, should that country happen to be conquered? Such a right is as foreign as is the territory. His advice and consent on such a subject should, on principle, be an obtrusion and an impertinence.

SECTION II.—THE POWER, CONSTITUTIONALLY, OF THE HOUSE OF COMMONS TO LEGISLATE FOR POSSESSIONS BEYOND THE LIMITS OF THE UNITED KINGDOM.

With regard to the House of Commons and its right to share in the legislation of a conquered or

ceded territory, it would appear from its history and
the theory and practice of the constitution that, if it
have any such right, it can only be *by purchase*, in
each particular instance.

In the early period of the British monarchy, after
the conquest, there was, as before noticed, no such
thing as a money tax levied with the consent of the
great council. What money the sovereign got from
his subjects was either from his vassals and the
tenants of the crown demesnes, under the powers
which the feudal tenure conferred on him as
superior lord, or was extorted without law or right
from his other subjects. In early times, those who
were not connected with land, either as superior,
vassal, or villein, were few in number, and still more
insignificant in wealth and consideration. In the
progress of ages, however, trade, handicrafts, and
manufactures improved, and with their improvement there gradually sprung up a portion of the
community possessed of the greater amount of
available wealth, but which was out of the pale
of feudality and the exactions which it sanctioned.
It naturally occurred to the sovereign to inquire
whether he might not make this manufacturing
and trading portion of his subjects a source of
revenue.

The crown vassals had never heartily brought
forward the contributions which their titles authorized

from them, and it was difficult in these irregular
times to ascertain even the titles by which they
held their demesnes, and of course what their contributions ought to be ;[a] and when the men-at-arms
were assembled, they were bound to serve, and
were provisioned only for a limited number of
days. When these expired, they returned home,
perhaps at the very moment at which their services
were most required, leaving the undertaking on
which they had been assembled to shift for itself.
If the sovereign could in any way obtain money
instead of troops from his subjects, he might raise
and equip troops when he pleased, and maintain
armies for such a period as his occasions required.
But the crown vassals, though rich in broad acres,
had few broad pieces, and the feudal tenure suggested
no course by which the raising of money by the
sovereign could be attained, even if the vassals had
been possessed of available wealth. The device first
fallen on was to commute military services for money
payments. The exactions in this way, having no
legal limit, increased beyond endurance by those
who had little money for themselves, and they
encountered consequently so much resistance that
the sovereign, in his difficulties, was but too glad

---

[a] One bishop of Durham acknowledged services to be due by
him for forty fiefs, but disclaimed seven hundred others, in respect
of which they were demanded by the crown !

to discover some other source whence his wants might be supplied.

The riches of the burghers and townsmen suggested a source whence ready money could be raised, not only for warlike purposes, but for the supply of the increasing wants of the royal establishment, beyond what the tenants of the royal demesne lands could supply in kind; and the protection which this part of the community enjoyed from the state, without contributing any part of the expense, suggested the pretext which should be used for obtaining from it the supply of the desired specie. No doubt one of the sources of royal revenue had always been arbitrary exactions from the towns and burghs, which at the time of the conquest, were little better than what we now understand by country villages; yet when the increasing wants of the sovereign rendered it necessary to increase the frequency and amount of these demands, and the increasing importance of the towns and villages suggested the possibility of their resistance to them, it became evidently of importance to systematize and legalize these exactions, by giving them in some respects, the authority of consent.

Edward I, therefore, being much pressed for money to supply the expenses of his vast military preparations against Scotland and France, first fell upon the device of summoning the towns and burghs

to the great council, by issuing writs directing the
return of two representatives for each, "as," the
preamble of his writ said, " it is a most equitable rule
that what concerns all should be approved of by all,
and common dangers be repressed by united efforts ;"
an ingenious and specious way of flattering and
bribing the commons into the course which he had
designed. They were not called together simply to
tax themselves, the true motive of their summons—a
call they might have been slow to answer ;—but they
were summoned that they might approve of what
generally was done in the great council, taxation
being included, though not mentioned.

Hitherto, the great council had been feudal; thenceforth it was to be popular as well. Hitherto, the
expenses of the state had been defrayed from those
revenues which the feudal tenure supplied by its
own inherent power, without the aid of any other
authority and by unauthorized and arbitrary exactions
from the non-feudal part of the people, the illegality
of which had been overlooked from their near resemblance to the exactions under the feudal system.
Thenceforth, revenue was to be derived from taxes,
to be imposed and levied with the consent of those
who, though they had enjoyed the protection of the
state, had not as yet contributed to its expense,
except occasionally, when the rapacity or necessities
of the sovereign had induced him to levy contributions

from them, which had neither law nor authority for their justification. Thitherto, the expenses of the state had been contributed in money, or in kind, by those orders in the state which alone had existence, or at least consideration, when the machinery of the state was contrived. Thenceforth, they were to be borne proportionally by the merchants and manufacturers, classes which had gradually accumulated wealth and risen into importance.

As yet, the great council had consisted of one chamber, formed of the crown vassals, summoned in person, "*de arduis negotiis regni tractaturi et consilium impensuri.*" Now, there was to be added a second chamber, of commons, summoned, not like the peers, "*de arduis negotiis tractare et consilium impendere,*" but "*ad faciendum et consentiendum*" simply.

The representatives sent by the towns and burghs, upon this coaxing summons, "*ad faciendum et consentiendum,*" understood too well what was expected of them, and, at first, did no more than answer the object with which the summons had been given. They granted the sovereign a tax upon their own means and the means of those whom they represented; and forthwith, deeming their part performed, they returned to their homes, leaving the other house *de arduis negotiis tractare et consilium impendere.* They followed this course even after the lesser crown vassals, represented by the knights of the shire, had been added to their house.

As the town and burgh representatives perceived their growing importance, acquired by the constant struggles between the sovereign and the great crown vassals, who alternately courted their support, they gained courage to go beyond simply assenting to or refusing the imposition of such taxes as the crown required of them. They ventured, at first, to attach to the money bills, presented for their consent, petitions for redress of grievances. In time they made redress of those grievances a condition precedent to the granting of the taxes. In the further progress of time, they took a prominent part in the general legislation of the country, and ultimately they have drawn to themselves, if not the chief, at least the most active share of this power. In the commons' house, most measures of legislation do now, in fact, originate, and are there elaborated. In the lords' house, they are but criticized and perfected; and the sovereign has lost all power of originating legislation. His ministers, no doubt, propose and, with the leave of the houses, introduce bills, but they do so, not as ministers, but as members of the house, and as representatives of that part of the kingdom which has sent them there. Simply as ministers of the crown they have no *locus standi*.

Notwithstanding the undoubted possession by the

commons of this power, which—however excellent in itself when properly worked, and however necessary for the due operation of the constitution—was gained only by encroachment on their part, and by concession on the part of the sovereign, yet the present only support of this power, as it was its original foundation, is the correlative power of granting revenue to the sovereign. The sovereign may levy armies, and equip fleets, and declare war either upon his own subjects or upon other states, and make conquests, and govern them, too, at his pleasure, *if* he can provide the means for doing this and for defraying the other expenses of his government and household. There is no power in the constitution which can stay his hand.

The power of dissolving parliament resides in the crown, and, from the moment of dissolution, each member of either house is remitted to his original individual condition. The peer retires into private life, with all those accessories of social power and consideration which the possession of hereditary titles and estates can bestow, but stripped of every iota of legislative or administrative power; and the commoner returns into the general herd of the people, no other ways distinguished from them than as his accidental possession of wealth may enable him to exhibit the enjoyment of greater luxuries, but stripped, like the peer, of every iota of power. From the moment of the dissolution of parliament, therefore, the sovereign of Great Britain is such in every sense of the term, with power as absolute, so far as there exists any opposing power, as the autocrat of all the Russias, if he can only command the necessary pounds, shillings, and pence. But inasmuch as the sovereign of Britain has little or no hereditary revenue, and taxes are voted only for a limited period, he is restrained, or rather his ministers are restrained, in the exercise of his power by the reflection that for everything he does, or which they in his name may do, they must one day, never far off, summon the parliament, to whom they must render an account; otherwise, .the whole machine of government must be brought to a stand still for want of funds wherewith to carry it on.

In this power of the commons, there is nothing savoring of the monarchical, any more than there is in that of the peers; indeed, there is much less, for individually, and without respect to their being members of the House of Peers when it is assembled as part of the parliament, each peer is an hereditary councilor of the sovereign, and, as such, may demand an audience, not only while the house is sitting, but while the parliament is dissolved; but the commoners, after the parliament is dissolved, are all equally indistinguishable, and, even while it is sitting, they enjoy individually only the power which their constituents have conferred on them, a power which they can render effective only through the collective power of the House of Commons; but they have no individual power.

Though the House of Commons, when assembled, has now the unquestionable power of considering, perfecting, and consenting to such laws as may be submitted by the ministers of the crown for its consideration, and has the equally unquestionable power of originating measures of its own suggestion, without regard to whether these measures, directly or indirectly, affect the taxation of the subject, and though the House of Commons, when assembled, may now undoubtedly require of the crown, through its ministers, an account of its administration, in regard to any particular which, in its judgment, may call for this inquiry, and may pass resolutions approbatory or condemnatory, which the crown will find it difficult to disregard, yet these powers proceed not from any inherent right in the commons, as part of the governing authority of the kingdom, but from the simple fact that the commons, keeping in their hands the strings of the national purse, have been able gradually to assume them.

These powers of the commons are too well established, and are obviously too salutary in the mode of their operation, to make it likely that the crown will enter into any discussion as to their origin ; yet, in their present extent, which embraces almost a share in the administration, as well as in the legislation of the empire, they are undoubtedly comparatively modern, and have been yielded much more as a matter of convenience than they have been gained as a question of right, and they have often been withdrawn; for, in the times of the bad Tudors and of the first of the Stuarts, both houses of parliament possessed but a shadow of power. They had become little better than the parliaments of France—courts for registering the edicts of the sovereign.

Fortunately for the state, the commons have held tenaciously to the power they always had of regulating the amount and mode of taxation. They have never, even in the most humiliating times of political degradation, parted with this engine; and, through it, they have always been able to regain their former station, and ultimately to establish their present almost super-eminent position in the state, as the principal member of the legislature, and controller, even, of the administration of the empire. Still this collective power of the House of Commons, great as it undoubtedly is, is referable to the source whence it flows, and cannot go above it. It is just the aggregate power of so many hundred individuals, delegates of the people, to give or to refuse so much money to the government, but who, neither individually nor collectively, have one scintilla of sovereign or administrative power. The result may, in effect, give the house administrative power, but, on principle, it directly gives none. If this be conceded, it is sufficient for the present purpose.

Each member sent to the House of Commons is sent there to protect, by his vote, the lives, liberties, and estates of the inhabitants, not only of the burgh or county which may have sent him, but of the whole United Kingdom ; to resist the passing of such laws as may tend to affect them injuriously ; and to condemn any administrative act of the government which may have worked in this way directly, or which may have a tendency to operate thus indirectly, by lowering the empire in the esteem and respect of other nations. In discharging this duty, each member is bound to consider, not only what he owes by his allegiance to the sovereign, but what he owes *loyally*, in the old French signification of the term, to his fellow-subjects. He sits in parliament as one of the community of persons who inhabit the United Kingdom, to represent their interests. By fiction of law, the whole commons of England are individually present in the House of Commons, for the protection and due administration of their common rights and interests, as subjects of the king of Great Britain, though, for convenience sake, only a portion of their number is actually present to represent them. But these representatives are still subjects, as much as their constituents, and have no right or authority beyond that which would be possessed by their constituents, if all were personally present, and that right would be simply to protect the lives, liberties, and estates of all those who live within the limits of the three kingdoms.

Beyond these limits, no individual commoner of Great Britain, nor any representative of any number, however great, of such commoners has any power or right in, or out of, parliament. What he owes to himself and his fellow-subjects is the beginning and the end of each individual's power in sending a representative to the commons' house of parliament, and this is equally the beginning and the end of the individual power of each representative, and of the united power of all the assembled representatives.

What right, then, can a subject of Great Britain, or a representative of any given number of British subjects, or an assembly of any given number of such representatives, have to interfere either in the legislation or in the administration of a country without the limits of the United Kingdom? What does he owe to himself, or what do they owe to each other, in respect of such a country? What community of interest have they to protect in respect of such a country? If the sovereign of Great Britain have conquered a foreign territory with the blood and treasure of British subjects, the British House of Commons may have committed a blunder in allowing him to do so, if they have given their consent to such an application of the power of the realm, or, if they have not so consented, they may have a right to impeach the advisers of the crown, for such a misapplication of what was intended solely for the protection and good of the three kingdoms. But what right has Isaac Jacobs, smith in Truro, as a subject of the king of Great Britain, to interfere in the government or legislation of this conquered territory? or what right has the representative of Isaac Jacobs, himself a subject of the king of Great Britain, or what right have all the assembled representatives of all the subjects of Great Britain, to say what shall be the laws for this conquered territory, or to interfere with the administration of these laws?

If they have any such right, it cannot be as subjects of the king of Great Britain, for the right of each subject, and of each representative, and of the assembled representatives, of such subjects, is based upon their common interest as subjects, with reference to the sovereign, to protect their laws, their liberties, and their estates; but they do not live in this conquered territory, neither have they any estates in it, and their common interests, not being co-extensive with the brotherhood of all mankind, but limited to the inhabitants of the three kingdoms, they cannot have any common interest with the inhabitants of the conquered country, any more than with the inhabitants of any other part of the earth, conquered or unconquered.

If, then, the subjects of the king of Great Britain have any right, by themselves or their representatives, to interfere with the legislation or government of a territory, conquered by the king of Great Britain with the blood and treasure of the inhabitants of Great Britain, it cannot be as subjects of the king of Great Britain, for to such interference there are wanting the very first elements which give the right to the commons of England of interfering in the legislation and government of the United Kingdom itself, namely, a common interest to protect their lives, liberties, and estates. Having neither lives, liberty, nor estates to protect in the newly-acquired territory, all they could have to assert by such inter-ference would be a right of dominion, a right by purchase, in respect of the British blood shed and the British treasure spent, to be co-sovereigns with the king of Great Britain. But such a right, by the constitution of England, does not exist in a subject of Great Britain, within the realm of Great Britain, and still less beyond it, if it can exist, even in the sovereign, beyond the limits of the three kingdoms.

But even if the commons could have any right to legislate for a territory, acquired at the expense of their blood and treasure, what right can they possibly have to legislate for a settlement, made by a portion of their own body, at the expense and risk of that portion, unless, at least, the settlement is to be treated as a mere local extension of the United Kingdom, the inhabitants of which are to enjoy all the rights and liberties enjoyed in the United Kingdom, parliamentary representation included?

CHAPTER IX.

WHETHER THE BRITISH SOVEREIGN ALONE, OR IN CONJUNCTION
WITH THE HOUSES OF PARLIAMENT, MAY CONSTITUTIONALLY
GOVERN POSSESSIONS BEYOND THE LIMITS OF THE UNITED
KINGDOM, CONSIDERED PRACTICALLY WITH REFERENCE TO
THE CONSTITUTIONAL POWERS OF THE DIFFERENT ORDERS OF
THE STATE.

IF the observations which have been presented in
regard to the power of the sovereign of Great Britain,
either alone or in conjunction with the houses of
parliament, to rule over a transmarine territory, be
well founded, the inevitable result, however startling,
apparently is that, *constitutionally*, or keeping
within the principles upon which the constituent
parts of her government are founded, Great Britain
has no power wherewith to govern any country
situated beyond the boundary of the United
Kingdom, and that if she do retain any under
her power, she cannot govern it otherwise than
upon the same arbitrary principles which prevail
in unlimited monarchies and which are utterly repugnant to her own constitutional doctrines, unless
there be a modification of her constitution, so as to
admit the foreign country to the full benefit of it.

However monstrous, and absurd, and unpalatable

such a doctrine might have appeared some ten years since, when our notions of exclusive trade and of colonial government were somewhat different from what they may be presumed to be at this day, possibly it may be found to be rational, and even palatable, now that we have abrogated the navigation laws, removed the restrictions upon trade, and very considerably changed our mode of governing our colonies.

But, before attempting to show how these changes bear upon the colonial part of the empire, it will be worth while to consider the practical working of the doctrine, contrary to that which has just been broached, namely, the doctrine that a foreign territory (*i.e.*, foreign as to locality, whether acquired by capitulation from an enemy, or by cession from a friendly power, or by voluntary settlement of British subjects) may constitutionally be acquired, and can constitutionally be governed, if not by the king, at least by the imperial parliament of Great Britain, including the sovereign. This subject has already been considered almost sufficiently, with reference to the sovereign, when speaking of his power to rule any territory out of Great Britain,[a] and little remains to be added to what has been said, as being irreconcilable in principle to the notion of the peers having any authority beyond this kingdom.[b]

[a] Vide supra, pp. 151 and 171.   [b] Supra, p. 190.

If the House of Peers do, on principle as well as in fact, represent the great land interests and aristocratic feelings of Great Britain, what voice can the land interests of a remote colony, or its aristocratic feelings, if there be any, raise in that house? So far as regards such a colony, the British House of Peers must be purely a *caput mortuum*.

When a baron of England, sitting in the House of Peers, learns that any measure has been introduced into the house affecting either land within the kingdom or his order, his alacrity is awakened to see that it shall not do this prejudicially, or more prejudicially than the occasion, which is suggested as the origin of the measure, requires; or, if the measure should affect neither land nor the order of the peerage generally, but only the interests, in these respects, of one of the body in particular, every peer has the reflection, that what has been done to-day to another may be done to-morrow to himself, to stimulate him to protect the individual in jeopardy.

But what individual interest has any baron of Great Britain, necessarily, to watch over a measure brought into the House of Peers, to affect land in a colony in the antipodes? or, what interest, in common with his order, can he necessarily have in such a measure? It may be that there is a stray peer, who happens to have a friend or a relative in the distant settlement, who has been able to gain his ear and indoctrinate him with his private notions, and that this peer may endeavor to make his voice heard in the house, in support or in condemnation of the measure proposed. But what assurance has the state that this individual peer is not advocating prejudiced and erroneous views? In those instances which affect the legislation of Great Britain itself, the state has the implied, if not the actual, security that each peer has his own interest, as well as his honor, to guide his judgment in legislating; but in the instance supposed of legislating for a colony, the sanction of self-interest is totally wanting.

Accidental interest there may be to induce even a number of peers to take part in the discussion of a colonial measure, such as those of religion, philanthropy, or morality. An active agitator from the colony, who has any scheme of his own or of his friends in these or other respects to promote, may succeed in enlisting a larger or smaller number of peers to adopt and advocate his views; but these peers cannot have either local knowledge or local interest to protect them from imposition and from advocating what may be not only useless, but positively injurious. Yet personal interest is the very foundation of every peer's right to sit in parliament and take any part in legislation.

It must be obvious that every necessarily self-acting guard of the interests of the subject is a-wanting when the House of Peers is sitting to legislate for a distant possession, and that so far as these are concerned, the passing of a bill through that house must, in many, if not in most cases, be an operation *pro forma*,—it may be of the minister of the crown, it may be of some enthusiast from Exeter Hall, or it may be of some interested party come from the possession itself; and that if discussion or opposition should arise, it must be occasional and accidental only.

If the peers of Great Britain, in legislating for a distant possession, or for a possession however near, yet still beyond the boundaries of the United Kingdom, lack that individual and general interest, which is the very title of their right to legislate for the United Kingdom itself, is the question more favorable for the legislation of a possession by the commons of England?

The title of a commoner to his seat in parliament is somewhat different from that of a peer to his seat. The commoner has no right to consider his own personal rights or interests. These may be protected or affected, no doubt, by the result of his vote; but that can only be consequentially; for, directly and immediately, he must lay aside all his private feelings and interests. The commoner sits in parliament, not for himself, but as the representative of others, not merely of that portion of the United Kingdom which the law has given the power to elect him, but for the whole common people of Britain.

Upon principle, the whole people of Great Britain should take part in the election of each of the members of the House of Commons. It has been only for convenience sake that the right of election has been parceled out in districts; and any member who should imagine that he may confine his views, in the votes he gives, to what benefits the district which elected him, completely misconceives his position. He is bound to dismiss from his mind not only his own private interests, but the individual and local interests of his constituents, except only in so far as his own interests and theirs are in common with those of the nation at large, and may, consequentially, be benefited or prejudiced by what is voted to be done for the nation at large.

But the interests of the nation at large are just an aggregation of the interests of all the individuals who go to make up that nation, the representatives included; and the guarantee, which the constituents or electors have, that the representatives will not betray the trust committed to them is, that their interests are common to the representatives. But how stands a foreign possession in respect of either representation or community of interest?

The political franchise, or right of electing

representatives to parliament, is not enjoyed by every individual in Great Britain, nor is it necessary, for any useful purpose or principle, that the franchise should be so enjoyed; for if all interests are fairly represented in parliament, and by such a number of representatives as makes tampering with them next to impossible, every useful purpose is answered. Though, *in theory*, it be true that "in the multitude of councilors there is safety, and purposes are established," yet there must be some limit to the numbers of "the multitude;" and it is equally true, *in practice*, that within any limits as to the number of councilors, the power of these councilors must be abstracted by, and rest in, one individual, or at least a very small number of individuals. Whether the councilors be electors resolving on the representative to be elected, or representatives resolving on measures to be passed, the power of the one or the other body, however large it may be made, will always be found to come round to a few individuals, either legitimately, through the mere effect of superior talent, energy, and general force of character; or illegitimately. through the obscene working of bribery, corruption, or family influence.

When the number of representatives is made so great as to render these illegitimate means of acquiring power nearly inoperative, then every useful

purpose of numbers is gained. All beyond that
may be very good in theory, but is injurious in
practice. It may be very sound in principle to
argue that every individual in the community has
a right, not only to partake in the franchise of
election, but even to sit in parliament personally.
On abstract principle, there seems no reason why
he should not have even that right. But what
advantage is there in having a right if it cannot be
enjoyed? and what enjoyment of the right of voting
could any individual have in an assembly of all the
inhabitants of Great Britain? It is, therefore, upon
the principle of necessity, more urgent than the
right to give personal attendance, that individuals
are not allowed to act for themselves in the councils
of the nation, but are required to send their representatives only. If every interest is represented,—and
on sound political principles, every interest ought to
be represented, if a healthy, easy, working of the
constitution is desired,—then every end is answered.

But to apply this to the colonial possessions of
Great Britain,—how are they represented in the
British parliament, either actually or virtually? What
interest, in common, have the farmers of Great
Britain with those in Australia or the Cape of Good
Hope? Both bodies produce corn and wool, and
they both wish to sell their produce as dear as
possible; but each will be defeated in this object

by how much the other succeeds. If abundance of Australian or Cape wool is brought to the London market, sufficient to supply the wants of the trade, and of superior quality to the Yorkshire wool, then the latter must be driven out of the market; and *vice versa.* England is overburdened with population, and is at her wits' end to know what to do with her criminals, the scum of that population. Hitherto, she has sent them to her penal settlements and to some of her colonies. These settlements and the colonies have at last grown strong enough in population to think they can do without so unhealthy an increase to it, and they refuse to receive more convicts. Here, again, the interests of the inhabitants of the mother country and of the colonies are in direct opposition. The colonists of Van Diemen's Land wish, for their own reasons, to make a new settlement on the main land. The Secretary of State for the Colonies tells them no, they must not, as Great Britain does not wish to extend her possessions. The colonists say very well, Britain need not go out of her own way, we will make the settlement ourselves; they do so, and Port Phillip is established, and becomes a thriving colony,—so thriving that the Secretary of State cannot see it slip from the power of Great Britain, and forthwith it is made a British colony. If the colonists of Van Diemen's Land had not been able, by their own resources, to accomplish this object of theirs, what interest would a farmer in East Lothian, or a shopkeeper in London, have had to urge upon the minister that he should give the sanction and support of the government to it? and, failing his compliance, what inducement would he have to bring the influence of the House of Commons to bear upon the minister? The inhabitants of the western division of the Cape of Good Hope desire to have the mountain passes between the interior and the coast opened up, for the passage of produce to the ports of exportation. The inhabitants of the eastern division object that too much money has already been expended upon such objects in the western division, and insist that the attention of the government should in future be directed more to the eastern division. What interest can any man who has never been out of the United Kingdom have in such a question as this? In these two instances the inhabitants of the mother country are indifferent to, and have no interest in, the wishes of the colonists.

If the inhabitants of Great Britain have no interest in common with the colonists in these questions, or have interests which are in conflict with those of the colonists, how are the interests of the colonists represented in parliament? As the members of the parliament represent only the interests of the inhabitants of the mother country by whom alone, and for whom alone they are elected, it is obvious that these members do not necessarily represent, and will not necessarily protect, the interests of the colonies in the House of Commons. If they will not do so necessarily—not accidentally, but necessarily—then the House of Commons, in legislating for the colonies is acting beyond its province, practically as well as theoretically, since the very end and object of its institution is to protect the lives, liberties, and estates of those whom it represents, of whom the colonists, *ex hypothesi*, form no part.

Mr. Pitt, in the course of the debates upon America, said, "Our legislative power of the colonies is sovereign and supreme. When two countries are connected together, like England and her colonies, without being incorporated, the one must necessarily govern,—the greater must rule the less; but so rule it as not to contradict the fundamental principles belonging to both." "The gentleman" Mr. Pitt afterwards said, "asks when were the colonies emancipated? But I desire to know when they were made slaves?" It is not difficult to conjecture what was passing through the mind of this champion of liberty when he made these observations. But it would have been difficult for him to have reduced them to practice.

There does not, in the first place, appear to have been any necessity why England should have ruled the

American colonies; there might have been another arrangement, as profitable to herself, as it would have been more congenial to the feelings of the Americans. But assuming that there is a necessity for England to rule the colonies, Mr. Pitt says, they are to be ruled "so as not to contradict the fundamental principles common to both." But how is this to be done? He speaks of "*fundamental principles* common to both." By the expression "fundamental principles," he must have meant to convey the principle of representation in the House of Commons and the right of the representatives there to stand upon Magna Charta, the statute *De Tallagio non concedendo*, the Bill of Rights, and the other instruments of British liberty. But when he speaks of these as being *common* to the inhabitants of Great Britain and to the inhabitants of the colonies, he is not so intelligible.

That these rights and liberties had *in fact* been common, Mr. Pitt could never have meant to assert, for the very subject of the debate in which he uttered the sentiment negatived such an assertion. It is, no doubt, true that one of the American colonies, Maryland, enjoyed a constitution, which made it virtually and in fact independent of Great Britain; but with that exception the closest resemblance which the most favored of the other American colonies had in their government to that of Great

Britain was, that they had assemblies composed of members elected by the people. To have told the Americans that this circumstance gave them the enjoyment of the " fundamental principles " of British liberty, in `" common " with the inhabitants of Great Britain, would have been a mockery and an insult in the face of the fact that the very subject of the debate in which that assertion was made, was the legality of an act of the *British parliament,* imposing a tax upon the Americans, which their assemblies had rejected, and, in the face of those other facts, which drove the Americans to attempt and achieve a successful rebellion.

What Mr. Pitt must have meant was that the colonists, having been Britons, were entitled, or *ought* to enjoy the " fundamental principles " of British liberty, in common with the inhabitants of Great Britain, and therefore it was that he, and the House of Commons in concurrence with him, voted the abrogation of the British act of parliament imposing a stamp duty on the Americans. In expressing this sentiment, Mr. Pitt repeated what had been enunciated by the minister of one of the Stuarts, those sturdy assertors of the royal prerogative. Speaking of the charters to be given to the North American colonies, Lord Halifax had said " there was no room to doubt that the same laws under which we live in England should

be established in a country composed of Englishmen."
In these opinions Lord Halifax and Mr. Pitt have
been followed by most politicians who have spoken
on the subject since their time. How far politicians
have *acted* upon these opinions is another matter,
which shall be considered presently.

Lord Mansfield said, it "was absurd that in the
colonies they should carry all the laws of England
with them; they carry only such as are applicable
to their situation."[a] These expressions had the
appearance of being more cautious and precise than
those they were substituted for, and they have, in
consequence, been adopted by all lawyers since Lord
Mansfield's time; for lawyers feel more sensibly than
politicians that any vagueness or inaccuracy of
expression is sure to revert upon themselves, and
therefore, by habit, they are more cautious in what
they say. But the caution here exists only in
appearance, for the question "which of the laws of
England are applicable to the situation of colonists"
has been discovered to be as vague as any other
question connected with colonial polity, and the
doctrine involved in it to be almost incapable of
application.

But, let it be assumed that the rights of the
colonists exist to the extent asserted in the absolute
terms of politicians, or only to the limited extent

[a] Howell's State Trials, vol. xx, p. 289.

admitted by lawyers, what then becomes of Mr. Pitt's other maxim, that "our," that is, the British, "legislative power over the colonies is sovereign and supreme." This assertion may be necessary, in order to support the other assertion, that "where two countries are connected together, like England and her colonies, without being incorporated, the one must necessarily govern,—the greater must rule the less;" but it contradicts the other maxim, that this "rule" must be "so as not to contradict the fundamental principles *common* to both." If the commons of England refuse to tax themselves, the "fundamental principle" of the British constitution is that no power on earth can compel them; but, according to Mr. Pitt, if the colonists refuse to tax themselves, the British "legislative power," being "sovereign and supreme," can compel them. If it may, then the "fundamental principle," that the subject cannot be taxed without his consent, is either not common to the colonists with the inhabitants of Great Britain, or the rule of Great Britain is such that it cannot be exercised without contradicting this fundamental principle.

It may be said that Mr. Pitt speaks of the "legislative power" as opposed to "rule," or rather as a component part of the power to rule, because he elsewhere says, in a passage which has been already commented on, that taxation is no part "of the legislative or governing power ;" and in the same debate he said, "When in this house we give and grant, we give and grant what is our own ; but in an American tax, what do we do? We, your Majesty's commons of Great Britain, give and grant to your Majesty, what? Our own property? No. We give and grant to you the property of your Majesty's commons in America. It is an absurdity in terms." And so, no doubt, it was, in fact as well as in terms, if it were not something worse. And yet, when Mr. Pitt said that " our legislative power was sovereign and supreme over the colonies," that "the greater must rule the less," there must unconsciously have been lurking in his mind a suspicion that " a sovereign and supreme legislative power " and the " rule," which England necessarily must have over her colonies, must include the right to tax ; else, if such a right were not included in the rule, why did he qualify his assertion of the right to " rule," which he used synonymously with the " sovereign and supreme legislative power," by the addition, " but so rule as not to contradict the fundamental principles common to both." If the right to tax, the question then in debate, was not included in the power to " rule," then why make this qualification as to the mode in which that power should be exercised.

The truth seems to be that Great Britain cannot constitutionally " rule " a foreign territory inhabited

by British subjects, who are entitled to enjoy the
"fundamental principles" of British liberty, by
exercising over them a "sovereign and supreme
legislative power," through the three estates of the
British realm, king, lords, and commons (whether
that power include the power to tax or not), without
necessarily contradicting the "fundamental principles" which, in the postulate, are asserted to be
"common to both" the inhabitants of the mother
country and the inhabitants of the foreign territory;
since the inhabitants of the foreign territory are not,
like the inhabitants of the mother country, represented, either virtually or in fact, either in the House
of Peers or in the House of Commons; and this
position is all the clearer and stronger, if the power
to tax be *not* included in the "sovereign and
supreme legislative power;" for then the colonists
lack the possession of that strong engine of power
wherewith alone the inhabitants of the mother
country have, as already shown, been able to with-
stand the power of the crown and of the peers,
whether single or united, when directed against their
liberties.

If this "fundamental principle" of the British
constitution,—that the commons are not to be taxed
but with their own consent,—that they may give or
refuse taxes until their grievances are redressed, or
such measures of executive government adopted as

they approve of, be not included in "the sovereign
and supreme legislative power" of the imperial
parliament,—then where does it reside? In the crown
it cannot be, for no such political heresy may be
uttered as that the crown may tax the subject. Is
it in the colonists? If so, how are they to use it?
By election of representatives to sit in colonial
councils and assemblies? Very good, if they have
them. But *cui bono?* To what purpose shall the
colonists use the power to give or refuse taxes. They
may exercise it, to the effect of preventing themselves
being overburdened by taxation, as the inhabitants
of the mother country may use the same power; but
this is just the last purpose to which the inhabitants
of the mother country have themselves put the
power; witness the £800,000,000 of national debt
which they have, by their representatives, authorized,
and for the interest of which they have annually to
tax themselves. The use to which the inhabitants of
the mother country have put this power, to regulate
the taxation, has been the protection of their liberties,
by controlling, through it, both the executive power
of the crown and the legislative power of the crown
and of the peers. But if the crown, the peers, and
the British House of Commons possess a "sovereign
and supreme legislative power" over the colonies,
how can the colonies exercise the power of taxation,
so as to control this legislative power over them. Of

course they cannot. If they could, the legislative
power would no longer be " sovereign and supreme ;"
and if they cannot, how, then, can they control the
executive power of the crown, when that is backed
by the sovereign and supreme legislative power of
the three estates? And if they cannot, then Britain
cannot *by possibility* rule her colonies, by the
exercise of " a sovereign, supreme legislative
power," without violating the first and fundamental
principles of her constitution, that the subject shall,
by his representatives, have a control, both of the
executive and legislative power, through the power
of giving or withholding taxes.

But, though the colonists have as clear and
irrefragable a right to be represented in parliament,
as to anything done by that assembly, which affects
their rights and liberties, either public or private, as
ever Ireland, or Wales, or Chester, or Durham, had,
ere they were allowed to send members to parliament, there is a difficulty in the way of a concession of this right to the colonies which seems
insuperable ; and that is, their distance from the
mother country.

If it were possible to overcome that difficulty,
there cannot be much doubt that our colonies would
then be ruled much more effectively and harmoniously
than they have been.

Burke says of Ireland, " We are sure that almost

every successive improvement in constitutional liberty,
as far as it was made here, was transmitted thither.
Your standard never advanced an inch before your
privileges. Sir John Davis shows beyond a doubt
that the refusal of a general communication of your
rights was the true cause why Ireland was five
hundred years in subduing ; and, after the vain
projects of a military government, attempted in the
reign of Queen Elizabeth, it was soon discovered
that nothing could make that country English, in
civility and allegiance, but your laws and your forms
of legislature. It was not English arms, but the
English constitution, that conquered Ireland."[a]   And
of Wales the same philosophic politician says, " You
find no less than fifteen acts of penal regulation on
the subject of Wales."[b]   " But our ancestors found
that the *tyranny of a free people* could, of all
tyrannies, the least be endured.   Accordingly, in the
27th of Henry VIII, the course was entirely altered.
With a preamble, stating the entire and perfect rights
of the crown of England, it gave to the Welsh all
the rights and privileges of English subjects."[c]   But
that " a nation should have a right to English
liberties, and *yet no share in the fundamental
security of these liberties*—the grant of their own
property—seemed a thing so incongruous, that eight
years after, that is, in the thirty-fifth of that reign,

[a] Vol. iii, p. 82.   [b] Vol. iii, p. 85.   [c] Vol. iii, p. 86.

*a complete and not ill-proportioned representation
by counties and burghs was bestowed upon Wales* by
act of parliament. From that moment, as by a
charm, the tumult subsided ; obedience was restored,
peace, order, and civilization followed in the train of
liberty—

> " '————Simul alba nautis
> Stella refulsit
> Defluit saxis agitatus humor
> Concidunt venti fugiuntque nubes
> Et minax (quod sic voluere), ponto
> Unda recumbit.' "

The same evil of discontent and accompanying
turbulence existed in parts of the present United
Kingdom, the inhabitants of which, at the present
day, would be surprised to think that they ever, at
any time, were unrepresented in parliament, and had
to submit to laws and to pay taxes, without having
had a voice in framing the one or in the imposition
of the other. The counties palatine of Chester and
of Durham were, at one time, without the pale of
the constitution, and were not admitted within it,
until they had expressly petitioned parliament to that
effect, when it was done by statute, expressly recognizing the justice of their demand.

But, if we could overcome the difficulties which
local distance offers to making the colonies, not mere
dependencies of the empire, but integral parts of it
in every sense of the word, it is by no means clear

that this would be a prudent step to take, or one that would add strength to the empire. It is much more probable that it would be productive of weakness. But this is a subject which will be touched upon by-and-by, in speaking of what should be done with our colonies.

CHAPTER X.

WE have seen that the minister of even so arbitrary
a monarch as Charles II, considered that English
colonists should enjoy the rights and privileges of
Englishmen;[a] and that all our statesmen after him
have endorsed this opinion with their own; that our
lawyers have ignored a right in the crown to legislate
for British settlements, or at least to tax them, except
with their own consent; and that Lord Mansfield,
one of the greatest sticklers for the royal prerogative,
while he was of opinion that the crown had power
to legislate for a colony acquired by conquest, was
further of opinion that it held that power sub-
ordinately to the power of the imperial parliament,
notwithstanding that the existence of the power in
the crown had been argued before him to be free
and independent "as a part of the prerogative."
We have seen, moreover, that, in Campbell v. Hall,
it was solemnly decided that so soon as the crown

[a] Vide supra, p. 172.

gave a constitution to a conquered colony, it ceased
to have any power to legislate for the colony. That
decision was obtained after an argument which, from
both sides of the bar, admitted that the crown could
not legislate *for a colony of Englishmen voluntarily
settled* in an unoccupied country ; and the decision,
by necessary inference, affirmed the argument.

Nay, we have a statement from the bar in that
case, not contradicted from the bench, that in
March, 1749, a declaratory act was introduced into
parliament, " in order to make the king's order law
in the colonies ; but that was petitioned against by
every one of the colonies, and was thrown out."
The vote throwing out such a bill was equivalent to
a declaration by parliament that the king's order
was " *not* law in the colonies." But if there could
be any doubt as to that, 6 Geo. III, cap. 2, declares
expressly the power of legislation and taxation over
the colonies to be in the king and the parliament,
without making any reference to the king's sole
prerogative. Its words are, " The king's majesty,
by and with the advice and consent of the lords
spiritual and temporal and commons of Great Britain
in parliament assembled, hath had, and of right ought
to have, full power and authority to make laws and
statutes, of sufficient force and validity to bind the
colonies and people of America, subjects of the crown
of Great Britain, in all cases whatsoever."

Though it be difficult to perceive upon the arguments which have been already offered,[a] how even the imperial parliament can legislate for British subjects settled abroad, consistently, at least, with the due operation of those constitutional principles which regulate the machinery of legislation for the United Kingdom, yet upon those abstract principles, which are laid down by Vattel,[b] that a colony becomes part of the state which settles it, and with reference to the *physical power* of the imperial parliament, it may be said that the parliament has power to legislate for the colonies.

But if the arguments which have been used,[c] have failed to show that a legislative power over the colonies cannot reside in the British sovereign, the statute 6 Geo. III, cap. 12, has put that question to rest, by declaring that that power resides in the imperial parliament—in the lords and commons— acting along with the sovereign, and consequently that it cannot reside in the crown *alone*.

The American colonies almost ridiculed the right and the power asserted by the crown to legislate for them, and they denied the right even of the imperial

[a] Vide, supra, p. 190, et seq.

[b] " Lorsq'une nation s'empare d'un pais eloigné, et y établit une colonie, ce pays, quoique separé de l'établissement principal, fait naturellement partie de l'état, tout comme les anciennes possessions."

[c] Vide, supra, p. 151, et seq.

parliament, and ultimately, by their rebellion, success-fully contested its power. The charter, which had been granted to the Americans by the last of the Tudors and by the Stuarts, had recognized the rights of the subject in the colonies to be those of English-men, carrying with them the rights and privileges they had enjoyed at home. Under these charters, an amount of freedom had been enjoyed, which was as nearly analogous to that enjoyed in Great Britain as circumstances would admit. The colonies were represented in legislative assemblies, which were elected annually. These assemblies voted the sup-plies annually and controlled their expenditure, and through this engine of power, the colonists, like the inhabitants of the mother country, had been gradually encroaching upon the power of the crown, which had been thitherto exercised through the governors appointed by it.

These encroachments had produced sore heart-burnings in the local officers of ·the crown, who represented the colonists to the executive at home as turbulent and factious, and determined to subvert all constituted authority. On the other hand, the colonists thought they had grievances against the local officers, which ought to be redressed, and these they represented to the home executive, as strongly and as frequently as they could. Unfortunately, the Board of Trade and Plantations had then the duty of regulating all matters within the colonies; but that board had neither the power of enforcing its regulations nor the responsibility of governing the colonies. This power and responsibility rested in the Secretary of State for the Southern Department. The board, like all inferior and irresponsible bodies, was not over careful to consider the effect of the measures it recommended, nor of the means it suggested for enforcing them ; and encountering opposition from the colonists which, in its transmission through the local officials, got that coloring which the irritated feelings of the latter suggested, the board allowed themselves to be mixed up in the irritation. Instead of considering the claims of the colonists through the medium they would have viewed similar claims, if made by the inhabitants of the mother country, the board kept their attention fixed on the spirit of encroachment and insubordination as it was represented to them, and overlooked the matters out of which that spirit had arisen, and the remedies which would have allayed it. The consequence was, naturally enough, an increase of dissatisfaction on both sides, which in time became so aggravated that it only required the active interference of the home government in support of the officials to fire it into rebellion.

Unluckily, the British minister of that day, the Duke of Newcastle, was better fitted to take part in a personal squabble about official power and patronage, than to weigh the political and social rights of a great rising community. Through him "the sovereign and supreme legislative power" of the empire was brought to bear upon the colonists, and the flame of rebellion was immediately kindled, to be extinguished only by recognition of the independence of the colonists, who severed themselves from their mother country in anger and hatred, to form for themselves, in "the United States of America," a dominion more vast, and which promises to become, in time, but for their own suicidal acts, more powerful than any that the world has yet seen. Did Britain retire from the ignominious and unnatural contest chastened and instructed, and resolved to improve for the future, in the management of those colonies which still remained to her, or which might thereafter be formed by her subjects? Let the civil rebellions which have since happened in Jamaica and other West Indian colonies, and the military rebellion in Canada answer that question.

It is impossible to read the English and American official correspondence preceding the American rebellion, without perceiving that the colonists pointed at having the same government in every respect as was enjoyed at home, including the control of the executive and legislative power through their representatives in the assemblies, and that the passing of the stamp act was only the torch which lighted the combustibles already collected. As Smith had said, in 1766,[a] "their great distance from Europe had alleviated more or less their dependency upon the mother state. Their situation had placed them less in the view, and less in the power of their mother country. In pursuing their interests their own way, their conduct had upon many occasions been overlooked, either because not known or not understood in Europe; and upon some occasions, it had been fairly suffered and submitted to, because their distance rendered it difficult to restrain it."

The taxes levied upon the Americans were confined to raising the money necessary for defraying the expenses of their civil government, and were so light that to govern three millions of people cost only £64,700 a year;[b] and their *internal* government, till the unfortunate stamp act was passed, was not interfered with further than that the governor and all the civil functionaries were appointed by the home authorities, and the colonists had to struggle with, or submit to, the tempers and caprices of these individuals. But in their *external* relations, they were fettered by the navigation act, and could not export to any but the mother country, certain specified commodities, which were technically called

[a] Wealth of Nations, vol. II, p. 402.   [b] Ibid, vol. II, p. 413.

the "enumerated articles." These were articles which the mother country did not produce, and could not well do without, such as molasses, coffee, cocoa-nuts, tobacco, pimento, ginger, &c., and therefore she forced the colonists to bring such of them as they produced to her market, and prohibited them from taking them to any other. The non-enumerated articles, such as corn, cattle, &c., which England did produce, and therefore did not choose to expose to a competition with the produce of the colonies, she allowed the colonists to take to the nearest and the highest market, wheresoever they could find it.

It was as much to get the better of this selfish and unprincipled exercise of the "sovereign and supreme legislative power" of the imperial parliament, and to obtain a remedy for many minor grievances, as it was resistance to the stamp act, that induced the Americans to do those things which Smith says were "overlooked, either because not known or understood in Europe, and on some occasions had been fairly submitted to, because their distance rendered it difficult to restrain it." It was these causes which induced them, when once they had raised the standard of rebellion, not to stop short in their career for emancipation, when the imperial parliament was terrified by the thunders of Pitt's eloquence, and by the bold front of resistance which the colonists had shown, into granting the repeal of that act which had been the immediate cause of the rebellion.

If the North American colonists had, from the beginning, been ruled by governors sent out from England, to rule either by their own arbitrary will, or assisted by an executive council, composed of officials also sent from the mother country,—if they had never known greater liberty than was afforded by this mode of government, modified as it was by the possibility of appeal to the imperial parliament when the grievance was general and not individual, —the rebellion of America would not perhaps have occurred till fifty years after the time at which it broke out. It was the legislative councils and assemblies popularly elected that had done the mischief in America, by the opportunity they afforded to the colonists of expressing their opinions to each other and of forming measures for giving effect to their opinions.

With a knowledge that the law allowed a power of legislating for colonies acquired by conquest to be in the crown, as part of the prerogative, only until the crown had given a new constitution to them, but not after, and that that power could be exercised only in subordination to the imperial parliament, but that the law altogether denied a power of legislation over colonies voluntarily settled by English subjects to exist in the crown, and at the very utmost allowed it to reside in the imperial parliament, exposed even there, in its exercise, to many serious anomalies and inconsistencies, as has been attempted to be shown in these pages,[a]—and with the rough and sad experience in the American rebellion of the consequences of the denial by a group of powerful colonies of a right of legislation, to be either in the crown or in the imperial parliament,—what has been the system of British colonial government since the conclusion of the American rebellion? This question shall now be considered.

[a] Vide supra, p. 190, et seq.

CHAPTER XI.

In considering the question with which the preceding chapter concluded, it will be convenient to separate the colonies, which we already had previous to and at the date of the declaration of American independence,[a] from those which we acquired or settled subsequent to that date, for the purpose of more clearly discerning how the powers of colonial government and legislation have been wielded since that event.

The colonies which we possessed at the date of the declaration of American independence, at least those worth mentioning, were our West Indian islands, and our North American colonies of Canada, New Brunswick, Nova Scotia, Newfoundland, and Prince Edward's Island.

All of our West Indian colonies had received charters from the crown, giving them legislative councils and assemblies with the exception of St.

[a] Our administration of the colonies which now form the United States may be gathered partially from what has been said above, p. 43.

Lucia and Trinidad, which two colonies, according to what law does not appear, were governed by orders in council.

The North American colonies, also, were administered by governors, exercising legislative powers with the advice and consent of legislative councils and assemblies.

It is no doubt true that some, both of our West Indian and of our North American colonies, had been acquired by conquest, and that others of them had been formed by voluntary settlement; but it is not necessary to distinguish them in these respects for the purpose of ascertaining whether the power of legislating for them resided in the crown or in the imperial parliament, because, on the authority of the decision in Campbell *v.* Hall, it may be asserted that, after the crown had given them a constitution by governor, legislative council, and assembly, the crown had parted with, and could not resume, the power of legislation.

In considering, therefore, our government of these different colonies, it must be apparent that our North American colonies, which now form the United States, were not the only colonies which possessed vents for the expression of public opinion, since all of these other colonies, with the insignificant exception of St. Lucia and Trinidad, possessed legislative councils and assemblies, equally with the United States.

It was to be expected, therefore, that, with the same means of resistance and combination at the command of the colonists, the same causes operating in our remaining colonies that had operated in the United States, would in time produce the same effects. The remaining colonies possessed forms of government, based upon the same recognition of the right of the colonists to enjoy all the rights and liberties of free-born Englishmen, as had been admitted into the local governments of the North American colonies, and it was only to be expected that the colonists would adopt every means open to them to obtain the full enjoyment of these rights.

A cursory notice of the past history of the administration of one or two of our West Indian and North American colonies will show that this is the course which things have taken, and that our government of them, far from being in harmony, has shown a constant conflict between the colonies and the home government, though backed by the sovereign and supreme legislative power of the imperial parliament. Upon this subject the world possesses information, in the work of no less an authority than Earl Grey, many years colonial minister, which, in this respect at least, is beyond cavil. Earl Grey gives a short summary of the later government of the colonies generally, and begins with that of the West India islands.

It will be convenient to follow this arrangement. But before noticing his lordship's account of the government of these islands, it must be explained that sugar had originally been one of the "enumerated articles," above referred to,[a] which, by the navigation act, required to be sent to the British market alone. In 1731, importation into other countries was allowed on a representation from the West India planters. The very high price, however, which Britain could always afford to give for the article, coupled with certain restrictions upon the importation into other countries, made the permission of such importation practically of no effect.[b] Great Britain continued to be, and always was, almost the only customer of the West India islands for the purchase of their sugar.

The "West India interest" was, for many years (nearly a century), very powerful in the British parliament, so powerful that, contrary to all justice and common sense, as it now appears to our statesmen, they were able to prevail on parliament (or rather on the minister, for in those days the parliament but echoed the will of the minister), to lay a much heavier duty on all sugar produced elsewhere than was leviable on sugar produced in the West Indian colonies. This was necessary, it was said, for the *protection*, as it was called, of the agriculture of these colonies. Towards the year 1846, among other

[a] Supra, p. 254.   [b] Wealth of Nations, vol. ii, p. 419.

fiscal discoveries then made, it began to be apparent
to the British legislative mind, that the difference
between the duty leviable on British sugar and
that leviable on sugar produced elsewhere, though it
had necessarily enhanced the price to the consumer
by a sum nearly corresponding with that difference,
and amounting, on a fair calculation, to several
millions sterling annually, had gone into the pockets
of the West India planters, or, more strictly speaking,
into the pockets of their mortgage creditors, and
yet this "protected" West India interest was as
hungry for "protection" as ever, and, what was
worse, was as much in need of it.

Protection, in short, was discovered to have been
a failure —to have been simply a means of taking
so much money out of the British consumer's pocket
to put it into the West India planter's, and enable
him thereby to bribe his mortgagee into permitting
him to live in luxury and independence in London,
while his plantations in the West Indies were being
mismanaged by agents, ultimately to fall into the
hands of the mortgagees themselves. So far as the
West India interest, strictly so called, was concerned,
the money represented by the difference between the
price that had to be paid by the consumer under the
effect of the high differential duty on all foreign
sugar, and the price that the consumer would have
had to pay if that differential duty had not existed,

and foreign sugar had been thus allowed to come into the market to compete with British West India sugar, was just so much money thrown away. It had been like water thrown upon sand; it had disappeared and left no good behind.

To protect this differential duty, and thereby to keep up the price of sugar, was, of course, of vital importance, not only to the planter, but still more to the London West India merchant, as he was called, or money-lender, as he might more appropriately have been designated, and these two powerful bodies —the planters and the merchants—had been able to compel the people to pay dearly for their sugar for nearly a century. Towards 1846 the delusion began to be apparent and to be acknowledged. It had long before been exposed, but there are none more blind or stupid than those that are determined neither to see nor to understand. The West India interest had now become not so powerful in parliament, and all the delusions about destruction of the colonies, deprivation of the luxury of sugar, and the like, wherewith the popular mind had been worked upon, having failed, and the minister, having given unmistakable evidence of his intention to do away with the differential duty upon sugar, along with similar duties on other commodities, every engine was put in motion to " bother " him into either receding at the outset, or retracing his steps after he had set out.

In spite of every opposition, however, Sir Robert Peel's government was strong enough to carry the passing of the act of the 8th of Victoria, cap. 5, whereby it was made lawful for Her Majesty to declare the sugar of any country, with which she should have a treaty of reciprocity, to be admissible on payment of duties after the same scale as was applicable to sugars, the produce of China, Java, or Manilla, *i.e.*, 28s. and 23s. 4d. per cwt., instead of 63s., the duty leviable on the sugar of countries not having treaties of reciprocity. All that remained now to be done was to set a-going such an agitation as might compel Sir R. Peel's successors in office to repeal that act. This unworthy step, it appears, the Protectionist party were not slow to adopt and unworthily to follow out.

SECTION I.—OUR GOVERNMENT OF THE WEST INDIAN COLONIES OF GUIANA AND JAMAICA, AND REFLECTIONS THEREUPON.

With this explanatory introduction, let us return to Lord Grey's account of the government of the West Indian colonies since 1846, in order to select the history of one or two of them. Let us begin with Guiana. In that colony, there exists what is called " The Court of Policy." " This court," Lord Grey says,[a] " in which the number of official and

---

[a] Colonial Policy, vol. i, p. 144.

unofficial members *is equal, the governor having a casting vote,* possesses the general power of legislation, but without the power of levying taxes, or making appropriations from the colonial revenue. These powers the Court of Policy can only exercise when sitting in the ' Combined Court' with the ' financial representatives.' Till lately, the financial representatives were chosen by about 800 persons only, out of a population of about 120,000, and *were really not the representatives of the people, but of the merchants, planters, and absentee proprietors.* In the Court of Policy, *the governor can always command a majority,* though this is never exercised without great reluctance. In the Combined Court, on the contrary, *the addition of the financial representatives leaves him without the power of carrying any measure, unless he can obtain the support of some, at least, of the elective members.*"

After giving this general account of the constitution of Guiana, Earl Grey narrates "the progress and consequences of the unfortunate differences between the governor and the Combined Court, *which for some time interrupted the regular working of the government.* It seems that the civil list of the colony had been provided for by an ordinance, which was not to expire until the year 1854, and was therefore, till then, beyond the action of the "Combined Court." But, in the year 1847, the

unofficial members of the "Court of Policy" suggested a diminution of twenty-five per cent. in all
salaries charged on the civil list, under the pretence
of relieving the distressed state of the colony, owing
to the great fall in the price of sugar, consequent
upon the removal of protection to that trade, by the
act of the imperial parliament of 8 Vic., cap. 5.[a]

The pretence was as shallow as it was unjust to the
holders of the offices, whose salaries were proposed to
be reduced, inasmuch as the revenue of the colony
had increased, instead of falling off, since the civil
list had been settled, with the concurrence of the
Combined Court. The governor, therefore, refused
to comply with the suggestion of the *non-official
members of the Court of Policy* for the proposed
reduction, and, as was anticipated, the *majority of
the Combined Court* refused the governor those taxes
which were necessary to defray the expenses of the
government not covered by the civil list.

"It was probably anticipated," says Lord Grey,
"that the embarrassment in which the government
would thus be placed would compel us," *i. e.*, the
ministers at home, "to apply to parliament for power
to continue to levy the usual taxes, *without the
sanction of the Combined Court*, or to have recourse
to some other expedient. *In the then state of the
House of Commons, we should, in either case, have*

[a] Vide supra, p. 263.

been exposed to a defeat, which would have greatly promoted the success of those who were struggling to recover for the British sugar-grower the monopoly of the home market, of which he had been deprived."

The minister at home very wisely defeated these anticipations, by adopting the more constitutional course of letting the colonists know that the government could not be carried on, if they would not vote the necessary expenses. He instructed the governor to discontinue those public services which he was refused the means of providing for, even if this should involve disbanding the police, shutting up the hospitals, the interruption of the administration of justice, and the withdrawal of the troops, and to intimate that no more liberated Africans would be sent to the colony.

Lord Grey says that, for his own part, while giving these instructions, which involved a possible dissolution of all society in the colony, he regretted the consequences they were likely to produce; he did not think that those who produced them ought to be relieved, " either by applying to parliament to set aside the constitution of the colony," or by yielding to their unreasonable demands : they ought to be made to feel the consequences of their own act. The result answered his lordship's expectation. In August, 1849, the Combined Court passed a temporary ordinance for the levying of taxes, and, in

December following, the governor reported the satisfactory termination of the controversy by the passing of all the usual financial measures.

Though the pretence made by the Combined Court, *(elected by eight hundred out of one hundred and twenty thousand inhabitants,)* for this controversy was relief to the colony generally, yet the true motive, it appears, was an attempt to promote the success of the efforts being made by the Protectionist party at home to overturn the tariff act of 1846. Governor Barkly, on the 18th March, 1848, wrote the minister,—" It seems to be the general opinion that the measures proposed to be adopted to stop the supplies *emanate from the West Indians in England* connected with this colony." One of the non-official members of the Court of Policy laid resolutions before the court, distinctly placing the refusal of the supplies on the ground *that protection had been refused the sugar-grower;* and Mr. Gordon, one of the principal planters in the colony, in his correspondence with the Colonial Reform Association, distinctly asserted that the attempt to cut down the civil list was, in the first instance, " *suggested by the Protectionists, as a part of a general system for embarrassing government, with a view of regaining lost protection.*"

This controversy, in which 119,200 inhabitants of the colony, out of 120,000, were made the sport of the representatives of the other 800, and *also of the Protectionist party at home*, cost the colony £150,000 in taxes not imposed or levied while the controversy endured, together with the disturbance of trade caused by the excessive importation of goods, during the cessation of taxation; an effect which produced little good to the consumers, as the chief advantage accrued to a few foreign importers of goods, who stored them until the prices should, on the resumption of the duties, rise sufficiently to answer their purpose.

But Lord Grey says, "the pecuniary loss" incurred by this struggle was "by no means the most serious part of the injury that resulted from it." This "most serious part" he describes to have consisted in the interruption that was given to measures for improving the colony, which were in contemplation before the struggle began, which have been adopted since it terminated, and which have now proved eminently successful and have brought the colony out of a state of hopeless despondency into a condition of most hopeful energy.

"During the continuance of the dispute," Lord Grey says, "an agitation was raised *in favor of the entire alteration of the present constitution, and the substitution of one precisely similar to those which exist in the older West Indian colonies, which possess representative assemblies, exercising in conjunction with the governor and council all the powers of legislation.* The state of society in Guiana, where there is an extremely small proportion of Europeans, the remainder of the population being made up of various different races, for the most part little advanced in civilization, and altogether deficient in the education and intelligence necessary for the safe exercise of political powers, rendered such a change in this colony, in my opinion, altogether inexpedient;" and so the change was not adopted.

The next colony mentioned by Earl Grey is Jamaica,[a] "which, for the amount of its population and the extent and richness in natural resources of its territory, is entitled to be considered as the most important of our former slave colonies."

This colony has, for two centuries, been in possession of a representative constitution, and its assembly not only exercises the ordinary authority " of a legislative body, but performs many of what are usually the functions of the executive government, the authority of the crown being more restricted than elsewhere by various laws, which have at different times been passed, and by usages which have grown up." It is not required in Jamaica, as it is in this country, in Canada, and in the Australian colonies, that every grant of money should be recommended by the crown's

* Colonial Policy, vol. I, p. 166.

representative, before it is voted ; but every member of the legislature proposes any vote which he considers to be advisable ; nor is there any person responsible for preparing an estimate of the probable receipts and expenditure of the colony, and taking care that the latter shall be covered by the former.[a]
" In the absence of any effective individual responsibility, it is too commonly the practice for each member of the assembly to push forward every grant for objects interesting to himself or his constituents, without much regard to the amount or comparative urgency of other claims upon the public purse, so that the appropriation of the revenue comes to be determined rather by a kind of scramble amongst the members of the legislature, than by a careful consideration of what the public interest requires."

The money got in this way is not, as in England, treated as a grant to the crown alone, but certain persons, known as " commissioners of public accounts," regulate both the collection and *the application* of the revenue, and have " frequently used the power of issuing, without the concurrence of the governor, sums in inconvertible paper, called island cheques." *All* the members of assembly *being ex-officio commissioners of public accounts*, and having, as such, a control over the audit of the accounts and the power of continuing to sit

[a] Colonial Policy, vol. I, p. 174.

and act, notwithstanding a prorogation of the assembly, are without any control by the crown, or any check from other authority.

Such being the nature of the constitution of Jamaica, the House of Assembly, on the 18th of December, 1846, addressed a memorial to the Queen, in which they craved permission " to re- monstrate against the many wrongs which we have sustained *by acts of the imperial parliament*." One of these wrongs, they said, arose from the question of slavery. " The establishment of slavery was *not our act, but that of the parent government*, and this policy was continued under the sanction of British laws equally sacred as those under which any other class of your Majesty's subjects hold their property. After having been most vigorously and profitably carried on for one hundred and fifty years by British ships, British merchants, and British capital, it was established by act of parliament." Lord Grey admits that " the abolition of the slave- trade was necessarily fatal to the kind of prosperity (such as it was) which Jamaica formerly enjoyed ;" and " this step once taken," his lordship says, " it became impossible for the island to enjoy durable prosperity, except by adopting an entirely different system." Instead of doing so, the colonists " were loud in their complaints, and ascribed all their losses and difficulties *to imperial legislation*. They offered determined resistance to the commercial policy which England had adopted, and acting under the same suggestions as had been made by the Protectionist party at home to the colonists of Guiana, those of Jamaica, in the summer of 1848, petitioned the governor to summon the legislature " to take into consideration the state of the country, and to deliberate and determine what measures ought to be adopted *to avert or ward off the baneful effects of imperial legislation.*"

The result was that the greater part of the taxes being voted only for a year, the assembly, as in Guiana, recommended a serious reduction, varying from *nineteen and a half to thirty-three and a half per cent.* in the civil salaries; and when the governor refused to sanction such a scandalous injustice to the civil servants, the assembly refused to vote taxes, which would provide *any part* of the salaries sought to be reduced. The course which Her Majesty's government followed was, in this instance, the same as they had adopted in the case of Guiana. They refused to confirm the acts proposed by the assembly, —they desired that body to be dissolved, and threw upon the colonists the whole responsibility of failing to provide for those services which were necessary for the maintenance and protection of society.

This course was as successful with Jamaica as it had been with Guiana. A new assembly made attempts to modify the objectionable acts, but failing in this, they finally abandoned them, and matters returned pretty much to their usual course; not, however, until after a great amount of injury had been done to the colony, which it is unnecessary to particularise, further than to repeat the expressions of Lord Grey, " An irreparable injury has thus been done to Jamaica, and an opportunity has been lost, which it may not, I fear, be easy to regain; nor can I look forward without very gloomy anticipations as to what may be the result of having allowed so many years to slip away without taking effectual measures to improve the condition, moral and physical, of the negro population."[a]

Here again, the colonists, besides having their own local difficulties to perplex and mislead them, have been the sport of a factious party in the imperial parliament, and concurrence in the commercial policy adopted by the home government, " has been accomplished only after struggles highly injurious to the colony."[b]

In the course of this last struggle, " a considerable number of the inhabitants of Jamaica"[c] suggested a change in the legislative council, and *also the introduction of the same system of government as had been established in Canada.* The home government refused the first of these suggestions, upon grounds

a Colonial Policy, vol. I, p. 190.   b Ibid, p. 170.   c Ibid, p. 414.

not necessary to be noticed, but they expressed their willingness to assent to the second, if the opinion of the colony in its favor should be unequivocally expressed by its representatives. Earl Grey, however, in his despatch expressed his doubt whether "those who have originated this proposal are aware that its adoption would involve the surrender by the assembly of much of that power which, in the process of time, it has acquired, but which, by the theory of the constitution, ought rather to belong to the executive government than to the legislature." This was a consequence which had never occurred to the agitators, and being too palpable, and such a loss of power being too unpalatable, thenceforth all suggestion about assimilating the constitution to that given to Canada was "tacitly abandoned."

Such is the account, given by the ex-colonial minister, of a colony " which has greatly the advantage of Guiana in the amount of her population, and still more in the comparatively advanced stage of civilization which that population had reached ;[a] yet Guiana, without these extensive powers of self-government, which it is the fashion to represent, as alone necessary for the welfare of a colony, and which Jamaica possesses has completely surmounted its financial difficulties. In Jamaica, on the contrary, the state of the colonial finances is getting from bad

[a] Colonial Policy, vol. I, p. 172.

to worse. There must have been serious errors in management of the affairs of Jamaica to account for so unfortunate a difference." These errors, his lordship says, are omitting to improve the moral condition of the population, reducing taxation without reducing expenditure, and want of system generally in the principal regulations.

Lord Grey concludes his notice of the West Indian colonies by quoting a passage from a speech of Mr. Disraeli, when Chancellor of the Exchequer, in August, 1852, wherein he demonstrated that the sugar cultivation of these colonies, so far from requiring protection, had actually improved since the passing of the act of 1846; the quantity of that article imported from these colonies being, in 1852, no less than 5,378,000 cwt., against 4,126,000 cwt. in 1851; while the importation of foreign sugar had fallen from 1,487,000 cwt. in 1851 to 814,000 cwt. in 1852.

After commenting upon such a convincing fact, Lord Grey concludes his notice of the West Indian colonies thus,—" But how much loss would have been saved to the unfortunate West Indians, how much better would the state of colonial industry have been at this moment even than that which the Chancellor of the Exchequer describes, if the party with which he is connected," meaning, of course, the Protectionists, " had, for the four years preceding February,

1852, taken a juster view of the prospects of the colonial planter. Had they done so, the colonists of Guiana and of Jamaica, instead of being encouraged to enter upon that unfortunate struggle with the government for the recovery of protection, which I have described, would no doubt have co-operated with us, in effecting the many much-needed improvements which we were anxious to assist them in accomplishing, and many an unhappy planter who has been compelled to sell his property for one half or one fourth of its real value, because the confidence of English capitalists in the possibility of his continuing his business with advantage was destroyed, would have obtained assistance that would have enabled him to surmount his difficulties."

The point of view from which Lord Grey gives this account, and from which his lordship wishes his readers to regard it, is his policy, or rather the policy of the ministry of which he was a member, in governing the colonies. In the circumstances in which Lord Grey and his colleagues in the ministry found the two colonies of Guiana and Jamaica, which he gives as a specimen of the condition of the other colonies, they could have adopted, perhaps, no more prudent course than that which they did adopt. Undoubtedly, it would never have done to allow the factious and selfish conduct of the assemblies, prompted by as factious and as selfish a party in the imperial parliament, to force the mother country from the course of policy it had deliberately adopted, and probably no quieter mode, or no mode less likely to be permanently injurious, than that which the home government pursued, could have been adopted; yet that course, if pursued with a more powerful and populous colony than either Guiana or Jamaica, might have been very perilous, and, even in their case, may have suggested in the breasts of the colonists ideas which may yet, at some future day, embody themselves into action.

In the case of Guiana the colonists may have asked themselves *whose* fault it is that their "financial representatives" are "chosen by about 800 persons, out of a population of about 120,000! and are really not the representatives of the people, but of the merchants, planters, and absentee proprietors!" If it were the home government which allowed this state of things to grow up, then it is that government, and not the colonists, who ought to bear the blame of "the unfortunate differences between the governor and the Combined Court, which for some time interrupted the regular working of the government," and which cost the colony a direct loss in money of £150,000, besides other consequential pecuniary losses of unascertained amount, while these pecuniary losses, great as they may be, were by "no means the most serious part of the injury that resulted from it ;" and though it might be very reasonable if the whole brunt of these losses and injuries had been to be borne by the financial representatives themselves, or even by the 800 " merchants, planters, and absentee proprietors" whom they represented, that they " ought not to be relieved from the consequences of their own conduct," which undoubtedly was most factious, yet, as the consequences did not affect these persons alone, but fell on all the colonists alike, *un*represented as well as *re*presented, it will not have been an unnatural question for the 119,200 *un*represented colonists to have put to themselves, why they should have been obliged to bear " the consequences of the conduct" of only 800 out of 120,000 persons !

It may have been to benefit these 800 " merchants, planters, and absentee proprietors," to the prejudice of the other 119,200 inhabitants, that the sugar cultivation had been *fostered* by these differential duties, which it was the object of the act of 1846 of the imperial parliament to remove, and it may have been that, if these 119,200 persons who are even yet *un*represented had been represented, this unwholesome bantling, the " protected " sugar trade, would never have been generated. If so, the occasion would not have existed which put it in the power of the " Protectionists " of London to lead the colony by the nose, to its own so serious loss and injury.

It is not improbable that these suggestions did occur to the colonists, for it seems that "during the disputes an agitation was raised in favor of the entire alteration of the present constitution, and the substitution of one precisely similar to those which exist in the older West India colonies, which possess representative assemblies, exercising, in conjunction with the governor and council, all the powers of legislation." It is not said by whom this agitation was raised, whether by the financial representatives and their constituents, with Jamaica before their eyes, and from a desire to gain the injudicious unconstitutional power there possessed, and abused, not used, by the representative assembly; or whether by the 119,200 *un*represented inhabitants, with the desire of gaining the same constitutional representation and power which has been granted to and has hitherto worked so admirably in Canada, according to all accounts.

If the latter were the agitators for a boon so reasonable in itself, the answer which, through Lord Grey's book, they must be satisfied with, is that the state of society in Guiana, where "there is an extremely small proportion of Europeans, the remainder of the population being made up of various different races, for the most part little advanced in civilization, and altogether deficient in the education and intelligence necessary for the safe exercise of political power, rendered such a change in this colony altogether inexpedient."

But the 119,200 *un*represented inhabitants may reply, and no doubt such of them as have thought a little on the matter have replied, but if the 800 represented " merchants, planters, and absentee proprietors" are "advanced in civilization," and are not deficient "in education and intelligence," as we are assumed to be, how is it that they have led the colony in such a dance of folly as to jeopardize the lives and properties of the whole inhabitants, and even the existence of its social arrangements. And if, on the other hand, they are as little " advanced in civilization," and are as "deficient in education and intelligence," as we are assumed to be, why was the power of doing this mischief ever given to them, and still more, why has it been continued to them, so that they may play the same game over again, should occasion arise.

Guiana is an instance of unhappy government under an oligarchy, such a form being assumed to be rendered necessary by the mass of the population being "little advanced in civilization and altogether deficient in education and intelligence." But Jamaica is an island "which has greatly the advantage of Guiana in the amount of her population, and still more in the comparatively advanced stage of civilization which that population has

reached." Does the picture which has been given
of the form of government in Jamaica and its
practical working with the home government, present
any more agreeable view than that which has been
shown of Guiana?

The colonists of Jamaica may ask whether it is
not the home government that has allowed the
constitution of the island to assume the motley that
it now wears. In one representative assembly are
engrossed all the powers of king, lords, and commons,
so far as the levying of finances and their appropriation is concerned. Each and every member of this
assembly has the power to propose a grant of money
for " objects interesting to himself or his constituents,"
without being responsible for adjusting the grant to
the means of providing for it, or for the " urgency
of other claims upon the public purse." Is it to be
wondered at that, with such a constitution, there
should not be any " careful consideration of what the
public interest requires," and that the revenue comes
to be determined " rather by a kind of scramble
amongst the members of the legislature?" But
where, the colonists may ask, has been the minister,
or how has " the sovereign and supreme legislative
power of the imperial parliament " been slumbering,
while such a state of confusion has been growing,
" under various laws, which have, at different times,
been passed, and by usages which have grown up?"

Yet, surely, this Jamaica constitution, under which it was only to be expected that confusion would be rendered worse confounded, is not " the power of self-government, which it is the fashion to represent as alone necessary for the welfare of a colony "! At all events, the colonists of Jamaica do not appear to have thought that it was so, for, so far from considering that they have had self-government, the assembly, though possessing all these extravagant and highly unconstitutional powers, does not think that even *it* has had self-government. The assembly complains to the Queen of the " many wrongs which we have sustained by acts of the imperial parliament ;" that " the establishment of slavery,"—the abolition of which it conceives, however erroneously, to be the cause of the island's difficulties—" was not *our* act, but that of the *parent government*," " under sanction of *British laws*." And, in order to procure the recall of the British act of parliament, which, after slavery had been abolished, repealed the differential duties, which they, however erroneously, supposed to be the last plank they had to hold on by, they allowed themselves to be made the dupes of the " Protectionist" party in the British parliament, and to be led through the same game in which the oligarchists of Guiana had taken so fruitless a part.

It may be very true that the colonists of Jamaica, under their ill-judged and ill-contrived constitution, for which the parent government would seem to be chiefly to blame, have had the power of misgoverning themselves among themselves, as children put into a nursery without nurse or parent, or with a nurse shorn of executive powers, are sure to do; but it never can be said that they have had the power of "self-government," either such as it is "the fashion to represent as alone necessary for the welfare of a colony," or of any other kind; for it is undoubted that the colony of Jamaica, with all its internal powers of self-misgovernment, has been subject to the external "sovereign and supreme legislative power of the imperial parliament," a power which has not been inert but active—whether for good or for evil matters not to be inquired here. Hence their complaint of "wrongs sustained by acts of the imperial parliament."

How the assembly intended that the Queen should redress the wrongs inflicted by acts of the imperial parliament is not shown; but it appears that "a considerable number of the inhabitants of Jamaica "[a] thought that a remedy against all evils, past or future, would be secured, "if the system of government now established in Canada should be introduced into Jamaica." That system is, as nearly as possible, the system enjoyed by the United Kingdom; it is the same, indeed, short of subjection to "the

[a] Colonial Policy, vol. I, p. 414.

sovereign and supreme power of the imperial parliament," in questions of external relations. In all matters of internal government, the colonists of Canada possess the exact form of government enjoyed by the United Kingdom. At all events the constitution of Canada is something very different from what appears to be the constitution of Jamaica, and, much more probably than it, possesses those powers of " self-government which it is the fashion to represent as alone necessary for the welfare of a colony."

Undoubtedly, Lord Grey takes the same view, for he prefers the constitution of Canada to that of Jamaica,[a] and tells the colonists of Jamaica that, though probably not aware the adoption of the Canadian constitution would " involve the surrender by their assembly of much of that power which, in the process of time, it has acquired, but which, by the theory of the constitution, ought rather to belong to the executive government, yet," if the people should, after this intimation, " by their representatives, either in this or in a newly-elected assembly, ask Her Majesty's sanction for the adoption of a similar mode of conducting the government of the colony to that which now exists in Canada," he was " not aware that any obstacle, which might not easily be overcome, would stand in the way of a compliance with their wishes."

[a] Colonial Policy, vol. i, p. 416.

The colonists of Jamaica, however, are not unlike the rest of mankind. Such is the secret charm of power, that no advantage, however obvious, will induce us to part with it. Being sensible that they have the power of electing their representatives, they, in this light, view as their own the power which these representatives have filched from the crown, and prefer the ruin and confusion in which their resources have been gradually wasting, because it has been produced by a power of their own creation, to the order and prosperity which, in other colonies, even without the constitution of Canada, is enjoyed under system and responsibility, because the control of that system would not be in their hands, but in the crown.

The folly of man is endless and inexplicable, and such is the folly of the colonists of Jamaica, that they have "tacitly abandoned" the request for the Canadian constitution, and have allowed the liberal and handsome offer of it by the home government to fall into abeyance. But, if there be truth, as undoubtedly there is truth, in the history of financial confusion which Lord Grey gives, and attributes justly to the preposterous constitution under which the island of Jamaica is tortured, it is the duty of the home government to compel the termination of such a mischievous state of things, and no more legitimate exercise of the " sovereign and supreme legislative power of the imperial parliament" could well be conceived than the passing of an act to compel the assembly to part with the exorbitant and unconstitutional powers which they have engrossed, and to force upon the colony the constitution of Canada.

But, passing that by, and taking things as they have existed—whether the wrongs, real or imaginary, of the colonists of Jamaica have been "sustained by acts of the imperial parliament," or whether the disordered and ruinous condition of the island[a] is to be attributed to its own evil constitution, the fact is avowed by Lord Grey, that the "successive changes" in the imperial policy, so far as these have borne upon these islands, "have been accomplished, only after struggles highly injurious to the welfare of the colony, and thus, for the last thirty years, the relations between the local legislature and the government at home, under successive administrations, have, with some brief intervals, continued to be on a very unsatisfactory footing. There has been little of that harmonious co-operation between these authorities, without which it is impossible that the affairs of the island can be properly and efficiently conducted."

So far as appears, the "very unsatisfactory footing" which has so long existed between the local

---

[a] The text was written in the year 1854.

legislature and the home government is to continue, and "struggles," as "highly injurious to the welfare of the colony" as any that have passed, may arise whensoever a subject to produce them shall occur. If the colony continue as depressed as it at present is, these struggles, like the past ones, may be comparatively unimportant to the mother country, and be injurious chiefly to the colony itself. But, should the colony avail itself of the "richness and extent in natural resources of its territory, which entitle it to be considered the most important of our former slave colonies," and becomes as rich and populous as these natural resources ought to make it under judicious government,[a] it may be a question whether the struggle between it and the mother country would be so easily overcome, as the struggles between them in the time past have been overcome, and whether either the negative indifference of the minister, or the active interference of the imperial legislature would be sufficient to allay them,—whether we should not have in Jamaica a repetition of the scenes, in Canada, of 1837 and 1838, which preceded the grant of the constitution which that colony now enjoys, and under which it is flourishing so pre-eminently, and, at the same time, so harmoniously with the home government.

[a] This, it is believed, is being realized since the text was written, i. e., 1854.

Section II.—Our government of Canada and reflections upon the changes which have been made in its constitution.

Let us now leave the West Indian colonies for those in North America, that we may see whether the system of government, founded on the implied and recognized rights of the colonists to enjoy the rights and liberties of free-born Englishmen, has worked any better in them than in our West India colonies. And, first, let us take Canada.

As Lord Grey's object, in his work, was merely to give an account of the imperial colonial policy, during his connection with Lord John Russell's ministry, it was not necessary for him to go further back in the history of Canada than to the statute of 1840, which gave that colony its present constitution. But, in the present inquiry, a short view of the previous constitutional history of this colony, and of the circumstances under which one of the most liberal of any of the constitutions which have been given to our colonies was granted by that statute of 1840, will be most instructive.

This colony, which was acquired by conquest from the French, was originally governed by the crown alone, under a royal proclamation. In 1774, this state of things was changed by the act of the 14 Geo. III, cap. 83, which was the first assertion of the sovereign and supreme legislative power of the imperial parliament. By the terms of that act, the colony was, in future, to be governed by a governor, with an executive council and a legislative council, both of these bodies being nominative.

In the year 1791, an act of the imperial parliament was passed, which separated the colony into two—Upper Canada and Lower Canada—and gave to each a constitution by a governor; an executive council, the members of which were appointed by the governor temporarily, as before; a legislative council, the members of which were also appointed by the governor, but for the term of life; and a legislative assembly, to be elected by the inhabitants of the colony, which, for this purpose, was parceled out into electoral divisions.

The course of government of Upper Canada, which is inhabited chiefly by persons of British origin, has been comparatively smooth enough. That of Lower Canada, in the population of which there is a strong admixture of persons of French origin, has been of a different character, and is that which is here to be noticed.

Under the constitution given to Lower Canada, by the act of 1791, a certain amount of revenue was raised within the colony, under previously existing laws. Previous to 1774, duties had been levied under laws having their origin during the French rule. These amounted on an average to about

£35,000 per annum. The act of 1774 abolished these old French duties, and imposed permanent taxes in their stead. There was also another source of revenue from fines and forfeitures, under the French tenure of land, which yielded annually about £5,000.

The revenue derived from these two sources, amounting to about £40,000 per annum, was not sufficient to defray the expenses of the local government. The deficiency, amounting to about £140,000, was supplied by the home government. This combined revenue was administered by the local government, on its own responsibility.

At the outset of the British rule, Lower Canada was inhabited almost entirely by persons of French extraction, speaking the French language, and having French habits and prepossessions. While this continued, which was for many years, the government of the colony was administered without opposition from the inhabitants. But, in process of time, there grew up " a considerable population of British race, having British habits, and possessing to the full the British love of enterprise."[a] Naturally enough, jealousies arose between the two races, and out of this sprung opposition to the government. To prevent this opposition from becoming overwhelming, the government most imprudently appointed chiefly

[a] Hansard's Debates for 1837.

persons of British origin to be members of the legislative council. Not only so, but persons who held official situations under the government, and therefore were in a double sense tied to it—by the prejudices of origin and by the motives of direct pecuniary interest—were appointed to be members of this council. The necessary consequence of this was to place the council appointed by the governor and his council of nominees in direct antagonism with the assembly elected by the people.

This spirit of contest put the members of the assembly, who had thitherto been little curious of inquiring into the powers given them by the act of 1791, upon looking into that statute, for the discovery of a weapon wherewith to combat their opponents, the governor and the legislative council. In the statute they found, to their satisfaction, the same lever wherewith the commons of England, to whom the assembly was analogous, had worked the protection of their rights and liberties against the crown. They found that with themselves resided the power of directing the assessment and the levying of taxes, with the exception of those levied under the authority of the imperial statute of 1774, and also the power of directing the appropriation of the taxes. But they, at the same time, discovered how this power in them had never been applied to by the government. The existence of the taxes levied under the act of 1774, and the contribution in aid, remitted by the home government, had made the local government independent of the assembly, by rendering it unnecessary to apply to it for the yearly vote of supplies.

The first step taken to destroy this state of independence in the government was to get the home government to discontinue their contribution to the colonial finances. The home government agreed to do this, and thus the assembly gained the control over their whole finances, by the necessity under which the local government was now put of resorting to it for an assessment upon the colony, to come in place of what the home government was thenceforth to discontinue paying, amounting, as before observed, to £140,000. Now began the tug of war between the governor, the legislative council, and the officials, both appointed by him, on the one hand; and the assembly, elected by the people, on the other.

From the year 1818 commenced a series of disputes between the government and the assembly, which continued down to the year 1828. It is not necessary to go into these disputes here, because the home government, in the year 1828, after a number of petitions from the colony for redress of grievances, real or supposed, had, as the colonists conceived, been disregarded, or ineffectually attended to, resorted to the House of Commons for power to control the colony in this protracted struggle; and with this view moved the appointment of a committee of the house to inquire into the matter.

This committee so far justified the complaints of the colony, for it made a report, which the house of assembly, in an address on the 21st November, 1828, described as "exhibiting a striking combination of talent and patriotism, uniting a general knowledge of public and constitutional law to a particular acquaintance with the state of both the Canadas;" and they pronounced upon its report that, "after solemn investigation, after deep and prolonged deliberation, it made a report, an imperishable monument of their justice and profound wisdom, an authentic testimonial of the reality of our grievances, and of the justice of our complaints, faithfully interpreting our wishes and our wants."

If the assembly had had rebellion and separation in their eye, in 1828, they would hardly have made such admissions as these to the government. Here, then, whoever might be to blame for past differences, was a starting-point for quiet and peaceful administration. The House of Commons had reported upon "the reality of the grievances" which the colony alleged, and upon "the justice of the complaints" which it had made, and the colonists, on the other hand, had admitted that the report "faithfully interpreted their wishes and their wants." Both parties, the home government and the colony, were now, it might be presumed, in a temper to work together harmoniously.

The governor, under instructions from home, set about redressing the grievances, but, unfortunately, not in a way that was satisfactory to the colonists. It is beyond the object of the present notice of these matters to inquire who was right or who was wrong, in the outset of the disputes which arose subsequent to 1828; but, as a specimen of one subject of contention, it may be mentioned that one of the grievances of the assembly was, that the governors had been in use to give a plurality of offices to one and the same individual,—the judges, even, being not exempted from this mode of influence,—and that they had appointed to be members of the legislative council persons holding official situations.

Whether this obvious and admitted grievance had, like the others, been "either settled, or proposed to be settled"—in which of these two categories this grievance was, in the year 1833, does not appear. But this *does* appear, that, in that year, the assembly passed a supply bill, tacked with conditions, providing that the persons holding certain offices should not be allowed salaries, *unless they ceased to hold certain other offices.* Now, this would not seem to have been a condition of taxation very unreasonable in itself, nor one beyond the duty of the assembly to make, nor was it so considered by the governor for the time, but *the mode* of making it was said by that functionary to be against rule; and so undoubtedly it was—a condition of any sort cannot constitutionally be tacked to a money bill. On this ground, the governor disallowed the bill, and the colonial minister of the day affirmed his disallowance. This was the last money bill that was presented, for allowance or disallowance, until one was presented in the year 1837, to be presently noticed.

Now, it does seem strange, unless the condition annexed to this money bill was conceived and begotten in one instant, without any discussion upon it by the members of assembly, either in private or in public,—unless its concoction was a matter kept secret from the governor, and wholly unknown to him, until he found it in the bill,—unless the governor could not put himself in communication either with the assembly, or with any member of that body, after he did discover it in the bill,—it does seem strange that some step was not taken to stop the course of this supply bill, until a declaratory bill should have been introduced and passed remedying the grievance. If this course had been adopted, the objectionable condition to the supply bill would thus have been rendered unnecessary as well as superfluous, and that bill would probably have passed the assembly in a form that the governor could have assented to.

Whether the redress of the other grievances was conducted in the same spirit does not appear ; but, if we may judge of the matter by the event, it would rather seem that the assembly had been either fretted out of, or had not been coaxed into, preserving that tone of conciliation and temper in which they had, in 1828, commented to the governor upon the report of the committee of the House of Commons of that year ; for, in the year 1834, the assembly passed *ninety-two resolutions*, " some of grievance, some of eulogy, some of vituperation, some directed against individuals, some against the governors, and some against the government at home ;" but all amounting to a long and vehement remonstrance.

After passing these resolutions, the assembly ceased to vote any supplies, until, three years afterwards, (1837,) in answer to an address from the governor, they said, " It is right we should tell you, and through you the British parliament and the British government, that, until you redress our grievances, which are of so important and so grievous a nature, we will not pay up the arrears, but, in order to show you how sincerely desirous we are that the machinery of government should go on, we will, notwithstanding the severity of the measures you now adopt towards us, vote the supplies for the current year, so that you may have sufficient time to write home to the colonial office, and to ascertain whether, in that quarter, there is any disposition to accede to those claims, which we deem just and reasonable." Acting upon this promise, the assembly, taking the estimates for 1833 as their guide, voted a sum of £54,640, for the expenses of the year 1837.

Whether the claims put forward were "just and reasonable," or unjust and unreasonable, here, at least, was £54,640 worth of willingness to be pacified; but this was given in such an exceptionable manner that it was not accepted, and no more was offered, either objectionably or unobjectionably. The assembly stood upon the vantage-ground which the power of taxation had given them, as it had given the commons of England when resisting the power of the crown; and what must have been the result, if the colony, like the commons of England, had had the power of the crown *alone* to contend with, it would not have been difficult to predict.

Whether the "sympathizers" from across the borders of the United States had begun, as yet, to instil their poison into the colonists, and to advertise "Five thousand laborers wanted at Indianopolis, Indiana, at from fifteen to twenty dollars a month. We wonder if we could be indicted for treason if we give it as our opinion that twenty dollars and board in Indiana are much better wages than sixpence a day, with the privilege of being flogged or shot, in the British army," as a seduction to desertion by the British soldiers stationed in the colony, does not appear. Either this had begun, or it had not yet occurred to the home government to pursue with Canada the very effectual course which, twelve years afterwards, and under the same circumstances, it adopted with regard to Guiana and Jamaica, as has been already sketched in these pages.[a] They did not desire the governor to stop the machine of government, by opening the prisons, shutting the hospitals, stopping the administration of justice, and withdrawing the troops. They resorted to "the sovereign and supreme legislative power of the imperial parliament" for removal of the obstruction.

The government removed one governor after the other, after having given each of them new instructions, and made various proposals to the colony, all to no purpose. The assembly was obdurate in keeping the purse-strings tied, and, to judge from the observations of the minister in the House of Commons, it would seem that, though the subjects of dispute might be legion, that upon which the controversy hinged was, whether the members of the legislative council should *continue to be nominated by the governor*, or *be elected by the colonists*. After noticing certain measures of redress which had been proposed to the

[a] Supra, pp. 265 and 272.

colonists, but which had been either rejected or
slighted, and among the rest an alteration in the
constitution of the legislative council, and a refusal
of the assembly to make any proposal of their own,
or to do more than consider any new proposal for
the modification of that body which the home government might make to them, Lord John Russell said,
" If we had introduced a plan for any change in the
elective" (*legislative?*) "council, the house of assembly
would have said, ' We rejoice that we have got rid of
the legislative council, as an obstacle to our desires,
but you have not fulfilled the whole conditions on
which we rest our case, and we must insist still upon
an elective council, as the only means by which
future harmony can be established.' "

The minister, at this time, seems to have considered
the notion of making the legislative council an elective body as utterly inadmissible, for he had just
before said that he had " stated expressly, that if any
mode of arranging the difference, which at that
period existed, could be pointed out, *otherwise than
by the appointment of an elective council*, we should
be ready to undertake the consideration of it," and
afterwards he asks triumphantly, with reference to
the answer he had put into the mouth of the assembly,
as insisting upon an elective council, " Is it not
obvious that such would have been the answer? Is
it not clear, from the spirit in which the controversy

had been conducted, that this would have been the reply of the Canadians, in answer to concessions volunteered by the government?" Perhaps "volunteered" was neither a happy, nor altogether an accurate expression, considering that the act of concession had been preceded by the long-continued withholding of the supplies by the colony, and the resolutions of the committee of the House of Commons of 1828. But, whether the concessions were forced or voluntary, it is evident that an *elective* legislative council neither had been, nor was intended to be, of the number. On the other hand, the colonists were determined to wring this from the government, and therefore, in August, 1837, they refused to comply with the request of the governor to grant the supplies, and persisted in their former demands; and, moreover, began to betray symptoms of *rebellion*, by holding seditious meetings, which in due time ripened into that crime.

In this dilemma, after putting down, by means of a military governor, the insurrectionary movements of the colonists, an operation which was not accomplished without the shedding of much blood and the infliction of great misery and hardship upon the colonists, government had recourse to the "sovereign and supreme legislative power of the imperial parliament," from which it obtained the act 1 and 2 Vic., cap. 9, which put an end to the constitution

given to the colony by the act of 1791, by repealing
that act, and giving the governor power to rule the
colony of his own authority, with a council of his
own appointment. The object of this step was not
to gain the power of tyrannizing over the colony,
but that of reconstructing its constitution, so as, if
possible, to make its rule more harmonious than it
had hitherto been.

Matters were allowed to go on, under the absolute
powers given by the 1 and 2 Vic., until there was
some reason to think that the angry feelings of 1837
and 1838 had subsided to such a degree as that the
contemplated measures might be entered upon. In
1839, ministers were of opinion that that time had
arrived. In consequence, they brought in and carried
the passing of the act 3 and 4 Vic., cap. 35.

The great change which this act made upon the
state of things as they had existed, prior to the
1 and 2 Vic., was to unite the two provinces of
Upper and Lower Canada into one colony. The
preponderance in the lower province of persons of
French extraction, and wedded to French customs
and opinions, was supposed to have been the great
source of the difficulty of government, and the cause
of the political dissensions in Lower Canada. To
counteract this, and give freer and more effective
action to British feeling, Upper Canada, inhabited
almost entirely by persons of British extraction, was

joined to Lower Canada, and of the two provinces were again made one colony.

This junction was the great leading feature of the act of 3 and 4 Vic., and upon its success, in controlling French feeling by British feeling, depended the efficacy of the statute to cure the past dissensions; for an *elective* legislative council was not conceded, neither was any other of the real or supposed grievances of the Lower Canadians remedied by the terms of this act.

Lord Durham, in his report on Canadian affairs, had suggested that there was an analogy between the government of the colony and the home government, and had recommended that the one should, like the other, be responsible to the legislative bodies, to the effect of its officers being dismissed when their measures should not be approved of by these bodies This motion was not approved of by the House of Commons, which resolved, on the motion of the minister, that " while it is expedient to improve the composition of the executive council of Lower Canada, it is unadvisable to subject it to that responsibility demanded by the house of assembly of that province ;" and the minister, still concurring in the wisdom of that resolution, and seeing nothing in Lord Durham's report to shake his opinion, the act 3 and 4 Vic. made no change in that respect by its provisions. The executive council, so far as the enactments of that statute were concerned, was in its action to remain independent of the legislative council and of the house of assembly.

But, notwithstanding the resolution of the House of Commons and the minister's re-assertion of the opinion which had induced him to move that resolution, it would seem that Lord John Russell, in 1839, announced to Mr. Poulett Thomson, then governor of Canada, that "for the future, the principal offices of the colonial governments in North America would not be considered as being held by a tenure equivalent to one during good behavior, but that the holders would be liable to be called upon to retire whenever, from motives of public policy, or other reasons, this should be found to be expedient." These expressions intimated the concession of responsible government and the executive council construed them as implying the further concession to themselves of the patronage to all colonial offices. Although not differing with the governor as to the course of policy to be pursued in the colony, and although they had a majority in the assembly in favor of that policy, the council, in order to strengthen themselves by anticipation against the governor, insisted that he should expressly transfer to them the whole official patronage of the colony, under the pretext that the council could not be of any use, unless they could conciliate the house of assembly to approve of such measures as they might recommend the governor to propose to them, and that one great engine for this purpose was the possession of patronage to colonial offices.

This motion was to place the council in the same position, and to give them the same weight in the administration of the colony, as the British ministers had in the government of the empire, and to reduce the governor, and through him the imperial government, to a mere cipher in the administration of the colony. But it appeared to Lord Metcalfe — an excellent man, and as excellent a governor—to be as novel in theory, as certainly it was new in colonial practice, and, moreover, to be, at the particular time, as unnecessary as it was novel, since there had not been any difference between him and the council, nor between them and the assembly.

It is obvious that this was an attempt of the assembly, with the connivance of the executive council, or, to speak more correctly perhaps, at the suggestion of that council, to bring about a responsible government, in spite of the refusal of the home government to assent to such a step. Lord Metcalfe apprehended this, and, under a due sense of the responsibility he owed to his sovereign and the parliament of Great Britain for every act of his government, whether originating with himself or with his executive council, he refused to comply with the demand of the executive council. All the members of the council, with a single exception, resigned. With this single councilor, Lord Metcalfe carried on the government till the close of the subsisting parliament, without the occurrence of any check to his administration.

The subsequent part of Lord Metcalfe's government was not so tranquil; for with the new council, which he formed after the close of the subsisting parliament, he found his government frequently in minorities with the new parliament. How he would have worked himself out of this dilemma cannot be conjectured, because private reasons compelled him to resign his government before that could be shown.

The Earl of Elgin was the governor appointed to succeed Lord Metcalfe, after a short interval of military governorship by Earl Cathcart. Lord Elgin came into office with the benefit of Lord Metcalfe's experience, and with instructions modeled after the pattern of those which, in 1846, had been addressed to the governor of Nova Scotia,[a] explained, no doubt, by the minister, so as to avoid, in the execution of them, the collision which had occurred between Lord Metcalfe and his executive council.

By these instructions, the governor was to carry on his government with the existing executive council, " so long as they possess the necessary

* Grey's Colonial Policy, vol. I, p. 209.

support from the legislature." But should they fail in having this, "it would then be your natural course, *in conformity with the practice in analogous cases in this country*, to apply to the opposite party." After pointing out, that if the governor should reject the advice of the executive council upon a matter in which public opinion went along with them, they would resign, the instructions continued,[a] "should it prove to be so, concession to their views must, sooner or later, become inevitable, since it cannot be too distinctly acknowledged that it is neither possible nor desirable to carry on the government of any of the British provinces in North America in opposition to the opinions of the inhabitants."

Before going further, it may be remarked that, if these instructions be taken in conjunction with the despatch of Lord John Russell of 1839, they show that, in the face of the resolution of the House of Commons;[b] and notwithstanding the re-assertion in equivocal terms, no doubt, by Lord John Russell, of the opinions he had expressed at moving that resolution, here is a concession, plain and unambiguous, of responsible government. Henceforth, the executive councilors are to retain their office only so long as their measures shall be acceptable to the assembly, and no doubt as a compensation to that body for the moveable character thus impressed upon their offices,

---

[a] Colonial Policy, vol. I, p. 212.   [b] Vide supra. p. 302.

the governor was directed to transfer official patronage from the home government to the executive council, for we learn that now "the government" (governorship?) " of Canada is literally the only civil office in that colony in the gift of the home government."[a]

But the history of concession to this colony does not end even here. By the act of 3 and 4 Vic., cap. 35, the taxes, levied under the authority of the local legislature, were to be appropriated by its authority, but only after payment of the sums which, by the act, were set aside for a civil list, and, in return for the power thus exercised over the colonial revenue, the crown surrendered, for the life of the sovereign, its hereditary revenues within the colony.

The colony pared down the civil list, fixed by the 3 and 4 Vic., cap. 35, and then said to the government, that, if it would agree to the list so modified, the legislature would pass an act of their own providing for its permanent payment. This could be done only with the consent of the imperial parliament. That consent the minister asked and obtained, and the 10 and 11 Vic., cap. 71, was passed, whereby so much of the act 3 and 4 Vic., cap. 35, as fixed the civil list, was repealed, and Her Majesty was empowered to consent to any act of the local legislature, making provision for it, which might be presented for her approval. This Her

* Colonial Policy, vol. i, p. 208.

Majesty has done, it appears, and now "the whole expenditure of the colony takes place under the authority, not of imperial, but of provincial legislation."

This concession was a gracious act, which government will feel the benefit of, so long as a grateful feeling for it survives, and the government of the colony is conducted harmoniously. After these conditions cease, there will be nothing to fall back upon but a re-enactment of the 1 and 2 Vic. Still, if the colony were to be retained, it was a gracious and a prudent step to consent to the colony paying its civil list, under the authority of its own legislature, and so by its own consent, rather than under the compulsitor of an imperial statute.

But, however gracious the next step in the progress of concession may be judged to be, it will be difficult to prove it a prudent one. In Lower Canada, as before observed, there is a strong admixture in the population of persons of French origin, speaking the French language, and cultivating French opinions and prejudices. As one means of wearing this out gradually, the 3 and 4 Vic., cap. 35, joined British Upper Canada to French Lower Canada; and as another means to the same end, its forty-fourth section enacted that all the proceedings of the legislative bodies, and all reports of these proceedings and all parliamentary writs and summonses and returns thereto should be in the English language only.

Under this enactment it would always have been an object of urgency with a parent, who desired to see his son enjoying the full franchise of a British colonist, that he should learn the English language, and this spirit, descending from father to son, and from son to grandson, a great part of the French population would, in time, have come to speak the English language. But, on a representation from the colony, so much of the 3 and 4 Vic., cap. 35, as made provision for this desirable end was repealed by the 11 and 12 Vic., cap. 56, and, now, so far as a knowledge of the English language is concerned, a man speaking French, or any of the Indian languages, is as well entitled to sit in the local legislature as one speaking the purest vernacular of England.

Earl Grey says this was a measure, "not of very great practical importance in itself, but considerable importance was attached to it by the inhabitants of Canada, as a proof of the confidence of the imperial government and parliament, and as removing the last traces of that distrust which the insurrection had necessarily left behind it."[a]   Surely no passage could be more replete with error than this, given as a reason for passing the 10 and 11 Vic., cap. 56.

So far from being a measure "not of very great

---

[a] Colonial Policy, vol. I, p. 236.

practical importance," it seems to be one of the *very greatest practical importance* to the home government that this act should *not* have been passed, and of all the greater importance, by how much the colonists viewed it as of "considerable importance" to them that it *should* be passed. Mr. Huskisson, at moving the committee of the House of Commons on Canada affairs, in 1828, used these expressions, " Whether Canada is to remain for ever dependent on England, or is to become an independent state—not, I trust, by hostile separation, but by amicable arrangement—*it is still the duty and interest of this country to imbue it with English feelings, and benefit it with English laws and institutions.*"

If there be sound philosophy, as well as true statesmanship, in these words, what more effectual step could be taken towards "imbuing" the French Canadians "with English feelings," and enabling them to comprehend and appreciate " English laws and institutions," than gradually to bring them into the knowledge and general use of the English language, in which these feelings are expressed, and these laws and institutions are written and commented upon. *Mais nous avons changé tout cela.* The 10 and 11 Vic., cap. 56, has destroyed any chance of a consummation so devoutly to be wished, and now, whether Canada "continue dependent on

England," or "become an independent state," the French Canadian will continue an alien in language, at least, as perhaps he will also in "feelings."

That the abrogation of the necessity to use the English language was desired, as "a proof of confidence," and as "a removal of the last trace of distrust" by the home government, however speciously it may read, is a pretence too flimsy to be believed.[a] The true and obvious ground was, that the colonists of French origin might, in a permission to use the French language, have a freer use of the political franchise. The more strongly they appreciated the use of this franchise, the stronger hold was there upon them to bring about the use of the English language, by allowing the use of the franchise, to its full extent, to those only who could speak that language. This hold is now entirely given up.

The other concessions to Canada by the home

[a] Kaye, in his Life of Metcalfe, vol. II, p. 567, speaking of how, against his nature, he was driven to adopt tactics instead of straightforward measures, says: "For example, being aware that the French Canadian party in the house intended to move an address to the throne, praying that the existing *restrictions on the use of the French language* in legislative proceedings might be annulled, the executive council proposed that they should anticipate the opposition by introducing the measure themselves. There were instructions from the imperial government forbidding such a proceeding, but it was expedient to disarm the opposition, and Metcalfe consented that the address should be moved by Mr. Papineau."

government tend, all of them, to bring the colonial
constitution nearer in principle and in action to that
of the mother country, and thereby tend undoubtedly
to draw closer the bonds of amity and good feeling
between the mother country and the colony; but
this last concession of the use of the English
language has a direct tendency in the opposite way,
and its injurious effects will probably become
apparent, so soon as the transitory emotions of
gratitude, by which it may have been followed, shall
have subsided.

But we may congratulate ourselves, so far as
matters have yet gone, upon the change from irresponsible to responsible government in this colony.
If there be any cause for regret, it probably is, that
the concessions, with the exception of this, as to the
use of the English language, have not gone far
enough, and, in the way they have occurred, have
not anticipated, instead of waiting upon, the demands
of the colonists. Lord Elgin assumed the government of Canada in 1847, and a dinner which was
given to him on his return from the colony in 1854,
in compliment to the success of his administration,
shows that he has ruled the colony harmoniously,
with an executive council, removable at the pleasure
of the assembly, as Her Majesty's ministers are at the
pleasure of the House of Commons. But it must
not be forgotten, that his lordship's government fell

in times of external peace, and followed the extraordinary exertions, to the hastening of his death, of
that singularly able, excellent, and ever-to-be-lamented
officer, Lord Metcalfe, to bring the machinery of the
new constitution into easy and smooth working; and,
during the subsistence of his government, there has
not been the occurrence of any measure, which the
home government required him to propose to the
assembly but which that body was resolute not to
pass.

Lord Elgin has had very stormy scenes within the
colony since he entered on his government. He has
had a parliamentary opposition upon a measure
strictly colonial, directed not only against his council,
but against himself, and against the home government;[a] he has had to encounter violent opposition
from the colonial press and serious riots of the people,
in the course of which he was obliged almost to
confine himself to his country residence, and he has
had to divert a movement for annexation of the
colony to the United States. But, being backed by
a majority in the legislative bodies, and by an executive council, acting in harmony with that majority,
he was able to refrain from putting down the
agitation by military force, and to allow the effer-
vescence to subside by self-exhaustion.

Lord Elgin's prudence and forbearance, throughout

[a] Colonial Policy, vol. I, p. 222.

this stormy period, accompanied as these qualities were by unswerving firmness in carrying out the measures which the assembly had resolved on, fully deserved the congratulations which he received on his return home, and present an admirable example for monarchs, as well as governors, to follow in similar circumstances. Yet the tower of his strength and the rock of his refuge was the *representative nature of the assembly and the responsibility of the council.* The inhabitants, who excited all the commotion, were sensible, by the votes of the assembly, that they were in a minority, and that, however they might bluster and storm for the chance of terrifying the governor, though backed by the majority, into yielding to them, they must, if that failed them, succumb in the end; and the governor and the majority, standing firm, they did succumb, " the authors of the movement, having apparently, on cooler reflection, become ashamed of it."[a]

But, had this agitation arisen out of a measure which the governor, with an irresponsible council, had followed out by command of the home government, but which the assembly, by a majority, disapproved of, and insisted on his abandoning, it is less than doubtful whether all the firmness of Lord Elgin, tempered as it was with so great prudence, would have carried him safely through such a crisis,

Colonial Policy, vol. I, p. 233.

and the possibility of this happening has not been provided for in the system of government which has been devised for this colony.

When Lord John Russell stated his reasons against making the executive council of Canada responsible to the house of assembly, he said, " The governor may ask the executive council to propose a certain measure. They may say they cannot propose it, unless the members of the house of assembly will adopt it; but the governor may reply that *he has received instructions from home, commanding him to propose that measure.* How, in that case, is he to proceed? Either one power or the other must be set aside. Either the governor in council must take the responsibility, or else must become a mere cipher in the hands of the assembly, and not attempt to carry into effect the measures commanded by the home government."

It is not very clear how Lord John Russell got the argument out of the dilemma in which he had thus placed it. " Either the one power or the other must be set aside," and he seems to have thought that the power to be set aside was the house of assembly, and that the mode of setting it aside was by refusing to make the executive council responsible to the assembly; but surely it was a *non sequitur* that such a step would accomplish the object. If the governor, with an executive council, responsible to him alone, and removable but at his pleasure, should, by command of the home government, propose a measure distasteful to the house of assembly, and which should, therefore, be rejected by them, who would be successful in case of a struggle? The governor, with his irresponsible council? or the assembly, with their power to withhold the supplies? In such a case, the position of the governor would, in no respect, be better than it was before the late rebellion. On the contrary, it would be much worse. Before the rebellion, the governor had the nomination of the legislative council, and the other official patronage of the colony, wherewith to influence the members even of the assembly itself, by the hopes of his letting some of the good things fall into their mouths. Since the rebellion, the governor has lost all this. He holds an office eminent, dignified, and lucrative enough, but one which, in the hands of an unwise or imprudent holder, would prove to be a mere empty pageant in any direct contest with the colony.

The junction of the two provinces into one colony may, by the drowning of French influence in British, make the recurrence of questions in which the government will differ from the colonists less likely or frequent, but it will not make that recurrence impossible for the future; and when it does happen, the power which then *must be* " set aside," as it was the power which before the rebellion was set aside, will be the government, unless, as at the rebellion, the troops of the mother country be again introduced, and the power of the sovereign and supreme legislature be again invoked to set aside the constitution of the colony, by a repetition of the 1 and 2 of Victoria.

So far from the concession of the responsibility of the executive council to the assembly being calculated to induce the lamentable state of things which has just been suggested, it would seem, on the contrary, well calculated to ward off, though perhaps not absolutely to prevent, such a crisis. So long as the executive council is responsible to the assembly, and the measures proposed to it are ostensibly those of the council and not of the governor, he may, through them, feel the pulse of the legislature, and thus delay coming to extremities, until public opinion has changed, or the home government has modified its commands; and, perhaps, in this way, he may altogether avoid the crisis, without having compromised either the power or the dignity of his office.

But, if the executive council should not be responsible to the assembly, then the measures proposed to the assembly must ostensibly, as well as in reality, be those of the governor. His intercourse with the assembly would then be direct, and conflict would be unavoidable should his instructions from the home government be peremptory and the opposition of the assembly be as determined.

But, as before observed, the responsibility of the executive council to the assembly may, for a time, ward off, and even eventually prevent, a collision between the government and the assembly, but it will not, in every instance and in every condition of circumstances, absolutely prevent it. And if it should fail in doing so, in two cases suggested by Lord John Russell when he opposed concession of this responsibility, in what a condition will the mother country be in with the colony? Lord John Russell suggested the case of the assembly, with the concurrence of the responsible executive council, desiring to enter upon war with a neighboring state, on questions of colonial quarrel, against the express instructions of the home government delivered to the governor, and he solved the difficulty no further than by saying that, in such a case, the governor must say, that " his duty to the crown and his general instructions will not permit him to take that course, and, therefore, he could not agree with the executive council to carry into effect the wish of the majority of the assembly."

But his lordship does not show what is to be done, if the assembly rejoin, " True, you must obey the orders you have received, and we must discharge our duty to our constituents : till the government

authorize you to concede this measure to us, we vote
no more taxes ; and if, under your instructions, you
stop the machine of government, we shall try if we
cannot hold society together and ensure safety to life
and property without you." That is the crisis in the
dilemma to which Lord John Russell should have
pushed the argument. Had he done so, it does not
appear how he could have answered himself.

The other instance, which Lord John Russell
suggested, to show the inexpediency of making the
executive council responsible to the house of
assembly, and as destroying the analogy between
that council and the home ministers, is in the matter
of trade.   His words were, " Neither could this
analogy be maintained with regard to trade between
Canada and the mother country, or Canada and any
foreign country." Having stated the difficulty, as
difficulty there would no doubt be, if the colony
should resolve upon a commercial policy opposed to
that of the mother country, and a difficulty, too, of
no slight magnitude, Lord John Russell leaves this
dilemma also unsolved.   He meant it to be inferred,
no doubt, that the case would not arise if the council
were not made responsible to the assembly ; but that
also seems to be a *non sequitur*, for, if the assembly
were bent upon the controverted policy, it would
matter very little to it whether the executive council
were responsible or irresponsible ; whether they had

to encounter the opposition of the governor, backed privately by his *ir*responsible council, or whether they had the concurrence of a *re*sponsible council, and had to encounter the opposition of the governor alone. In either case, the measures, open to the assembly, for enforcing their policy, in opposition to that of the home government, would be the same; and, in either case, all that the governor could do would be to fall back upon the home government, as the governor had to do on the occasion of the past rebellion.

Unless, in short, the responsibility of the council to the assembly would, in either of the instances put by Lord John Russell, suggest to the assembly the wish to go to war, or to adopt an objectionable mercantile policy, a supposition too absurd to be made, that responsibility adds as little to the difficulty of the governor's situation, in the case supposed, as it had any share in creating the situation itself; and the *non*-responsibility of the council would as little assist in removing the difficulty of the position, as its responsibility would offer any obstacle to such removal.

If there be any weakness in the Canadian government, as it now exists, it would seem to be in the constitution of the *legislative* council. The members of that body are nominated by the governor, acting in the selection with the advice of the executive council,[a] and since the executive council is as responsible to the assembly for the advice given in this selection as it is responsible for any other advice, it would seem that the legislative council must be little better than a mere duplicate of the executive council, and cannot have any weight in the colony.

If the legislative council were made elective, there would then be the check of one popular body against another. If the assembly should accidentally, from the temporary ascendancy of one or two members, gifted with fluency of speech, though not blessed with wisdom, be unreasonable in the measures it wished to force upon the government, the legislative council, not being under the influence of the same *cacoethes loquendi*, might be more rational and better disposed to concur with the government against the assembly and the executive council, or with the governor and the executive council against the assembly alone. In either case, the contest would be directly between the two popular bodies—the legislative council and the house of assembly,—and the victory would be to that one of them which should have the support of the people at large.

In this way, again, the governor might be able to test public opinion, and to shape his course so as to avoid conflict with popular opinion and a compromise of the dignity and efficiency of his office, by getting

[a] Since the text was written this has been altered, it is believed.

into the situation, "neither possible nor desirable, of carrying on the government, in opposition to the opinions of the inhabitants."

But, without speculating further on the future history of Canada, if we except the short period since 1847, the past history of the government of that colony shows that the same expressions may be used in regard to it as Lord Grey has used in regard to Jamaica, "the relations between the local legislature and the home government have been on a very unsatisfactory footing," and there has been little of "that harmonious co-operation between these authorities, without which it is impossible that the affairs" of the colony "can be properly and efficiently conducted;"[a] and there may be made this serious addition to so unsatisfactory an account of a colony, that the colonists of Canada have actually proceeded to open rebellion. The rebellion has, no doubt, been put down, at the cost of more or less blood and treasure to the parent country and the colonists, and of much misery to the colonists;[b] but, after all this, the colonists, having previously an assembly popularly elected, which had the power of giving or refusing taxes, have retained that assembly with this power, and have been successful in likewise obtaining the patronage of all civil offices, the nomination of members of the executive council included, and the

[a] Colonial Policy, vol. i, p. 170.   [b] Hansard, 1839, p. 2642.

governorship alone excepted,[a] together with the removal of the executive council so often as its measures
shall be unacceptable to them. All this has been
conceded, in recognition of the principle that "it is
neither possible nor desirable to carry on the government of any of the British provinces in North America
in opposition to the opinions of the inhabitants ;"[b] and
still there is the risk, at some future day, of the occurrence of the two instances which Lord John Russell
has suggested, and others might be suggested, as
likely to bring the colony into collision with the
mother country.

Canada is making such rapid strides in population
and wealth that the day cannot, in probability, be
very distant when it will refuse to be controlled by
the policy of Great Britain, and will assert for itself
a right of independent action. For such a contin-
gency there has been, apparently, neither anticipation nor provision.

Would not the erection of this and the neighboring
colonies into an independent monarchy be a noble
provision for one of the princes of the blood royal
of Great Britain, and be an acceptable boon to the
colonists? If that were done, Great Britain would

---

[a] This, though not stated by Earl Grey, seems a necessary
inference from the other circumstances mentioned by him, that the
appointment of governor is " the only office in the gift of the home
government." Colonial Policy, vol. I, p. 208.

[b] Colonial Policy, vol. I, p. 212.

be reproduced in North America; and, in the strife of nations, who can doubt upon which side Great Britain and this her eldest daughter would be found.[a]

SECTION III.—OUR GOVERNMENT OF NOVA SCOTIA AND NEW BRUNSWICK, AND REFLECTIONS UPON THE WORKING OF THE CONSTITUTION CONCEDED TO THESE COLONIES.

Lord Grey says[b] of Nova Scotia and New Brunswick, that "the same system of government which has been established in Canada has been brought into successful operation" in these colonies. Whether this has been done in consequence of agitation in them, similar to what took place in Canada, as was hinted in the parliamentary debates upon that colony,[c] and which, in Canada, ripened into rebellion, Lord Grey does not say. Whether Nova Scotia and New Brunswick have had an elective assembly and a responsible executive council conceded to them, in

[a] Since the text was written, (in 1854,) Canada has offered, and Great Britain has accepted from it, a regiment, fully equipped. This truly gratifying fact, so far as it shows the spirit of the Canadians, while it fortifies the arguments for the course proposed by this work, suggests the possibility of a frequent repetition of such a colonial compliment destroying the efficiency of the Mutiny Act, and jeopardizing the liberties of Great Britain.

[b] Colonial Policy, vol. I, p. 274.

[c] Hansard, 1837, p. 1,031, Mr. Leader, in the debate on Canada, asked: "Have ministers heard no whisper of grievances unredressed in Nova Scotia and New Brunswick? The whole of British North America is in a state of uneasiness and distraction."

consequence of their own agitation, or because of the
example shown by the concession of these matters
to Canada, and in apprehension of disease, from
sympathy, in these members of the body politic, does
not appear in "Colonial Policy;" but there *does*
appear in that volume a specimen of the working of
the constitution in Nova Scotia, which gives a good
example of the collisions which may possibly occur
between the home government and the North
American colonies, even after the grant of so liberal
a constitution as has been established in them.

When Lord John Russell said that the analogy
between the responsibility of the British ministers to
parliament and of the Canadian executive council to
the colonial legislature could not be "maintained,
with regard to trade between Canada and the mother
country, or Canada and any foreign country," he
evidently confined the impossibility of the analogy to
the external trade of the colony,—to its exports and
imports. But, in a subsequent part of the same
speech, in which this language was used, his lordship
said, " I can conceive, and I think it would be the
part of wisdom and of justice to say, that there are
matters affecting the internal affairs of these provinces
—that there are matters in which neither the imperial
parliament nor the general government need interfere,
and on which they should be anxious to consult the
feelings of the people of the colonies. It seems as

much a rule of sound sense as of generosity to say that there are some questions on which it would not be desirable that, on the opinion of the Secretary of State for the Colonies, the opinion of the House of Assembly should be put on one side."

From this language, it is apparent that interference, even in the internal affairs of the colonies, was contemplated to be *the rule*, and non-interference *the exception*. It is not said that the colony, having the regulation of its own affairs, it nevertheless is possible to conceive cases in which the home government *should* interfere to deprive them of this self-management. But that, having a constitution which, although in terms it implied self-government, was so far from being intended to give this power, it was necessary to say that it was possible to conceive cases in which the home government should *not* interfere.

This construction of the relations between the colonies and the home government very soon received practical application, in the case of New Brunswick. The legislature of that colony passed an act, granting a bounty for the cultivation of hemp within the colony. As the act was of limited duration, the home government did not refuse the royal assent to it; but they instructed the lieutenant-governor to refuse his assent to any future act, having a similar object. The house of assembly, in an address to the sovereign, represented that the question was one "*purely local*," on which "the legislature of New Brunswick might safely be left to the free exercise of its discretion." But the home government, after full deliberation, did not agree in this view of the subject, nor recall their instructions to refuse the royal assent to all bills having a similar object; and they informed the assembly that the measure contemplated would be injurious, not only to the empire at large, by interfering with the policy of free-trade, which it had finally adopted, but to the colony itself, by diverting capital from those investments in which, if left to itself, it would naturally be placed, as the most profitable, to one that, *ex concessis*, was not advantageous without the assistance of a bounty.

The colony did not agree to this view; they considered the imperial prohibition of differential duties and bounties as a capricious interference with their right to regulate their own taxation and dispose of their own money, for purposes of internal government. The same despatch which communicated the view which the colony had thus taken of the government's instructions to the governor, transmitted a minute which the executive council had passed, expressing a wish that the colony *should be allowed to impose differential duties* on imports from the United States, in retaliation for differential duties imposed by the United States on imports from the colony.

In November, 1850, the home government transmitted a despatch, explaining their views upon bounties and differential duties, and adhering to their determination not to accede to the wish of the colonists, in either respect. In April, 1851, the assembly passed strong resolutions in assertion of its right to pass measures of the kind objected to, and the ministry, of which Lord Grey formed a member, went out of office before the matter was adjusted.

It is quite immaterial to the present inquiry which party was in the right, as to the particular policy in dispute—the home ministry or the colonial legislature. But it is most material to inquire how the dispute is to be ended under the constitution which this colony enjoys. If the dispute had occurred in Great Britain, the ministers must have given way to the parliament, however well convinced they might have been of the blindness of parliament in desiring the continuance of differential duties and of bounties (and both differential duties and bounties have had their day in the mother country, and a long day it was); and so, upon constitutional principles, the governor of the colony (who, in a contest with the colonial legislature, stands pretty much in the same relative position to it as the ministers in England do to the parliament) ought to have been instructed to give way to the colonial legislature; and so, no doubt, he would have been instructed, but for the interference which such a step would have created to the imperial policy of free-trade. But, if the colony should refuse ultimately to acknowledge the urgency of this reason, and should adopt the same steps to compel the colonial government to accede to their views which the House of Commons, in a similar case, might adopt to coerce the home government, and which Canada did use to coerce the same authorities, what is then to be done? Here, again, would be a dead lock, which nothing could remove but a repetition of what occurred in Canada, by the passing of the 1 and 2 Vic., to suspend the constitution of the colony, with all the possible attendant dangers of such a step.

SECTION IV. — OUR GOVERNMENT OF NEWFOUNDLAND, AND REFLECTIONS UPON THE WORKING OF THE CONSTITUTION CONCEDED TO THAT COLONY.

It does not appear, from Lord Grey's work, what is the particular nature of the constitution enjoyed by Newfoundland, where "the policy of the home government, until within a comparatively recent period, was not to promote, but as much as possible to discourage, regular colonization;" but where settlements grew up, in spite of " what was done to prevent them." It seems that, " only about twenty years since, a form of representative government was established in the island. At first, the experiment was so little successful, that parliament was compelled to interfere, and partially to withdraw *the privileges* which had been *conceded* to the colonists. In 1847, the constitution originally given to the colony was, with some amendments, restored to it, and placed on a permanent footing. Newfoundland was not, therefore, considered by us as yet ripe for the system of government now established in the other North American colonies."

Here is another instance, after Port Phillip, of settlements formed by British subjects, " in spite " of the home government, over which the power of that government has been shed by forming them into colonies. The original constitution given to this colony of Newfoundland was " a representative " form of government, " conceded," not as the " birthright" of British settlers, but as a " privilege," which was afterwards " partially withdrawn," as the colony was not considered to be " yet ripe " for the system of government established in the other North American colonies.

Without stopping to inquire, for the present, into the necessity for the government submitting to have a colony thrust upon it, or whether representative government should be designated to be " the right " or " the privilege" of British subjects, where their home government follows them into a foreign settlement of their own establishing, in order to put them under its power, it may naturally be asked what it was which constituted the ripeness of the other North American colonies for the liberal system of government which they now enjoy?

Lord Grey probably intended to intimate that society in Newfoundland was not in so advanced a state as in the other North American colonies, and, *in this respect*, Newfoundland was not yet ripe for the system of representative government. But, unfortunately, the more liberal system of government established in the other North American colonies was not *voluntarily* conceded to them, because of any improvement in the state of society, or any greater capacity shown by society for self-government. It may be that the minister was of opinion that the state of society in Canada did show such a capacity, but, if that were so, the opinion was not to be discovered, either in the debates in parliament, or in the despatches to the colony which were made public, and it was not acted upon till after an actual rebellion, by which the *free action* of self-government was attempted to be obtained, had been put down by force, and the constitution itself had been suspended for several years, and been replaced during that time by arbitrary government.

If, therefore, the concession of the liberal government which Canada now enjoys was a concession because of the advanced state of society, the mode and the time of making it gave it, unfortunately, very much the appearance of a concession to force, after having, for the time, put down that force, in order to save appearances.

Reasoning upon this, and connecting the effect with the ostensible cause, the colonists of Newfoundland might not unreasonably say that they were not considered "yet ripe" for representative government, because their aspirations for free government had not "yet" blown into rebellion.

But, passing by these speculative observations, which are perhaps out of place here, and have been introduced only as an illustration of the arguments which will presently be used to suggest what ought to have been, and in future ought to be, the principles according to which British settlements should be founded and established, let us see how the particular form of representative government which Newfoundland was considered ripe enough to enjoy, has worked practically, with a view to ascertain how the system of government established in the other North American colonies will work in Newfoundland, when it shall become, what it has not yet been considered, ripe for such a system.

It is well known that the principal source of the

wealth of Newfoundland, as it was the original inducement to the settlement, is the deep-sea fishings, within a certain distance of its shores. Fishermen from the United States of America have, it seems, been encroaching upon these fishing grounds, stimulated to do so by a bounty, given by the United States government, for all fish caught by citizens of the republic. The inhabitants of Newfoundland, naturally enough, are jealous of this foreign interference with what they conceive to be their rights, according to international law, and they have called upon the home government to interfere, and exclude the United States fishermen from their waters.

Lord Grey uses very cogent arguments, and states them very lucidly, for showing that the Newfoundland *fishermen* have little to complain of in this matter, as, in all probability, the effect of the bounty given by the United States to their own fishermen may be the same as was the effect, on the coast of Northumberland, of a bounty given by France to its fishermen. The French fishermen, finding sufficient profit in the bounty given by their government, and in the price they procured for the fish in their own market, to allow them to buy fish from the Northumbrian fisher, took that course. They bought of him instead of spending time, labor, and discomfort in catching fish for themselves. Accordingly, they did not do that which it was the very object of the bounty to induce them to do—catch their own fish.

It may be that the bounty given by the United States government works in this way with Newfoundland, and that the Newfoundland fishermen do, in fact, as Lord Grey suggests, actually get the benefit, or at least an important part of the benefit, of that bounty, in the price they receive for their fish from the United States fishermen : they have this market beyond their own.

On the other hand, the Newfoundland fishermen may say, and say correctly, that if the United States did not give a bounty to their own people, so as to induce them to leave their own shores, none of them would find it worth their while to do so, as the wages of labor are so high in the States. In that case, the fishermen of Newfoundland, where wages are not so high, might find it to be worth their while to leave their own shores and go to the United States market, where they could make their own price, being without competitors, instead of being obliged, on the fishing grounds, to make a stiff bargain with the United States fishermen, under the threat by the latter of dropping their lines if their terms are not acceded to.

There may be as much truth in this view of the case as in the other, and, if the fishermen of Newfoundland are able to convince their representatives

in the colonial government that their view ought to
be given effect to, and every impediment be thrown
in the way of the United States fishermen, and if
these representatives, having the purse-strings, should
insist on keeping them tight until the home government should agree to remove the fishermen of the
United States from the banks of Newfoundland, even
at the risk of going to war with that power, how
could such a dilemma be got out of?

It may be said that the fishermen are too unimportant a body in the colony of Newfoundland to be
likely to produce such crises, especially if their
fellow-colonists should concur in Lord Grey's view,
that they rather gain than suffer by the bounty. But
there are other bodies still involved in the discussion,
and these are the *fish-curers* and *fish-merchants* of
Newfoundland. Even Lord Grey does not deny
that those persons are injured by the Americans
carrying off the fish to be cured in the States, and
be consumed there, or exported thence. Considering
the prodigious export of Newfoundland cod to the
Catholic countries of Europe and Asia, the amount
of capital invested in this trade by the colonists of
Newfoundland must be very great, and as agriculture
within the colony seems to have been comparatively
neglected,[a] and there is no other local trade, the
probability is that "the fishing interest," if not the

[a] Grey's Colonial Policy, vol. I, p. 301.

most important interest in the colony, may be made so by the addition of the fishermen.

If the fish-curers and traders, backed by the fishermen, were to prevail on the local parliament to pursue the course with the home government which has been suggested, must the dilemma be got out of by suspending the constitution in this colony also, and bringing the " sovereign and supreme legislative power of the imperial parliament " to bear upon the colony ? That might be done once, and successfully, as in Canada; but will once be sufficient? While fishing continues, the cause of complaint may endure, and with it successive attempts to force redress. The constitution may have to be suspended once, and again, and again. Surely, a body politic cannot be either in a sound or a safe state, where such a violent and dangerous remedy has so frequently to be had recourse to.

CHAPTER XII.

CAUSE OF THE EMBARRASSMENT WHICH OCCURRED IN THE GOVERN-
MENT OF SUCH OF OUR PRESENT COLONIES AS WERE FOUNDED
PREVIOUS TO THE DECLARATION OF AMERICAN INDEPENDENCE.

THE cursory specimen of the rule of our North
American colonies, given in the preceding pages,
shows that the recognition, contained in the constitutions of these colonies, of the right of Englishmen to
liberal institutions has not worked more harmoniously
in these colonies, than it has done in the West India
colonies. In both sets of these colonies there has
been a struggle for independence. The difference
has been only in the result of that struggle. The
West Indians thought to gain their point by passive
resistance to the home government, and failed. The
North Americans chose active resistance, and failed
also. But the danger of the contest was too great to
allow of its being repeated, and the home government
has yielded everything that the colonists have demanded which has stopped short of independence.
When *that* also is asked, it will be difficult to refuse it.

It seems impossible to avoid the conclusion that
giving our West Indian and North American
colonies constitutions, having some analogy to the

constitution of Great Britain, has led the successive
governments of the mother country into all the difficulties which they have had to encounter in the
administration of these colonies. The unavoidable
tendency of constitutions of so liberal a nature, if
they are worked out to their legitimate results, must
be to produce ultimate independence of the mother
country, as the short summary which has been given
of the administration of Canada shows. If the
minister were prepared to assist in this—if he
foresaw rather an advantage, than a disadvantage,
to the mother country in her colonies standing upon
their own strength, instead of being dependent upon
her,—at all events, the people of Great Britain were
very far from being in a disposition to concur in
such a view.

So long as the British nation thought that its
navigation laws and its system of differential duties
were the main foundations of its naval and commercial supremacy, it would have been hopeless for
any British minister, however far in advance of his
age, to have hinted at anything like independence
being conceded to the colonies. It was not until
1848, that the nation became sufficiently enlightened
to see, and acknowledge, and allow its rulers to act
upon the fallacy of these notions, by abrogating the
navigation laws, and introducing freedom in trade,
whether with our colonies or with foreign nations.

Accordingly, the administration of those of our colonies which already possessed constitutions based upon a recognition of popular rights could not well have been other than it has been. It has not repudiated these constitutions, indeed, but, on the other hand, it has not heartily acknowledged them and been forward to perfect them by practical application. Each successive colonial minister has seen no other course open to him, without stultifying himself before the nation, than to give effect, as much as possible, to the monarchical instead of the constitutional principle.

CHAPTER XIII.

ADMINISTRATION OF OUR COLONIES WHICH WERE FOUNDED BY
VOLUNTARY SETTLEMENT OF BRITISH SUBJECTS *SUBSEQUENT*
TO THE AMERICAN REBELLION.

THE colonies which had no existence at the date
of the declaration of American independence, but
have been acquired or formed by us since the commencement of the present century, with the benefit
of the experience we have derived from the American
rebellion, as to the form of constitution we ought to
give them, in order to steer clear of the questions
out of which the rebellion arose, may next be
considered.

The same motives have operated with the home
government, in framing the constitutions which have
been given to those colonies which we have either
acquired or formed since the declaration of American
independence, as actuated the government in administering the colonies which had obtained constitutions previous to that event. The warning
which the American rebellion gave, should have
induced us, if we meant determinedly to keep our
other colonies for ever dependent upon us, to recall
the liberal constitutions which the colonies then in

existence already possessed, and to abstain from giving similar constitutions to such colonies as we might thereafter acquire, or form; or rather, that is the course which was pointed out to us, if we meant to maintain our navigation laws and our exclusive system of trade.

So long as the nation was convinced that we must force the trade of our colonies through our channels, it was impossible that liberal constitutions could be allowed fair play, with any hope of maintaining our illiberal commercial policy. The minister was, therefore, in a degree, compelled to give our new colonies such constitutions as he could well administer, without running counter to the received notion, become almost an irrefragable doctrine, that British colonists have a right to enjoy the rights and liberties of free-born Englishmen, and at the same time give them constitutions so illiberal in form as would make it possible for him to enforce against the colonists our exclusive commercial policy.

It is upon such reasoning as this that the form of constitution given to such of our colonies as have been acquired or formed subsequent to the declaration of American independence can alone be accounted for. Whatever doubt might have existed as to the power of the crown to legislate for a colony, which the sovereign had acquired by right of conquest, no question had ever been raised as to *the*

*non-existence of such a power in the crown with
regard to colonies settled by British subjects.* The
very argument of the question, in regard to conquered or ceded colonies, had assumed that such a
power did not reside with the crown, but that
Englishmen, settled in a colony of their own forming,
were entitled to be governed, as nearly as possible,
after the fashion of government existing in the
mother country, namely, by a government acting
under responsibility to a popular assembly.

Upon whatever grounds the proceeding may have
been rested, the fact is, that in none of the colonies
we acquired or formed since the beginning of this
century, was a popular form of government established at the outset. In all of them, the crown was
omnipotent and irresponsible, save to the imperial
parliament. The best evidence of this is to be found
in the minute of the privy council of the 1st of May,
1849 : " In those ancient possessions, which at present form so large a part of the United States of
America, and in all the other British colonies, there
prevailed, until the commencement of the nineteenth
century, the almost invariable usage of establishing
a local legislature consisting of three estates—that is,
of a governor appointed by the sovereign, of a council,
and of an assembly elected by the people.

" But during the nineteenth century, the British
crown has acquired, by conquest and cession from

foreign states, three Transatlantic colonies, one colony in South Africa, and four colonies to the eastward of the Cape of Good Hope. During the same period, the British crown has acquired, by the occupation of vacant territories, two colonies on the West Coast of Africa, three in New Holland, one in Van Diemen's Land, one in New Zealand, and one in Falkland Island. *In no one of these sixteen colonies has the old colonial polity of a governor, council, and assembly been introduced. In no one of them, except New South Wales, has any electoral franchise been granted to the colonists, or any share in the local legislation to their representatives.*

"In all these conquered colonies the ancient system of internal government remains such as it was at the time of the respective conquests, excepting that by letters patent, under the great seal, a governor and a council appointed by the crown have in each of them been authorized to make local laws.

"In all the colonies acquired during the nineteenth century *by the occupation of vacant territories*, the same system of internal legislation by a governor and a council appointed by the crown has been introduced *by the authority of parliament*.

"In colonies so acquired, the royal prerogative was *competent only to the establishment of systems of civil government, of which a legislature composed, at least in part, of the representatives of the people, formed a component part. To dispense, even for a while, with such a legislature, parliamentary aid was requisite.* But in sanctioning that departure from the general type or model of the earlier colonial constitutions, it has been the practice of parliament to recognize the ancient principle, and to record the purpose of resuming the former constitutional practice, so soon as the causes should have ceased to operate, which, in each particular case, had forbidden the immediate observance of it."

There is in these passages unequivocal evidence of the fact that, in all our colonies, acquired in any way during this century, popular representation formed no part in the form of government under which they were put. It is not said where the recognition of the principle of popular representation, and " of the purpose to resume it, so soon as the causes which in each particular case had forbidden the observance of it should have ceased," was recorded. But if it were so recorded, the colonists had this record to appeal to, as well as the other records, in regard to the rights of Englishmen, which have already been mentioned, and which are recognized in the passage of this minute, where it is said that it required parliamentary aid to dispense " even for a while " with a popular legislature.

Without stopping to inquire whether even parliamentary aid could, constitutionally, place Englishmen
under the absolute government of the crown,—that is
to say, absolute so far as any control from themselves
was concerned,—it may be remarked that Englishmen,
with these records of their rights and of the fact that
they were intended to be suspended only for a time,
would not be slow to claim the enjoyment of their
rights, and to make the period of their suspension as
short as possible.

SECTION I.—OUR ADMINISTRATION OF THE SOUTH AUSTRALIAN
COLONIES.

It would occupy too great space to go minutely
into a history of the administration of our colonies
acquired during the present century, in order to
show how constitutions, from which the principle of
popular representation was excluded, and in which
the monarchical principle was enforced, have worked.
It will be sufficient to give such a notice of these
colonies as will show how the colonists have relished
the suspension of their right, as Englishmen, to
popular representation for the short period which has
elapsed since the acquisition or formation of these
colonies.

To New South Wales a constitution has been
granted, by 13 and 14 Vic., cap. 59, but after much
internal disturbance and agitation. Even the liberal

provisions of that statute, in which popular representation is unequivocally recognized, have not prevented a protest by the legislative council, which was in existence in the colony at the time the statute was passed.

This protest, as it represented the past intercourse between the colony and the home government, will make any further account of that superfluous, as the view taken by the colonists of their past government, whether correct or erroneous, does not concern the present inquiry.

The protest says, " After the reiterated reports, resolutions,, addresses, and petitions, which have proceeded from us, during the whole course of our legislative career, against the schedules appended to the 5 and 6 Vic., cap. 76," (being a land sales act for the colony,) " and the appropriations of our ordinary revenue, *under the sole authority of parliament*, against the administration of our waste lands, and our territorial revenue thence arising; against the withholding of the customs department from our control ; against the dispensation of the patronage of the colony at dictation of the minister for the colonies; and against the veto reserved and exercised by the same minister, in the name of the crown, in matters of local legislation,—we feel that we had a right to expect that these undoubted grievances would have been redressed by the 13 and 14 Vic., cap. 59, or that power to redress them would have been conferred on the constituent bodies, thereby created, with the avowed intention of establishing an authority, *more competent than parliament itself*, to frame suitable constitutions for the whole group of the Australian colonies. These our reasonable expectations have been utterly frustrated. The only result of this new enactment is that all the material powers, exercised for centuries by the House of Commons, are still withheld from us,—that our loyalty and desire for the maintenance of order and good government are so far mistrusted that we are not permitted to vote our own civil list, lest it might prove inadequate to the requirements of the public service,—that whilst in defiance of the 18 Geo. III, cap. 12, a large amount of our public revenue is thus levied and appropriated by the authority of parliament, we have not even the consolation of seeing that portion of it which is applied to the payment of the salaries of our public officers, distributed, as it ought to be, among the settled inhabitants,—and that, as a fit climax to this system of misrule, we are not allowed to exercise the most ordinary legislation which is not subject to the veto of the colonial minister."[a]

This is the statement of a body, which consisted partly of nominees of the crown, and partly of the

[a] Grey's Colonial Policy, vol. II, pp. 314 and 317.

representatives of the people, and whether the grievances alleged were real or imaginary, justly or ill founded, matters not. The protest shows the discontented view which the colonists took of their past government, and the nature of the changes in it which they desiderated; and that, as before observed, is alone material here.

This protest for New South Wales may be read for Victoria, South Australia, and Van Diemen's Land, to all of which the 13 and 14 Vic. applies.

No doubt, that statute was introduced and passed on the authority of the opinion expressed in the minute of the privy council, from which extracts have been taken, that the time had arrived for conferring the franchise on these colonies, as they were able to fulfil the condition "on which alone such a grant ought to be made," that of sustaining the expense of their own civil government.

Assuming this to be the only condition on which the franchise of popular government ought to be granted, we have already a proof of the use which has been made of it, in the instance of New South Wales, by the exercise of the power which the 13 and 14 Vic. gives the colonists, of amending and altering their institutions almost to the fullest extent.[a]

That statute did not purpose or profess to make

a Grey's Colonial Policy, vol. II, p. 322.

a constitution for the colony—it was intended only to effect a separation of Port Phillip from New South Wales, but, while doing so, it gave the powers of amendment and alteration which have been mentioned. These the colonists have exercised, by preparing for themselves a constitution, on the mode of that established in Canada, and after doing so, if report speak truly, they have exceeded the civil list proposed by the government, and, for one item, have voted a salary to their governor, which would be princely even in Europe.

How far this constitution will be accepted by the home government, and the act establishing it be confirmed, has yet to be ascertained, but there can be little doubt of either of these events happening; and then, after years of civil turmoil and agitation, these Australian colonies will have obtained a constitution, which, if it do not make them absolutely independent of the mother country, places them, at least, on the highest spoke of the ladder whereby independence is to be reached.

SECTION II.—OUR ADMINISTRATION OF THE COLONY OF THE CAPE OF GOOD HOPE.

The Cape of Good Hope is another colony which may be referred to, as an instance of our colonial government of colonies acquired during this century, and of the spirit which prevails in most of these colonies. This colony was acquired by conquest from the Dutch, in 1806, but was allowed to form the subject of cession in the convention between Great Britain and the Netherlands of 13th August, 1814. From 1806 downwards, till the year 1825, it was ruled by a governor alone, without a council of any kind whatsoever. His fiat was law, and the only appeal from the courts of law was to himself and the lieutenant-governor. In 1825, the government was so far altered that the governor was henceforth to be " advised and assisted " by a council composed of six officers of the government. In January, 1834, the government was again altered by the creation of two councils—one executive, the other legislative : the executive to consist of four official persons ; the legislative to consist of twelve, or not less than ten members—five being official persons, and the remaining five or seven, as the case might be, being unofficial persons. Discontent and dissatisfaction, if not engendered, were, at all events, aggravated by the admission of members taken from the people, but not elected by them to this legislative council. Matters went on from bad to worse, till something very like a rebellion arose, on the subject of sending convicts to the colony. No doubt the confusion upon that occasion was greatly attributable to willful or very culpable mismanagement

by the local government, but the success of the
colonists, in resisting the local government, and
through it the home government, upon this subject of convicts, revived, with increased ardor,
an agitation for popular institutions, which had
previously occurred, but was apparently slumbering
for a time.

The home government, influenced by exaggerated
accounts of the disturbed state of the colony,
received from those in authority, or more probably
acting upon the opinion expressed in the minute
of the Privy Council, to which reference has
already been made, granted the colony, in the
year 1850, a constitution, consisting of a governor
appointed by the crown, a legislative council,
and a house of assembly, both of them elected
by the people, with power to appropriate its own
revenue, after permanent provision for a fixed civil
list.

The colonial parliament has met under this
constitution, and already, in its first session, a motion
has been made for an address to the crown, praying
the establishment of a responsible government, in
other words, for a government under which, as
already exists in Canada, the colonists may have the
same power as exists in the mother country, namely,
the power of removing, by a parliamentary vote,
those civil officers through whom the government

is administered. This motion has been postponed in the meanwhile, with every prospect of its being renewed next session.[a]

This colony, likewise, is within one step of the top of the ladder which reaches to independence.

[a] Since the passage in the text was written, *i. e.*, 1854, the colonial parliament has met in its second session, and this motion has been renewed in the form of one for the appointment of a committee to consider how responsible government can be best introduced. This motion has been carried, and the committee has been appointed.

CHAPTER XIV.

IT does not seem then, that, in the result, the administration of these colonies, which we have established or acquired since the beginning of this century, with the benefit of the experience derived from the American rebellion, and the consequent exclusion from the constitution which we gave them of the principle of popular representation, and the substitution for it of regal government, has been very different from the administration of those colonies which had obtained constitutions prior to the American rebellion, wherein the principle of popular representation was already distinctly recognized. If there be a difference, it is only in the superior quickness with which our new colonies have run the race, not merely for the recognition of popular representation, but for its complete establishment and enjoyment. Though these colonies were neither in existence, nor thought of at the beginning of this century, they are as close to the grasp of independence as are our North American colonies, in whose constitutions popular rights have been recognized for centuries.

There has, in all the colonies, been a perpetual encroachment, on their part, with the view of obtaining the full enjoyment of popular rights, and gradual concession, on the part of the government, without any apparent distinct view of what *might* be given and of what *must* be withheld; but with every appearance of an apprehension, which has been more manifest in later years, that the colonies were forcing on the government to the recognition of independence—that the lowering sky of colonial agitation shows independence looming on its horizon.

Private adventurers seized upon parts of America and the West India islands, and some of them, possessing influence at home, procured from the crown charters of government, whereby they were to rule the district embraced by the grant, assisted by a council of their own election; but, "so soon as the state and circumstances of the said colony should admit thereof, they should, with advice and consent of their councils, call general assemblies, *and make laws,* as near as may be agreeable to the laws of England."

Whether these words to be found in the charters of Charles II, or similar ones which appear in other charters, were introduced by the grantees, in order to reconcile their fellow-colonists to this mode of gaining a title to rule, without having any right to it, or whether they were introduced by the minister at home, from some generous and gratuitous emotion for those of his countrymen who, by his act, (so far as that act could be available for anything,) he was about to place under the authority of one of their fellow-subjects, without any of those safeguards for the protection of their lives and liberties which are afforded by the British constitution under which they had hitherto lived, does not appear. But, however that may be, it seems certain that the ministers, who put their signatures to the warrants by virtue of which the seal was affixed to these charters, never could have calculated beforehand what would be the necessary effect of the words which have been quoted, should the colonies embraced by these grants ever attain to any internal power, either in population or pecuniary resources.

Out of this recognition of a right in the colonists to be governed after the model of the British constitution, has sprung all the doubt and difficulty which have perplexed our courts of law and our statesmen from that time downwards. Hence sprang the American rebellion, the West Indian, Australian, and Cape of Good Hope agitations, only stopping short of rebellion, and the Canadian rebellion, which has ended only short of independent government.

If the British sovereign had taken possession of

all the territories which our beloved Queen now holds as her colonies, and the three estates of the realm had determined to rule these possessions after any given, determined mode of government, even though that mode had amounted to an absolute despotism, there would have been a simple, intelligible state of things, under which both the rulers and the ruled would have known what they were about,— simple in principle and intelligible in action, for nothing can be more simple, in both of these respects, than the rule of despotic power; whereas our colonial government has been an inconsistency, an eccentricity, and an anomaly, from its very beginning,—liberal in the outset in the promise of British liberty, but most backward and niggardly in the performance, and for an obvious reason, the impracticability of performance.

The people have been told by the government that they were to be ruled as British subjects, and the courts of law have decided, and statesmen have acknowleged, that, though removed from the mother country, or born out of it, they were still to be considered as within it, and to be entitled to all the rights and liberties of free-born Englishmen. The colonists have taken them at their word, and whenever they have been strong enough to speak out, have insisted on its performance.

Whether performance were possible or impossible,

no one has ever stopped to consider. Each colonial minister has struggled with the difficulties of his time, as best he could, keeping as much power to the crown as he could, and giving as little constitutional power to the people as he durst not well refuse. Trying a government here by the governor of the crown, with a council of nominees,—there by a governor and a council, partly of nominees and partly of elected members,—here by a governor, nominee council, and an elective assembly,—there by a governor, and executive council *ir*removeable, and an elective legislative council and assembly,— here by a governor with an executive council *re*moveable, and an elective legislative council and assembly,—here the crown has the appropriation of the revenue,—there the colony has the appropriation. except as regards a fixed civil list, and there the colony has the unlimited power of appropriation; such are specimens only of the varieties in the mode of English colonial government : Joseph's coat had not so many colors.

But in the midst of all this change and diversity, two things have been constant and never varying,— a spirit of encroachment on the part of the colonists, and of concession on the part of the crown. The colonists have stuck to the text. They were told they were free-born British subjects, having all the rights of British subjects, and they have steadily and

consistently insisted upon obtaining the enjoyment
of these rights without troubling their heads to
inquire how that could very well be accomplished ;
and they have quarreled with, and bullied, and
threatened, and fought with the government to gain
it, accusing each successive minister with the love
of power and patronage whenever he has refused any
particular demand having that direction. On the
other hand, the ministers, however varying in their
tempers and politics, whether Tory or Whig, Liberal
or Conservative, have always found themselves in a
false position. They could not deny the text, yet
they found it impossible to act up to it. However
scandalously, and with however little regard for the
feelings and rights of the colonists, our colonies may
in former times have been managed, the most unruly
colonial spirit cannot but admit, that within the last
twenty years, every attempt has been made to come
as near to the text as possible,—at each step the
attempt has been bolder to bring the constitution of
the colonies nearer to the constitution of the mother
country.

It would be sad, as well as absurd, to think that
the many eminent statesmen who have held the
office of Colonial Secretary, have not seen where the
true root of their difficulties lay. The only apology
which can be offered for their not having followed
it out in all its ramifications, so as to apply the axe

effectually, is that the pressure of official business while in office did not allow them time. The temper and opinions of the inhabitants of the mother country would not have admitted the application of the proper remedy, and these made it still more hopeless for the ministers to attempt any remedy when out of office and reduced to the position simply of independent members of parliament, than this would have been while they enjoyed the power and prestige of office.

In Canada, the colonists have now their parliament by popular election. The governor, not the crown, has the power of appointing to all the colonial offices, and their parliament has the appropriation of the taxes and the power of controlling the executive, as to the appointment to offices and in every other respect, by the possession of a power to compel him to change his executive council. They enjoy a constitution as nearly resembling that of Great Britain as possible, and are, in short, all but entirely independent of the mother country. This is the boldest attempt to conciliate a colony which has yet been tried, and it would only be wood-cocking to try to conceal that it has been the fruits of the Canadian rebellion. But for that violent pressure upon the home government,—but for that fearful shadow of an event, which might be coming, if it were not anticipated, the Canadians would not at this day in all probability, be enjoying the rights they now possess. But their constitution was not given them apparently from any enlarged or enlightened view of what ought to be the colonial policy of Great Britain, abstractly from a consideration of the power or temper of any particular colony. It was given, if we may judge by the self-congratulation of ministers after the success of the experiment has been so far tested, merely as an experiment:

> ——." In extremes, bold counsels are the best,
> Like empirics they last are tried,
> And by the event condemned or justified."[a]

"The event" has not come yet, nor will it probably till the colony has some individual interest, either in conjunction with, or in opposition to, the neighboring states of North America, of New Brunswick, or of Nova Scotia, which the mother country may find it necessary, or for her interest, to combat. Then will come " the event," and what that may be, it is needless to speculate upon. Yet, the experiment of a liberal constitution has been so far tested as to justify the minister in congratulating himself and the colony upon its success. The *internal* government of the colony we have every reason to expect will continue to be administered " with that harmonious co-operation between the

[a] Dryden, Aurengzebe.

authorities," which, " for the last thirty years," has
not existed in Jamaica. When that co-operation
in the *external* government shall be found to
be wanting, then some bold " empiric remedy"
will be tried, " by the event to be condemned or
justified."

In this respect, Canada is neither an exception
nor an anomaly. The same observation may be
made as to all the other colonies, which have been
mentioned. Some of them are advancing more
rapidly, and others more tardily, to the attainment
of that internal strength, which is sufficient to ensure
compliance with a demand for external independence. But all of them show that no well-digested
or profoundly-considered scheme of colonial government has ever been laid down in the mother country,
which each succeeding minister could refer to as
having guided his predecessors and as the compass
for his own political voyage, either in regard to the
colonies generally or in regard to any one colony in
particular.

CHAPTER XV.

DEFECT IN THE SYSTEM OF ADMINISTERING OUR COLONIES, ARISING FROM THE NATURE OF THE OFFICE OF SECRETARY FOR THE COLONIES.

WHY should the state of circumstances indicated in the close of the preceding chapter exist? Government is a science. Human nature is known, and its principles of action understood. The same men do not change their feelings and aspirations with their personal locality. Why should it be supposed, then, that that can be endured in colonies which will not be tolerated in England? In England, the minister must rule conformably to the wishes of the people, as expressed by their representatives, and there it is assumed that this mode of governing is that which conduces most to the prosperity and happiness of the country. In the colonies, the minister has ruled according to his notions of what is best, and it has been assumed that the colonists were unfit to judge for themselves, and therefore that this mode of governing conduced most to their prosperity and happiness. But if the colonists are not fit for the degree of self-government enjoyed at home, until

society in them has advanced to a certain stage, both
as to numbers, wealth, and experience, approaching
that of the mother country, in what respects is the
colonial minister qualified to supply for them these
defects in the meanwhile? However uncourtly or
unpalatable this question may appear, it is not these
pages which suggest it; colonists have *already*
asked it in more than one instance, and have
answered it for themselves in the negative. And
it must be confessed that it is difficult to contradict them.

The changes of colonial minister are constant, not
from circumstances having reference to colonial
government, but almost always from circumstances
of a totally different nature; arising either out of
home or European politics. No minister can depend
upon retaining his office for any given time.
He is, from the moment he enters upon it, a
tenant at will, and at a most capricious will,
no less than that of a popular assembly; and,
during his tenancy, he is so persecuted with the
constant demands of detail, that he has no time
to devote for the general; he is so pestered with
the concrete that he can never get a view of the
abstract.

The fault of our colonial system, if error there be
in it, is not in the men who have been our colonial
ministers. It is not to be ascribed to want of ability

in the ministers to devise a philosophical system of rule, nor yet, probably, to their want of inclination to grapple with the difficulties of their position. So far as the minister is concerned, it is attributable to the short and precarious tenure of his office. He has often run his course before he has got well into the saddle. He has hardly grappled a survey of all the details of his office, so as to obtain a comprehensive and abstract view of the system, when he is ejected from office, to make way for a successor, who has to go through the same preparation, with the same uncertainty as to its being fruitful; and should either of them return to office, it is much more likely to be to another department of the government than to that of the colonies. But, if the individual should resume the colonial portfolio, he will hardly have taken up the thread where he laid it down, and have unraveled the clue, before he will again be ejected from office, from some cause having, as before, little or perhaps no reference to, or any connection whatever with, his previous or present, good or bad, administration of the colonial department.

It is impossible that the colonial government can be administered according to any fixed, enduring system, so long as the administrator is to be thus constantly changing, or that, assuming the colonies to be unfit for self-government, the minister can be in a condition to supply their defects.[a] If the colonies, therefore, are to be retained, a radical change in this respect would appear to be necessary, by the appointment of a permanent colonial minister, and perhaps there would not be so much difficulty in accomplishing this as at first view may appear.

It would not be necessary to change the system, by which the ministry are constantly varying, according to the acceptability of the men or their measures with the House of Commons. That, no doubt, produces some inconveniences in all the departments of government, but these inconveniences are greatly overbalanced by the advantages, and, at all events, there has not, as yet, been devised any

---

[a] The author met, one day, a French missionary, who has lived for twenty years with the Bechuana tribe of Kafirs, of whom Moshesh, who fought with Sir G. Cathcart, is paramount chief. The missionary observed, " The Kafirs, with whom everything is stationary, cannot understand how the government of the Cape of Good Hope is always changing. Moletsani, one of their chiefs, with whom I reside, said to me, ' Tell me how it is that the great chiefs, whom you tell us the Queen of England sends to the Cape, are always changing their plans; what one does to-day is undone by the one who comes to-morrow.' ' Oh,' I said, ' when any of your people are ill you send for a doctor. If the medicine he gives cures, it is well; if not, you send for another, but you do not make him use the same medicine, you let him use his own.' ' Oh yes,' said the Kafir, ' I see, I see; the Cape is sick, and the Queen sends these great chiefs ' (his name for governors of any kind) ' to make it well;' and as each new governor has sincè come, he asks, with a smile, ' Is this the doctor who is to make the Cape well ?' "

other feasible scheme whereby the will of the people can be made to act upon the executive, and whereby this constantly recurring change of ministers could, at the same time, *be* avoided.

Though the system be retained as to the rest of the cabinet, there seems no necessity why it should, likewise, be retained as to the Secretary of State for the Colonies. There was a time when there was no such secretary in existence, and when the management of the colonies was entrusted to the " Board of Trade and Plantations." So far as precedent goes, therefore, there is no *necessity* for the officer who administers the government of the colonies having a seat in the cabinet, and there seems as little necessity, either upon principle or expediency.

The constant change in the members of the cabinet undoubtedly produces great inconvenience by the constant change in measures, as well as in men ; but, of all the members of the cabinet, there is no one to whom this observation applies so strongly as to the Secretary for the Colonies. The Lord Chancellor, in the administration of equity, may undoubtedly take a different view of rules and precedents from his predecessor ; still, he is bound to act according to rule and precedent, and, in a great degree, the administration of the judicial branch of the chancellor's office, to which the objection of change in the officer peculiarly applies, is controlled by these rules and precedents, in spite of the temperament and peculiar qualities of mind of the man who may, at any one time, hold the office. If the Chancellor of the Exchequer, the Home Secretary, or the President of the Board of Trade, adopt in his department a system very much opposed to that of his predecessors, and in any respect prejudicial to the community, or to any particular branch of it, those affected by the change are at hand, and have their representatives to appeal to in the House of Commons. The aberration cannot, therefore, be very great, nor very far in the wrong direction, before a remedy is applied. So, if the First Lord of the Admiralty strike out a new and eccentric course in any part of his department, the appeal and the remedy are at hand. The Foreign Secretary can hardly indulge in such a course, from the very nature of his office. He cannot prejudice foreign powers, for they will soon make their complaints heard in a very audible and effective manner; and he cannot depart from the broad line of policy which had been pursued by his predecessors, to the injury of his own country, without its being known to the community, and affecting the most sensitive part in the social system,—jealousy as to the state's external intercourse with other states.

In regard to other members of the cabinet, with the single exception of the Secretary for the Colonies, so far as the administration of their particular departments is concerned, the officers administering them, probably, might be changed as often as there are months in the year, without much prejudice to the country being the result.

But the Secretary of State for the Colonies is an officer *per se*, removed by distance from those whose most vital interests he is to rule over, and still more so by the absence of all *immediate* responsibility for his acts in administering them.

The secretaries for the home and foreign departments live in the country whose interests they are to protect; they have the benefit of their own eyes, and ears, and intellects, in regard to what comes within the scope of their own observation, for the purpose either of original information, or of correcting or modifying that information which may be given them, and they have all the various channels of private and public information ready at their command. The secretary for the colonies lives at a distance, it may be of thousands of miles, from the colony he is to govern. He is not necessarily a person who has, at some time, resided out of the mother country, and he cannot, by possibility, be one who has resided in each of the colonies; he must, therefore, be a person ignorant in some degree, if not to a great degree, of the habits, customs, and peculiar ways of thinking of the inhabitants of each colony, as well as of the social, municipal, and commercial requirements of the colony. For all these, he must trust to the eyes, ears, and intellects of others, and these others, being almost necessarily official persons, are not those who, from their position, are best calculated either to acquire, or to give him, impartial and valuable information; especially in any dispute in which the local government may happen to be involved with the colony. If the information be in itself incorrect, or if the opinion formed of it be inaccurate, and the measures of the minister should be prejudicial to the colony, there is no community at hand, as respects the home government, to whom to express the complaints of the colony through the public press. There is no public press in the mother country identified with the colony in which to make such expression; and if the minister should ignore the complaints of the colony, when made privately through correspondence with his department, there are no representatives of the colony in the House of Commons through whom to make these complaints, to be both heard and felt, as the mother country can do when the minister adopts any line of policy obnoxious to it.

If it be difficult in the mother country to wean individuals from the pursuit of their selfish individual interests to the consideration of a public grievance, so as to form a body large enough to justify its resolutions being called the voice of the people, without which the minister would not be bound to treat, as he would not be justified in treating any matter as a grievance, contrary to his own opinion upon the subject. If there be a difficulty to accomplish this in the mother country, where the community have the parliament and the government under their eyes, how much more difficult must it be in scantily-inhabited colonies, at the distance of thousands of miles from the home government, to warm up the scattered population, however crying the grievances may have been, to make complaints which cannot reach the government until the expiry of months, and which cannot be answered until the expiry of as many more.

And if, for his country's good, the public-spirited individual, who has taken the matter up, should have succeeded in enlisting his fellow-colonists in the cause, so far as to make a general expression of complaint to the home government, should the minister, acting either from misinformation, or misrepresentation, or from erroneous opinion, reject the complaint, what hope could the patriot have of reviving the enthusiasm of complaint, which, during the months passed in the transmission of the complaint and the re-transmission of the answer, had long since died out.

If, hoping against hope, he should succeed in

resuscitating public feeling and united action out of private suffering and individual complaining, so as to procure a petition to the home parliament, who is there, in that body, whose duty it is to present even, or, still more, who is there whose duty or whose interest, (a more effectual stimulant,) it is to advocate such a petition? If the colony employ an active agent, or send home an energetic deputation, members of the House of Commons may be found who may accidentally have made the colonial government of the empire their study, and who may take a proportionate interest in the local affairs of the colonies, or there may be members who think that the colonial office is the tender part of the government of the day, and that a little sparring in "the colonial line" may bring them into notice, and lead the way to parliamentary fame. Among such members there may be found some to advocate the interests of a complaining colony in the British House of Commons. But what is the body to whom such advocacy is to be addressed? What interest has a Yorkshire fox-hunting squire, an admiral in Her Majesty's navy, or a lawyer in Lincoln's Inn? What interest can such members of the House of Commons take in the local affairs of Australia, or New Zealand? or what interest can the growers of Norfolk wheat, or the fleecy breeders of Lincolnshire and Salisbury Plains, or the mine-owners of Cornwall,

Northumberland, and Wales, take in the sheep-walks
and wheat-farms of Australia and the Cape of Good
Hope, or in the Burra-Burra mines of Australia, or
in the Namaqualand mines of the Cape, unless to
defeat their prosperity ? Or if Australia should
become, as in time it no doubt will become, a
manufacturing country, what interest could the
Manchester or Glasgow cotton-spinner or weaver
take in the rising manufactures of Australia but to
check their growth ?

The truth is, it is not in the nature of things that
a colony can be got to complain, except as to
grievances of magnitude, nor until these grievances
have become so intolerable that the colonists have
presented to themselves the alternatives of redress,
or of separation and independence. It is equally
true that they have never procured redress until they
have presented their complaints to the home government under these alternatives. And, to our shame
be it said, they have procured redress, even under
these alternatives, in proportion only as they were
likely to be able to enforce the latter alternative—
separation and independence. For proof of this let
Canada and Jamaica witness. However far wrong
Jamaica may have been as to protective duties, and
however much the home government of the day may
have been justified in adopting the steps they did to
bring the colonists to their senses, it never can be

said that to leave the inhabitants to struggle on amid the ruin and disaster in which their affairs are undoubtedly involved without a stronger effort than appears to have yet been made to destroy that Babel of a local government, is what a home government should do, if it take interest in regulating the local government for the welfare of the inhabitants; more especially as the existing state of things could never have grown up had the home government, by its governors, interfered to prevent it.

Not only, therefore, is the Secretary for the Colonies necessarily in a position which precludes him from forming any general comprehensive scheme for colonial government, or from having all the local information which would enable him to be certain that he was governing any particular colony according to its social requirements; but there is nothing in the system which will ensure the correction of his mistakes. It is no doubt true that the colonial minister may consult the other members of the cabinet, and that, in some cases, he is bound to do so. But these cases are only those in which the general colonial policy of the government is likely to be affected by the particular measure. The great routine of colonial government goes on with very little resort to this power of reference; and, when it is used, it probably is a greater source of mischief than of benefit. The other members of the cabinet cannot take the colonial minister's office upon them, and go minutely into all the details connected with any measure; they must trust to that minister's account of these details, prepared according to the medium through which he may have viewed them, without there being any one between him and the cabinet to present the reverse of the picture he may honestly, but erroneously, have drawn. It is just possible, therefore, that a reference to the cabinet may confirm the minister in an error rather than withhold him from its commission.

Even if the minister and the cabinet should be right in adopting any particular measure, there is no certainty that it will be carried out. Their instructions may hardly have reached the colony before a change in home politics has produced a change of the minister and of the cabinet, and, with them, of the particular measure; for the new minister may disapprove of his predecessor's policy. The only course which is open in such a case is to recall the measure and substitute another for it. But the first may have had the approbation of the colony, and the second may have to encounter its hostility, in the shape of violent and threatening remonstrance, and the remonstrance may reach the mother country just in time to be received by a third minister, differing in his views from both his predecessors.

These hypothetical instances are by no means

fanciful,—they are based upon past experience, which some years since suggested, as a remedy, the appointment of Mr. Merivale to a permanent office in the colonial department. That appointment has produced a very perceptible increase of system and unity in the administration of the colonies in minor matters. But, inasmuch as the office is subordinate to that of the minister, and is very much occupied with matters of detail, it falls short of the remedy required for securing a broad, well-considered, philosophical, as well as constitutional, system of colonial policy. And, even in regard to those matters of detail which come within its scope, its efficiency has been so far marred by the continued change in the person of the minister; each successive minister feeling at liberty to chalk out for himself his own course of policy, even in matters of detail. Hence the many varied forms of constitution given to uneasy, impatient colonies.

If the super-eminent officer in the colonial department held his office during good behavior, and independently of changes in the cabinet, there would be an opportunity, as well as a motive, for devising a general scheme of colonial government; and still the force of parliamentary opinion might be brought to bear upon the office as effectually as at present upon the Secretary of State for the Colonies. There would then be a fixed permanent responsibility to which the colonists, in case of any grievance, real or supposed, could appeal, instead of finding, as they at present often do, that while they have been maturing their remonstrance or complaint, the person who occasioned the grievance has ceased to be minister, and that the person who has succeeded him is as innocent of any knowledge of the matter as of any participation in the infliction of the grievance.

CHAPTER XVI.

But let the colonial minister's tenure of office be
perennial or ephemeral, and as consistent, broad, and
liberal a scheme of government for her colonies be
devised by the government of Great Britain as is
conceivable, it will ever be impossible to retain and
govern the British colonies in harmony and in consistency with the British institutions.   Despotic and
constitutional principles have hitherto had a constantly recurring conflict in the administration of the
British colonies, and this must continue.   Either the
minister has ruled them after his own arbitrary will,
(not using that word " arbitrary " in an offensive
sense, but simply to express the will of an individual
exercised without any responsibility to, or control
by, the people,) or, if the colony has become too
strong in its opposition to this, the minister has had
recourse to the sovereign and supreme legislative
power of the imperial parliament to control the
colony, and when the colony has kicked even against
this authority, which in fact has oftener than other-

wise been another mode of enforcing the minister's
fiat, and when it has exhibited a degree of strength
and stubbornness which it would not be prudent to
contend with to the uttermost, then its own *internal*
government has been handed over to the colony's
own self-administration, and control over only its
external relations has been reserved. But there is
no reasonable expectation why this last and inner
fence should not also be broken down, so soon as an
occasion of difference, in regard to external relations,
shall arise between the mother country and a colony
strong enough, and head-strong enough, to enforce
compliance with its own views of what is most conducive to its own individual interest, without regard
to the general British colonial policy.

In the use of general and abstract terms, we are
very apt to lose sight of the subject we are talking
about; at least, we almost invariably leave the details
out of our view. When we say that Great Britain
has given to many of her colonies liberal constitutions, so liberal that they as nearly as possible
approach to her own constitution, few people take
any other view of the subject than to congratulate
themselves on the generosity of their country and
on the assurance it gives that the colonies, themselves
also feeling this, will be governed with greater ease
and with more harmony to the home government
than formerly. But this is all delusion.

In the first place, no British-born subject can look upon the grant of self-government to a colony, in which he has gone to live, as a boon. Far from it; he looks on it, as a more or less tardy concession of a right which should never have been withheld. Parish elections and parliamentary elections at home indoctrinated him from his infancy with the notion that Britons can only be governed with their own consent, expressed through their representatives. Of course, when the right of self-government has been conceded, the colonists have not been so ungracious as to express themselves otherwise than as if it were a boon; but that they do not think it to be in fact otherwise than the concession of a right, and that they will so view it, should ingratitude ever be upbraided to them, in the event of any collision with the home government, is what every one must feel convinced of who has lived in a colony to which a free constitution has been accorded.

But, in the second place, when it is expected that the colonies will be ruled with greater harmony to the home government, under the operation of a free constitution than they have hitherto been, under the rule of a governor, appointed by the home minister, acting with the assistance of a council composed of government officials, it is forgotten what has in fact been done by giving a constitution.

Under the former state of things, each resident in

a colony had his own individual importance, in proportion as his occupation happened, in colonial estimation, to be more or less genteel, or in proportion as he might have earned more or less money, which in colonies, as in mother countries, gives power and importance among individuals. But under a constitution, which hands over the government of a colony, in all substantial respects, to the inhabitants themselves, this is entirely changed. The legislative council and house of assembly are elected by the inhabitants at large—each member of the community will, thereby, be raised in his own importance, and look upon himself as a constituent part of the local government. He will identify the local legislature with himself, as bodies of his own creation, and he will be as jealous of the respect shown to them by the executive government, whether home or colonial, as is any inhabitant of Great Britain of the respect shown by the executive government to the imperial parliament, which the colonist will look upon as the prototype of the colonial parliament.

And, as to the members of the legislative council and house of assembly, each of these will, in his own fancy, and in fact also, fill a station much higher than he filled before, or ever even dreamt of. From mere merchants, farmers, journalists, tradesmen, attorneys, and surgeons, each honestly pursuing his individual modest avocation, they have been transformed into statesmen and legislators, dealing with abstract and general questions, embracing political, social, and commercial objects. They are no longer engrossed solely by their own individual pursuits, either of gain or of humble ambition, but have been elevated into public characters, with more or less just or extravagant anticipations of what is to be achieved by their legislative labors for the country of their adoption.

Hitherto, the leading men in a colony have wrestled with the government, and, in this way, have built up their self-importance, so dear to every man. In future, this will very much cease. As the administrative power will be under the control of the elective legislatures, there is not likely to be individual combats with the executive. The field and the combatants are changed. The life and soul of a free government is domestic faction, and the life and soul of faction is the desire of men to build up their importance with each other. No man can exalt himself with others without trenching upon the self-importance of some other who is as anxious to be exalted in the estimation of their neighbors as himself. Disputes and parties, therefore, are sure to arise between the members of the colonial legislatures, during which the government, if prudently managed, will probably have only to stand by and look on.

This will be a source of ease and strength to the

government, which was not looked for in the times
when it was judged politic to keep the reins of
government tight, and to refuse any approach to
self-government. But this state of things will last
only so long as the executive assumes little better
than the part of bottle-holder in the play of colonial
faction, and discovers in that character neither
temper nor partiality. The internal government
of a colony under a liberal constitution is likely
to go on peaceably enough, as far as the mother
country is concerned, if reasonably prudent men
be selected to wield the executive power. So far
the mother country has gained instead of losing
by the concession of liberal constitutions to the
colonies.

But, should the crown or the imperial parliament
be brought into direct conflict with the colonial
legislature, upon a matter, either of internal government, as in Canada,[a] or of external policy, as in
Newfoundland,[b] or of internal policy, as in New
Brunswick,[c] it is not difficult to foresee how very
different that struggle will be from any that has
occurred between a colony and the mother country,
while as yet the colony had not obtained a free
constitution. As much from vanity as from affection,
the colonists call their legislative bodies " The Parliament," and frame everything connected with them

[a] Vide supra, p. 300.   [b] Vide supra, p. 332.   [c] Vide supra, p. 326.

after the model afforded by that assembly in the mother country, even to the naming of their officers. They have their " speaker," their " usher of the black rod," and their " serjeant-at-arms," in utter ignorance, probably, of the origin of these names and of their applicability. This is an amiable and a harmless vanity, no doubt, if it would end there. But can it be thought that these colonial scions of the British stock will be careful to preserve the analogy between their parliaments and that of Old England in trifles only, and be indifferent about it in essentials? That they will be content to look upon their parliament as a toy to be rattled in their ears, and will not regard it as an instrument wherewith to achieve freedom and independence? Not more surely does each member of the colonial legislature look upon himself as a modern Solon, a Lycurgus, or a Somers, than does each and every one of them consider that legislature to be as important in every respect as the parliament of Great Britain, and to have, on principle, as much right to respect and independence of action as that imperial assembly. The dignity and authority of the colonial legislature each member will regard as the source of his own individual importance, and he will watch over and protect its independence as feverishly as he will guard his own individual personal respect.

The colonists would be unworthy of self-government if they did not feel in this way. Individual vanity and self-importance, individual thirst for power and public estimation, are the springs which keep the state machine in motion in the mother country. But for the gratification of these appetites, few men would be found to take on them the burden either of the executive or of the legislative business of the empire ; and it is well that it is so, for patriotism unalloyed is as rare as virtue unalloyed. The same motives which produce public men at home will do so in the colonies, and the same feelings will govern the colonial statesmen in their public conduct.

Should, therefore, any question of internal or external colonial government arise, in which the crown and the colonial government, on the one hand, and the colonial legislature, on the other, should take opposite and conflicting views, an appeal to " the sovereign and supreme legislative power of the imperial parliament" will be much more doubtful of effect and more dangerous in its consequences than such an appeal has been when directed against a colony without a constitution, or with a constitution not purely elective, or with a constitution purely elective, but which has not been long enough in operation for the inhabitants to have ascertained their position and power, with reference to the local or imperial government and parliament. They will not bow with that deference which, in old days, used to be shown to the despatch of a minister, nor obey in silence the dictates of an act of the imperial parliament; but will set up their own judgments and their own wills against both, as having equal pretensions to reason, justice, and sound policy, and as equally entitled to deference and to obedience.

In such a contest, how different will have become the position of the mother country from what it was before the grant of liberal constitutions. Then the minister had but to encounter, in his chamber, or it might be in parliament, the energetic remonstrances of one, or two, or more individuals in the character of personal complainants, or of deputies, exposed even in the colony, and still more in the mother country, to those sneers and imputations of bad temper and interested motives which the indolent and selfish, the greater part of a community, throw out against those who attempt to reform abuses, while the reform is yet unachieved, but who, when the reformation *is* achieved, are the loudest in lauding it, and the first and the most eager to profit by it. Should a contest hereafter arise between the minister and a colony, it will be one between his individual opinion and that of the whole colony, having a palpable and substantial expression in the vote of its parliament. In such a contest, the minister must give way, or have recourse, as in Canada, to the " sovereign and supreme legislative power of the imperial parliament," in the meanwhile, only to retrace his steps afterwards, as in Canada, by a concession of all that the colony had asked.

CHAPTER XVII.

WHY should so great an empire as Great Britain be kept in such a constant struggle against humiliation, as she has hitherto had to maintain, and is still likely to be obliged to maintain, with her colonies? Strong against all Europe in arms, she has been feeble against *them*. Why not forisfamiliate at once all those sons of Britain who have gone forth from her? Why not, by emancipation, make them at once feel their own weakness, and turn them from factious, rebellious remonstrants against reserved authority into earnest petitioners for protection, by the resumption, so far, of abdicated power?

If Great Britain, now probably at the very pinnacle of her strength and grandeur, were, of her own accord, to declare the inconsistency of her past colonial government with her own domestic institutions, her regret that, in the outset, she had not followed the example of the ancient Greek republics, by allowing the foreign settlements of her subjects to be independent and self-acting from the beginning,[a] and her determination, for the future, to give them

[a] Vide supra, p. 13.

that which she should never have withheld,[a] there is probably not one of her multitudinous colonies that would not be alarmed at the prospect of being thus thrown upon its own resources, and that would not cling with tenacity to the mother country for the continuance of its protection, if not by a continuance of its government, at least by the framing of treaties of the most intimate alliance. The position of the mother country and the colonies would then be reversed, and be one, not only more consistent with their relative positions, but of much greater mutual strength. The weaker, sensible of its own inherent infirmity, would look up to the stronger with affectionate respect, glad to have countenance and protection, instead of blustering and wrangling, with scowling looks and angry mien, for still another concession of freedom, with a scarcely-concealed threat of recourse to foreign power, in case of refusal.

Should there be a colony confident enough in its own strength to rejoice at such emancipation, and to be indifferent in regard to its future relations with the mother country, the act of emancipation would not occasion the loss of such a connection; it would only anticipate it—it would only voluntarily concede that which, without it, would soon be taken. But there is probably no British colony, however prosperous

[a] The 18 Geo. III, cap. 12, gives the example of such a declaration in regard to the right and intention of taxing the American colonies.

and populous it may as yet be, which, if it were
emancipated to-morrow, would be either in a condition or in the humor to be independent of, or
unconnected with, Great Britain, even in its internal
government, and without regard to its weakness for
external self-action. However blusteringly a few
unruly colonial spirits may, in this colony and in
that, have talked about separation and independence,
there is no British colony, however populous and
wealthy it may yet be, which is not sensible of the
respect it derives, and, with that respect, of the peace
and security it enjoys, by being a member of the
British empire. Nay, there are few colonies which
are not sensible of the advantage to their social
manners and habits, and of the greater security to
their liberties and estates, which are produced by
the appointment of governors from among the
magnates of the mother country; and of their judges
and other functionaries from among the inhabitants
of the mother country, who have spent their youth
and manhood in the full enjoyment of its free and
vigorous institutions, and in the practice of the social
habits and manners of its more advanced, and therefore more highly cultivated, society, and that would
not receive, with regret and remonstrance, the
intimation that it must henceforth choose these
functionaries from among its own inhabitants, with
all the local feelings, prejudices, and personal motives

incident to the members of a limited community, whether that community be provincial or colonial.

At present, the home government, in the exercise of a material power which is undoubted, and of a moral and legal right which is very questionable, appoints to each colony a governor and subordinate functionaries of its own selection, and removes and substitutes them, at its own pleasure. How much more graceful would it be that these appointments should be made at the request of the colony. No doubt the request would not be made, if the colony felt that the state of its society justified making such appointments from among its own inhabitants; or, if the request were made at the outset, this would cease so soon as the colony should come to think that the improved condition of its society justified the discontinuance. But why should this be otherwise? Why should such a government as that of Great Britain expose itself to the unworthy imputation of keeping a colony as a patronage farm. Let the government, with benignity and just pride, select from the inhabitants of the mother country such functionaries as a colony may ask for, and as will do honor both to the government and to the colony; and let it congratulate the colony on its progress in social improvement when it finds that the colony has discovered that it can make the selection from among its own inhabitants. If the colony has been premature in making this discovery, it will soon find out its mistake. The evils of official tyranny or incompetency are too direct and obvious to escape discovery in the limited community of a colony. With popular self-government, the source of the evil would soon be discovered, and its remedy be as readily applied. In the mother country, with its redundant population, official situations are objects of great request, not only by the middle classes of society, but by the offshoots from the aristocratic body. Official abuse and incompetency, therefore, is there too often covered over and protected. In the colonies, this is otherwise. In them, much more money can be made in trade or by agriculture than the salary of any office will yield, and there is no redundancy of population. Official situations, therefore, are left to such emigrants from the mother country as are unfit for trade or agriculture, either from want of capital or defect in habits and education, and, under a free constitution, which brings the supervision of everything and everybody within the power of the inhabitants, the public officers will be looked upon, as they are in fact, as public servants, instead of public masters, which, in past times, they have too probably considered themselves.

This suggestion of Great Britain giving up authority over her colonies, and entering into treaties with them of the closest alliance, is not new. It will be remembered that it was recommended by Smith, in his "Wealth of Nations," in the passage, which has already been quoted,[a] wherein, after observing, ironically, that no country will ever take such a step, he continues, "If it was adopted, however, Great Britain would not only be freed from the whole annual expense of the peace establishment of the colonies, but might settle with them such a treaty of commerce as would effectually secure to her a free trade, more advantageous to the great body of the people, though less so to the merchants, than the monopoly which she at present enjoys. By thus parting friends, the natural affection of the colonies to the mother country, which perhaps our late dissensions have well-nigh extinguished, would quickly revive. It might dispose them, not only to respect for whole centuries together that treaty of commerce, which they had concluded with us at parting, but to favor us in war, as well as in trade, and, instead of turbulent and factious subjects, to become our most faithful, affectionate, and generous allies ; and the same sort of parental affection on the one side, and filial respect on the other, might revive between Great Britain and her colonies which used to subsist between those of ancient Greece and the mother city from which they descended."

In considering this subject, it should not be

[a] Vide supra, p. 51.

overlooked that sound reason and principle support
the assertion, in regard to all colonies, but especially
in regard to colonies founded by a government so
popular in its elements as that of Great Britain, and
by the inhabitants of a country enjoying such liberal
institutions as those of Great Britain, that sooner or
later they will achieve their independence of the
mother country. They will do it the sooner, if circumstances should rapidly increase their population
and wealth, and the later, if circumstances should
concur to retard these events. But not more certainly
does a young man leave his father's house so soon as
he has attained the strength of manhood, and gained
its knowledge and experience, and go forth into the
world to be the founder of his own fortune, than will
a colony shake itself loose from all trammels imposed
upon it by the mother country, whether for wise or
for selfish purposes, so soon as the colony feels itself
powerful enough to contest the continuance of these
trammels. Turgot, the French philosopher, said of
colonies generally, " They are like fruits, which cling
to the tree only till they have ripened;" and, he added
prophetically of our North American colonies, " So
soon as America can take care of itself, it will do
what Carthage did," make itself independent of Great
Britain, as Carthage did of Tyre.

CHAPTER XVIII.

LORD GREY admits that "the view is at least plausible," which says, "if the colonies are no longer to be regarded as valuable, on account of the commercial advantages to be derived from their possession, the country has no interest in keeping these dependencies; and it would be better to abandon them, thus getting rid of the heavy charge on the country, especially in providing the requisite amount of naval and military force for their protection." His lordship also admits that "the view is at least plausible," which, on behalf of the colonists, inquires whether, "if they are no longer to enjoy their former commercial privileges in the markets of the mother country, they derive any real benefit from the continuance of the connection?" But his lordship considers that the British colonial empire ought to be maintained, "principally, because I do not consider that the nation would be justified in throwing off the responsibility it has incurred by the acquisition of this dominion, and because I believe that much of the power and influence of this country depends upon its having large colonial possessions in different parts of the world."

In this passage, the maintenance of the colonial empire is rested upon two grounds : first, the responsibility we owe to the colonists ; and second, the power and influence which the colonies give to the mother country.

SECTION I.—THE DUTY OF PROTECTION WHICH WE OWE TO THE COLONISTS.

With regard to the first of these grounds, it is, no doubt, true that we owe a certain degree of protection to individuals who have gone to reside in distant colonies on the supposition, sanctioned by ourselves, that they were there to live under the shield of the British government.   But if it be advisable for us that we should cut off straggling and distant members of our empire, in order that we may husband and preserve the strength of the trunk, or main body, let us ascertain which of these members it is that desires to have the connection or dependence upon us as a colony maintained.   It by no means follows that because a settlement is not to continue a colony of Great Britain, and, as such, a constituent part of the British empire, it must, therefore, cease to have any connection with, or to receive any protection from, that empire.

If, by a declaratory statute, such as 18 Geo. III, cap. 15, in regard to abstaining from taxation of the American colonies, we should proclaim our intention to emancipate our colonies, unless in those instances in which we cannot do so without injustice to the colonists themselves, and if we should thus invite the colonies to express their wishes, whether for separation or for continuance of dependence, we may find that some of the colonies can establish such a claim upon us, for the continuance of their dependence and of our protection as it may not be possible for us to disregard.

Lord J. Russell says, many of our colonies " would be wholly unable to form prosperous, civilized, free communities, not having the means to preserve anything like independence or security, amidst the savage races by which they are surrounded." This seems applicable only to New Zealand and the Cape of Good Hope, and even as to them is, perhaps, overcharged. But be it that it is applicable to " many " of our colonies, and that it is understated : if they represent their inability to stand of themselves, and their desire to continue integral parts of the British empire, bound by allegiance to the crown, and subject to imperial rule, colonies then they must continue. But they will do so *not against their will*, but at their express desire. This will not only put us in the position, but give us the right of adjusting the terms upon which our protection is to be continued, with the benefit of all the knowledge and experience we have gained, in regard to what we can with safety give, and they can with justice require, instead of being, as we are at present, in a false position in both of these respects. We have had no unity or system in the management of our colonies, from inevitable causes which have been already explained;[a] but have been doing and giving to one colony something very different from what we have been doing and giving to half a dozen others. If we were to adjust the connection which should subsist between us and such colonies as desired the continuance of colonial dependence we should, in such a case, reconstruct, instead of continuing to patch and to mend.

On the other hand, we might find, on passing such a declaratory statute, some colonies to which, from consciousness of the acquired strength of manhood, the continuance of filial dependence had become irksome; which, however unruly they might have been while galled by the trammels of that dependence, were by no means disposed to disown their parentage and cut off all connection; but would gladly substitute for colonial dependence a treaty of alliance, such as Smith has described, to be followed probably by all the mutual beneficent consequences which he predicted.

[a] Vide supra, p. 353, et seq

Section II.—The power and influence which the colonies
        give to the mother country.

Lord Grey says,[a] " No alliance between independent states can be so close and intimate as the
connection which unites the colonies to the United
Kingdom, as parts of the great British empire," his
lordship having previously observed, that " the
possession of a number of steady and faithful allies,
in various quarters of the globe, will surely be
admitted to add greatly to the strength of any
nation." It is unquestionably true that the possession of a number of steady and faithful allies, in
various quarters of the globe, would add greatly to
the strength of the British empire; but so far from
that warranting the inference which Lord Grey seems
to intend to be drawn, that the possession of a great
number *of colonies*, in various quarters of the globe,
will add *still more greatly* to the strength of the
empire, because the connection which unites the
colonies to the United Kingdom is *more close and
intimate* than *an alliance*, it seems to do just the
reverse.

It is never questioned, in modern days, that an
alliance between Great Britain and the minor states
of Europe is a source of mutual strength to her and
to them, while it is as broadly admitted that the
right of the sovereign of Great Britain to the minor

[a] Colonial Policy, vol. i, p. 12.

kingdom of Hanover was a constant source of weakness to Great Britain while it lasted; and yet Hanover was a more favorable instance for the maintenance of connection than an ally can be, so far as closeness and intimacy was concerned. Hanover belonged to the crown of Great Britain, but was no part of the British empire, and, therefore, there was no obligation on the empire to protect it; yet, with this slight connection, British statesmen allowed it constantly to embroil the empire with European states, because of the possible imputation of weakness to the empire, if any attack upon the hereditary possessions of the sovereign were allowed to pass unresented by the empire. This is the only excuse that can be framed for the ministers of the first three Georges, in spending the blood and treasure of Great Britain upon Hanoverian quarrels.

Colonies are not " closely connected " with the empire, as was Hanover, because of the accidental coincidence of its sovereignty in the same person as the monarch of Great Britain, and as are allies, by virtue of the treaties formed with them. They are *integral parts* of the empire, and, as such, must be protected and defended to the last extremity, and with as much pertinacity and with as keen sensitiveness to national honor, as if the capital itself were in question. It is on this account,—it is on account of this identity of interest, *more close than the connection of any alliance,* however intimate,—that colonies may be sources of weakness rather than of strength to the mother country.

Lord Grey says that the tie which binds the British colonies to the mother country is, no doubt, of far greater importance to them than to her. " While still forming comparatively small and weak communities, they enjoy, in return for their allegiance to the British crown, all the security and consideration which belong to them as members of one of the most powerful states in the world. No foreign power ventures to attack or interfere with the smallest of them, while every colonist carries with him to the remotest quarters of the globe which he may visit, in trading or other pursuits, that protection which the character of a British subject every where confers, and can depend in any difficulties, or under any oppression to which he may be exposed, on the assistance of Her Majesty's diplomatic and consular servants, supported, if necessary, by the whole power of the empire."

How true and just are these observations, and how forcibly do they exhibit the moral and material strength conferred upon the colonies by their connection, as such, with the mother country ; yet the expressions are not one whit less applicable to the county of York or to the county of Northumberland, than they are to the colonies. The only difference is that, whereas an insignificant colony is very likely to draw upon the assistance of Her Majesty's diplomatic and consular servants and to ask the support of the whole power of the empire for the negotiation or enforcement of some measure, in which the empire is very slightly interested, the counties of York and Northumberland can have few interests which are not identical with the interests of the rest of the empire, or which can form a subject of separate discussion.

So much for the benefit, in moral and material strength, conferred upon the colonies by their connection with the mother country. But let us see the *per contra* in this account of mutual connection, never forgetting, as Lord Grey judiciously cautions us, "that the power of a nation does not depend merely on the amount of physical force it can command, but rests, in no small degree, upon opinion and moral influence;" in which respect, his lordship thinks, " British power would be diminished by the loss of our colonies to a degree, which it would be difficult to estimate." Lord J. Russell also says, " If the colonies were *abandoned* by Great Britain, they would, most naturally and most justly, apply to some other country for protection. They would say, We have been abandoned by those to whom we were bound by allegiance,—protection is now taken from us ; and we ask you to become our protectors and to receive our allegiance."

The force of these opinions may, perhaps, rest on
the use of the expression, " *loss* of our colonies," and
" *abandon* our colonies ;" and it may vanish on the
substitution of " *emancipation* of," and " alliance
with," our colonies. There is that alternative, surely,
between " allegiance" and either " loss" or " abandonment." If we expressed our intention to emancipate and yet to protect by alliance, why should the
colonists go to strangers for that protection, which,
in that case, we, one of the most powerful nations
of the earth, — if not on account of our naval
superiority, the most powerful to protect colonies,—
should never have given up, and should be ready
to continue.

Lord J. Russell continues, " One scheme is, that
we should altogether abandon any share in the
government of our colonies, and that we should
likewise refuse them any means of defence. Such a
system would very soon lead to this : these colonies
would say, ' If we are not to be defended,—if we
are to receive no support from Great Britain, let
us look for other protectors, let us ask other states
if they will assist us, with their arms and protect us
against any attacks which may be made upon us.' " If
there be any truth in what has been stated in previous
pages, we have been " abandoning any share in the
government " of some of our colonies so fast that
very little remains, and that little—while, by holding

them, they are kept in the humor to encroach—they will very easily force from us. But even if they forced the whole,—even if Canada refused to take a governor from us, pretty nearly the only hold we have upon her, why must we, of necessity, also " refuse " her " any means of defence ?" Why should it be assumed, as a general proposition, that discontinuance of our colonies, as such, must be accompanied by a refusal of all assistance for their defence, where from circumstances the colony is unequal to undertaking that burden ? What has enabled Portugal to maintain its existence as a separate state, but its alliance with Great Britain, by offensive and defensive treaty ? And what is there in the nature of things to prevent the adjustment of such an alliance upon fair, reasonable, and just terms with such countries as now form part of our colonies, after they should have been made as independent of us as Portugal has ever been?

But let us return to the inquiry, whence these observations of the ministers have made us digress. The moral, as well as material, strength conferred upon the colonies by their connection, as such, with the mother country being admitted, let us see the *per contra* in the account of mutual connection. Let us inquire what strength they return for that which is conferred upon them.

While it is conceded, on all hands, that the

mother country is a source of strength, safety, and respect to the colonies, in what one way have they returned her the compliment or the benefit? It is beyond all question that no one of the numerous British colonies has ever contributed a sixpence in the shape of direct revenue to the imperial treasury. Smith[a] says, Great Britain is, "perhaps, since the world began, the only state which, as it has extended its empire, has only increased its expense, without once augmenting its resources." What that eminent philosopher said nearly a hundred years ago is equally true at this day.

We attempted to tax the North American colonies, *not for imperial* but *for colonial* objects. Rebellion made us recoil from the attempt, and the 18 Geo. III, cap. 12, gave assurance to the colonies that the attempt would not be repeated. It never was repeated with these colonies, nor has it been repeated by the imperial parliament with any other colony, except perhaps during the short period during which the constitution of Canada was suspended. No doubt, what the imperial parliament did not venture to do, the crown has ventured, and achieved, too, in many of the colonies, but always for colonial purposes. The crown, by its governors, with their nominative councils, has levied taxes in many of the colonies, but always for colonial purposes; and the

[a] Wealth of Nations, vol. II, p. 482.

assertion, even against the crown, remains true that the imperial treasury has never benefited by a sixpence in direct revenue from the imperial colonies.

If the mother country has not received from the colonies money, one of the most material elements of imperial strength, has she received contributions of men, the element of imperial strength next in importance?[a] Which of all her numerous colonies sent Great Britain a single regiment—a single company of soldiers, to aid her in the last war that she maintained, almost single-handed, against nearly the whole powers of Europe, wielded by Napoleon, and against the United States of America, to boot? Not one. Nay, which one of Britain's numerous colonies undertook, during that fearful war, the defence of its own territory from foreign invasion; or even the protection of its inhabitants from any internal violence, exceeding the strength of civil police to cope with? Not one. If Canada has, as yet, undertaken the expense of its own internal or external protection, it is the only British colony of which that can be said. It is true that that and some others of the colonies, to whom representative constitutions have been accorded, have been told that they must, in future, take this burden on themselves;

[a] The text was written in 1854. When the Indian mutinies broke out, Canada zealously and loyally tendered a regiment, for the use of the empire, which has been embodied and is doing duty.

but it is well known, with what grumbling and bad grace they have received the intimation, and how slowly and reluctantly they have set about complying with it. When Canada has done this, when she has raised an army, and found its maintenance compatible with her rapidly increasing resources, are the United States the only power against which she will use it? Will she never shake her fist in the face of the mother country, should she attempt to back the governor against the local parliament, by such an imperial statute as the 1 and 2 Vic., cap. 35?[a]

SECTION III. — WEALTH DERIVED BY THE MOTHER COUNTRY FROM COLONIAL TRADE SHOWN BY A COMPARISON OF THE COLONIAL WITH THE HOME TRADE.

Great Britain, then, has not received from her colonies any direct contribution, either in money or in men,—the two great and only elements in the material or physical power of a nation. But, it will be said, the indirect contribution to her treasury from her colonial trade has been prodigious, and has, in truth, been one of the great sources of her colossal strength. This assertion is no doubt true, in some respects, but it is erroneous in many more; and, even if the assertion were true, in its integrity,

[a] In 1850, Lord John Russell considered the population of the British North American colonies to be not less than two millions.

it by no means follows that this flow of wealth from colonial trade is to be dried up, so soon as the colonies shall have been emancipated and an alliance shall be formed with them.

That the colonial trade of Great Britain forms an important item in the aggregate account of British commerce, is indubitable; but to assert that it forms the most important item in that account would be as indubitably erroneous. By far the largest, as well as by far the most profitable item in the account of British commerce, is the commerce which is confined in its operation *within the limits of the united kingdoms.* The materials which, within these limits, are grown, manufactured, sold, and consumed, are much larger in quantity, and much more profitable in the result of these operations, with a view to the wealth and power of the empire, than is all the foreign trade, whether to colonies or foreign states, put together. So long as this home trade is left free and unfettered, so long as the moral and political tone of the people is kept up by a vigorous and free press, and so long as the dealings of the people are enforced by a just administration of the law through lofty and independent judges,—so long, and no longer, will the little islands of Great Britain and Ireland maintain their present proud and honorable position among the nations of the earth, even were their supplies of mineral wealth dried up to-morrow, and, with them, the foreign trade which they chiefly support.

Greece had no minerals, and she had only a barren soil, but she enjoyed freedom and education, and, with the energy which these blessings infused into the spirit of her people, she laughed the hosts of Asia to scorn, and, doubtless, had she preserved freedom, as well as education, she would equally have derided the power of Rome, if she might not, indeed, have overwhelmned it, while as yet Rome had not made herself mistress of the world. Great Britain and Ireland have never halted on their onward march to national grandeur and supremacy since they established freedom of the press, trial by jury, and independence of the judges; and they will maintain the position they have achieved, so long as they maintain these palladia for freedom of thought and of action.

Hitherto, in maintaining its position, the British empire has been little indebted to foreign aid, and certainly not at all to colonial. It has drawn all its armies from the three kingdoms, and most of the treasure required for the support of these armies has been derived from the trade of her own subjects.

The trade next in importance to Great Britain, after her home trade, has been that which she has established with foreign countries; and the advantage to her of the trade with each country, *ceteris paribus*, has been in proportion to the nearness of the country to her territory. Capital is the main spring of trade, —it is its life's blood. Upon the regular and rapid circulation of capital depends the profits of trade. If a man have money enough to pay, *on the instant*, for all he buys, he can, of course, purchase on more reasonable terms than he could do, if he had to ask for *credit*. If a man have enough to pay for what he buys at *one* month's credit, he can purchase on better terms than if he had to ask for *three* months' credit. If he have enough money to pay at *three* months' credit, he can purchase more cheaply than if he had to ask *eighteen months'* credit. All this must be so, because the use of money is as valuable to the seller as it is to the purchaser. If the dealer in any particular article have only £5,000 in money, he can purchase but £5,000 worth of the article; if he sell the quantity on credit, he cannot buy more, unless upon credit, until the price of what he has sold is paid him. If, then, he do not purchase more upon credit, and yet have sold the £5,000 worth upon credit, his business is at a stand, until the period of that credit shall be run out,—all this time he is doing nothing,—the most unprofitable occupation which any body, and still more a merchant, can be engaged in.

To avoid this, a prudent dealer buys more goods *on credit*—that is, he purchases, perhaps, £5,000

worth more of goods, stipulating that he shall not
pay for them until the end of three, six, eight, or
nine months, according as the credit he may have
given for the original £5,000 worth may have been
short or long ; in fine, he gets for that time the use
of another man's £5,000, and, of course, he must
pay for it in the price that is bargained for. The
second £5,000 worth, therefore, is bought at a
higher price than was the first, by how much the
use of money may at the time be cheap or dear.

If a merchant in Liverpool send a hogshead of
sugar to a grocer, in Chester or Lancaster, for sale
by retail in his shop, the sugar reaches the shop in
the course of an hour or two, and it may be all sold
in the course of a week or a fortnight, if the grocer's
business be brisk. One month's credit may be all
that the grocer requires to ask, in order to be sure
of having got from his customers money to pay for
the hogshead, if the sales over his counter have been
for ready money ; at the end of the month, the price
of the hogshead would be in the Liverpool merchant's pocket, ready to be embarked in a second
speculation.

While as yet there were neither canals nor railways, an operation such as that which has been
described could not have been carried on between
a Liverpool merchant and a grocer of York or of
Lincoln. Each must have waited till the merchant's

traveler came round with samples to show the different qualities to be sold, because the grocer could rarely afford the expense of time and money required for a journey to Liverpool. If, then, the traveler came round only once in half a year, the grocer had to buy, and the merchant had to sell to him, a quantity equal to the demands of the grocer's business for six months; and if the transaction were done upon a credit, calculated as to length, with a view to the grocer being in funds to pay from the proceeds of his retail sales, the merchant must have allowed the grocer a credit of nine months, for at least a portion of the price. During this nine months, then, the merchant must have been deprived of the use of so much money.

In old days, therefore, trade between Liverpool and Chester, or Lancaster, was much more advantageous than trade between Liverpool and York, or Lincoln, not only because the Liverpool merchant had to give the Chester or the Lancaster grocer credit for *one* month, whereas he had to give the York or the Lincoln grocer *nine* months' credit; but because he had to trust the Chester or the Lancaster grocer with only *one month's supply*, whereas he had to trust the York or the Lincoln grocer with *six months' supply*. But railways have nearly annihilated space, both as to time and distance, and now the dealings of the Liverpool merchant with a York or a Lincoln grocer may be upon terms as advantageous for the grocer, so far as distance apart affects it, as may his dealings with a Chester or a Lancaster grocer. Hence one of the many benefits which railways have conferred upon Britain has been to make the home trade both more profitable as to terms, and more safe as to credit.

If a merchant of Manchester be asked to send a bale of cotton cloth to a merchant in Bordeaux, or Lisbon, or Alicante, or Marseilles, or Trieste, before he can tell what price to put upon the cotton, he has several considerations to take into account, beyond what the Liverpool merchant had, in the case of the transactions with the English grocer. He has to consider the length of the voyage to either place, and the risk of the voyage, and the uncertainty of his information as to the proceedings of his customer in the mode of conducting his business, whether prudently or incautiously. Everything that conduced to make the credit longer in duration and larger in amount, in the case of the York or Lincoln grocer, while railways had no existence, comes into operation more strongly. The place being more distant, and the means of communication more difficult, the quantity of goods sent, at one time, must be greater, and the credit for payment of them must be longer. In other words, the English merchant, in order to trade with the French, Spanish, or Italian merchant, must part with a larger amount of money's worth, and be out of pocket the money he paid for it a much longer time than he would require to do were he trading with a dealer in England.

By how much the English merchant must do so, by so much is his foreign trade less advantageous, than is his home trade. In other words, in the home trade, he can buy oftener, and sell oftener, and thus realize a profit, (as it is to be taken for granted that each operation yields a profit,) much oftener, within the year, than he can do in the foreign trade. This he can do in one foreign trade more than in another, exactly in proportion to the greater or less distance and uncertainty of communication of one place over another. Foreign trade between Britain and the states of Europe, therefore, is less advantageous than trade *within* Britain between its own subjects. But steamboats and railways have made this foreign trade more profitable than it used to be.

But, if the European trade be less advantageous than the home trade, then the American, Asiatic, and African trades are even less advantageous than the European; and in one or other of these quarters of the globe are all the British colonies situated. The most favorable in this respect, now-a-days, are the British North American and West Indian colonies, between which and the mother country the length of time for communication by letter has, by steamboats, been reduced from four and six weeks to sixteen and eighteen days; but still, as to them, goods, (of which only a small proportion is sent by steam conveyance,) require from four to six weeks for their transmission; and probably the capital which is expended by the English merchant in purchasing them is not returned to him from these colonies within six months, at the most moderate computation.

But, between the Cape of Good Hope and the mother country, steamboats take nearly six weeks for the voyage, and sailing vessels from two to three months. Between the Australian colonies and the mother country, steam vessels require nearly three months for the voyage, and sailing vessels about five months. And between New Zealand and the mother country, the voyage is still longer. It is probably pretty near the truth to say that the minimum time within which the English merchant who sends goods to these colonies can expect to receive back the money he expended in purchasing them will be twelve months, and the maximum two years, or longer. During all that time his capital is beyond his control, and its place must be supplied by money borrowed from others, at the heavy expense of discount, commission, and stamps.

The colonial trade of Great Britain, therefore, is the least profitable of all the three trades which have been mentioned—home, foreign, and colonial. Why, if that be the case, it may be asked, has not the colonial trade been abandoned, and the home and European trade been alone cherished. The answer is ready. The superabundance of British capital is such that it is constantly seeking new channels for investment, and it often falls into those which not only are not comparatively so profitable, but prove to be positively unprofitable. Hence the facility with which trade springs up between every new colony as it is established; and after money has been expended in purchasing goods, ships, warehouses, counting-houses, and dwelling-houses, with a view to trade with any place, it is no easy matter to dispose of these properties, after it is found out that the trade is not remunerative. The consequence is that a trade is often continued which does not yield more profit than the common interest of money, without leaving any-thing for profit, or even for tear and wear of material.

It was at one time thought that the trade with our colonies was the most profitable of any, because of the valuable nature of the produce of these colonies. Accordingly, by our navigation laws and our system of differential duties, we did everything to ensure a monopoly of the colonial trade to ourselves, as has been already noticed. But the fallacy of this has been discovered, and the monopoly has been aban-doned. It is no doubt true that, while that monopoly lasted, we derived a certain amount of direct benefit. " But," as was said by Smith one hundred years ago, " to obtain that there are very probable reasons for believing that England has not only sacrificed a part of the absolute advantage, which she, as well as every other nation, might have derived from that trade, but has subjected herself both to an absolute and to a relative disadvantage in every other branch of trade,[a] by forcing a great part of her capital from a foreign trade of consumption, carried on with a neighboring country, into one carried on with more distant countries, from which the return of that capital is tedious as well as uncertain."

Section IV.—Effect of abrogation of the navigation laws, and of the system of differential duties on the colony trade of Great Britain.

If the colonial trade of Great Britain were beneficial to her, while its monopoly lasted, as it indubitably was, though in a minor degree to her home and European trades, it was not in consequence, but *in spite*, of the monopoly. The abolition of the monopoly has not endured long enough to afford proof of this assertion, nor is it necessary for the present purpose to prove it. If the monopoly were the chief source of advantage in the colony trade,

[a] Wealth of Nations, vol. ii, p. 444.

that source has been dried up by the abolition of the monopoly, and it never can be re-opened, whether the colonies be retained or emancipated. The monopoly can never be re-imposed.

Engrossment of the colony trade having ceased, through the abrogation of the navigation laws and of the system of differential duties, if we are to retain that trade, it must be by some other means than, as in times past, by the force of these laws. "*By the repeal of the navigation laws,*" says Lord John Russell, "*I conceive we have entirely put an end to the whole system of commercial monopoly in our colonies.* We have plainly declared that, on the one hand, if we require productions, similar to those which our colonies produce, we shall be ready to take them from other parts of the world, and, on the other hand, we have left the colonists free to provide themselves with the products of other countries than our own, and to impose upon the manufactures of Great Britain equal duties with those imposed on foreign manufactures." If, therefore, we are to retain the monopoly, *in fact,* of the trade with those countries which at present constitute our colonies, after having abandoned it *by law,* it must be through other means than those by which we acquired, and have hitherto maintained, that monopoly. It must be by giving the colonies the best and the cheapest goods of our manufacture, and taking from them their produce on terms more advantageous for them than other nations can afford to give. The colony trade, in short, is now open to competition with Great Britain by all the other nations of the earth, and the monopoly of that trade has ceased to be the strong but delusive argument which it used to form against emancipating the colonies.

One other advantage, in the way of trade, which Great Britain has derived from her commerce with the colonies, has been that they have taken off her damaged, ill-finished, and ill-got-up goods, and goods which have remained on the merchant's hands until the fashion for them has passed by. These are all purchased at low prices and sent to the colonies, and are there sold at prices varying from twenty to thirty per cent. *higher* than they would have fetched if they had been sold to the dealers at home as good, merchantable wares. At the Cape of Good Hope, one cause of the defect in goods, it is believed, is that the colonists, particularly of Dutch origin, will not give above a certain price for goods, as they regulate their purchases more by what they have been accustomed to pay than by the value of the article. It may also be thus elsewhere; but it is much to be regretted, because the purchaser willing to pay a fair price cannot but suspect that he has been imposed upon when he gets an inferior article.

This trade has no doubt been very profitable to Great Britain, and, while the monopoly of her colony trade lasted, it was a pretty safe one. The colonists hitherto have taken these inferior goods, probably not in ignorance of their defects, nor without indignation, but because Great Britain would not allow any other nation to come with her goods and by competition put an end to this system, and during the time that has passed since the abolition of the monopoly, the colonists have continued to take these inferior goods at high prices, only because no other nation has, as yet, profited by the abolition of the monopoly to come in and offer its goods for competition with the British goods.

So soon as other nations shall be able to take advantage of the markets in our colonies, which have been opened to them by the abrogation of the navigation laws and of the system of differential duties, so soon will this branch of our colonial trade be at an end, unless our merchants shall take warning beforehand, by reminding themselves that "*character*" is as valuable in the colonies as it is at home, in all commercial transactions. The character of the British merchant, in transactions either with foreign countries or with the colonies, probably stands higher than, or as high, at least, as that of the merchants of any other nation, so far as regards the *monetary* part of commerce and the uprightness and liberality of his transactions, as to their form or terms. But, with regard to the quality of the goods he has hitherto thought it justifiable to offer for sale in the colonies, on the maxim, no doubt, that the colonist's " eye should be his merchant," probably the British merchant's character stands as low as, if not lower than, that of the merchants of any foreign country.

But, whether this imputation as to our exports be just or unjust matters little in the present inquiry. If it be just, other nations will in time find out the opening which the short-sighted covetousness of our manufacturers has left for them, whereby to edge themselves gradually into our colonial trade; and this they will do, whether our colonies continue such or be emancipated. If the imputation be unjust, our merchants will retain the colonial trade, so long as the colonists shall be convinced that it is for their interest to deal with them, rather than with the merchants of other countries. This, also, the colonists will do, whether the colonies continue such or be emancipated.

SECTION V.—EFFECT OF COLONIAL TRADE IN CREATING A MER-CANTILE MARINE FOR GREAT BRITAIN.

It may seem, perhaps, that one direct and unquestionable and unalloyed advantage which Great Britain has derived from the possession of colonies has been the creation of her enormous mercantile marine. By

her monopoly of the colony trade; by forcing all
the produce which came from the colonies to be
brought into her ports and to be re-exported thence,
before it could pass into other countries; and by
almost engrossing that re-exportation, Great Britain
made herself the carrier for the world. Yet the
question, if not of the fact, at least of the extent, of
this advantage, as arising from the possession of
the colonies, is more than doubtful, if we may judge
by the comparative increase of our already enormous
mercantile marine over that of other nations, *since*
the abrogation of the navigation laws and of the
differential revenue laws. The increase of our trade,
since trade in general became free, has occasioned
an unprecedented demand for shipping; but, so
far from British shipping having been thrown out
of employment by foreign shipping taking its
place, we have even more than our share of the
increase, and British ships were never dearer,
nor freights higher, since the termination of the
last war, than they have been since the trade of
our colonies and our home trade were thrown open
to the world.

But, whether free trade shall prove to be injurious
to British navigation or not, it *is* free, and therefore,
as the colonies can now choose, out of the ships of
all nations, those in which to export their produce
and import their articles of consumption, in this

respect, also, it must be indifferent to the present argument, whether the colonies continue such or be emancipated. While the navigation laws and the system of differential duties existed, we forced the colonies to employ our ships. Now that these are at an end, their employment of our ships must depend on whether they find it for their interest so to do, and that consideration will be unaffected by their position with us, whether as colonies or as independent allies.

We made our mercantile navy, let it be conceded, by making colonies and forcing them to employ our ships. If we had merely made colonies and never forced them to employ our ships, we should, *ex hypothesi*, never have made our navy; we must, in that case, have been indebted for our success in forming a marine to the excellence of our ships and the superior skill of our mariners. Now that that force upon the colonies has been withdrawn, if our colonies are also emancipated entirely, we shall not be in a worse condition, for the *maintenance* of that marine, than we were in when we contemplated its *formation*. On the contrary, we shall be in a much better condition, inasmuch as the colonies are ready formed and our mercantile connections with them are fully established. We may therefore *retain*, without the force of monopoly, what, on the supposition in question, we could not have *created* without that force. At all events, the force of monopoly has been withdrawn, and it cannot be *resumed*, so that if we are to retain our mercantile navy, so far as the colonies are concerned, it can only be by those means by which alone we could have created it, had monopoly of the colonial trade never existed, namely, by the superior excellence of our ships, the skill of our seamen, and the cheapness of our freights.

That certain countries are to continue British colonies, and that Great Britain is to trade with these countries, neither are identical propositions, nor parts of one and the same proposition. We may *retain* our colonies and *yet lose their trade*, as Spain lost the trade of her colonies, notwithstanding the most strenuous efforts to retain it; and we may *emancipate* our colonies, and *yet retain their trade*.

By planting British subjects in distant countries, for the purposes of agriculture, or of commerce, we not only created new sources of trade, but we gave that trade a British inclination. The colonists not only were of British origin, but they retained British connection, both family, social, and commercial. They speak our language, and it is to British capital that they have been indebted for success in their undertakings. Though, therefore, we had never been so unjust as to compel the colonies to trade with us and with no other nation, the probability is that we should naturally have engrossed the greater part of their trade, and now that we have abandoned the monopoly *by law*, the probability is that we shall nevertheless retain the monopoly *by nature*. In colonies of purely British origin, things must change very much with us, and with them too, and many things must happen before a foreign country could subvert our trade with them.

The colonists are of us; their forefathers were of us, and lie buried with us; they have relatives among us; they have friends among us; they have commercial establishments or commercial connections with us; they derive most of their capital from us; they speak the same language with us; the romance of our past history they share with us; and, notwithstanding occasional squabbles and some blustering, they are proud to be connected with us, and sorry would they be to be separated from us.

The passing of a few generations, no doubt, will loosen some, and change others, of these ties; but they give us a great start in the race of competition, which any foreign nation might attempt to run, for the trade of our colonies—so great a start as to make it very improbable that any foreign nation will attempt to enter upon such a competition, unless we, by retaining our colonial government, with all its inducements to fretting and fuming, and by a continuance of our present injurious and discreditable system of trading with the colonies, should induce the colonists to second such an attempt.

In colonies of foreign origin—such as Lower Canada, the Cape of Good Hope, and the Mauritius —our hold upon their trade may be more uncertain, now that we have abandoned the monopoly of it by law, especially in such of them as have a preponderance of colonists of foreign origin. But, even as to these countries, their separation from the country of their origin has continued so long that their connections with it have been dislocated, if not obliterated, and will not, in all probability, be resuscitated, unless we shall, by our own folly and misgovernment, lead things to take that course. At all events, the emancipation or retention of these colonies can have but small effect upon such a question, after the liberal constitutions which we have already bestowed upon them—so liberal that they stop only short of emancipation.

If Great Britain should emancipate all her colonies to-morrow, there is not the slightest reason to apprehend that this would immediately make the least change in her mercantile transactions with the colonies; nor would it do so ultimately, so long as Great Britain should, independently of colonial considerations, maintain her present mercantile position and character, and give the colonists good articles, at reasonable prices.

SECTION VI.—VALUE OF COLONIES IN AFFORDING HARBORS FOR
THE BRITISH MILITARY AND MERCANTILE MARINE.

But Lord John Russell says, "Every one will admit the value of that commerce which penetrates to every part of the globe, and many of these colonies give harbors and security to that trade which are most useful in time of peace, but are absolutely necessary in time of war." If we are to "lose," or to "abandon," our colonies, we may certainly, with them, "lose" or "abandon" these harbors, which possess all the advantages for our commerce that have been thus attributed to them. But if we neither "lose" nor "abandon" our colonies, but only "emancipate" them, does it follow that, in that event also, we must lose or abandon these harbors. May not an empire, at emancipating its colonies, form such an alliance with them as may enable it to retain all the benefit which it has hitherto enjoyed from these harbors, though not under the title of a right of sovereignty.

We might, while emancipating our colonies, stipulate, in a treaty offensive and defensive, not only that we should be as highly favored as other nations, *but that we should be more highly favored than any other nation,* in respect of harbors and every thing else. And what other nation could object, in such a case, to such a stipulation? Nay, we might, at the moment of emancipating them, retain a right of sovereignty over such harbors or places of strength within them, as might appear to be necessary for the purposes of military or mercantile marine. For instance, in the Cape of Good Hope, retention of the isthmus on which Cape Town and Simon's Town are situated, would secure to us everything in that colony which could be valuable to us in that respect. If to that retention were added that of Malta, Gibraltar, and of the island of Barbadoes, there would probably be no other retention worth our while ; but if there be any other harbors or islands worth retaining for imperial purposes than those which have been mentioned, they have only not to be overlooked in making the arrangement which has been suggested.

CHAPTER XIX.

IF, then, the British colonies have never contributed
any revenue to the British treasury, in times either
of peace or of war; if they have never contributed
to the armies of the mother country a single soldier;[a]
if the trade of the colonies with the mother country
has been profitable to her, but only in a minor
degree, when compared with her home and European
trade;—then, what is the strength which we derive
from our colonial possessions, and which should
make us pause, ere we think of parting with them?
If the assertion be just, which Lord Grey makes,
that "much of the power and influence of Great
Britain depends upon its having large colonial
possessions in different parts of the world," that
"power and influence" must depend rather upon
the character for strength which these possessions
give, than upon any *actual strength* which they
confer. The "power and influence" must depend,
not so much "on the amount of physical force," as

---

[a] With the exception as to Canada, already noticed.

upon " opinion and moral influence." Is this not
very much like the language of the man who keeps
up an expensive establishment of horses, carriages,
and servants, because of the *reputation for wealth*,
which this exhibition of what wealth—or the credit
of having wealth—can alone procure? But does the
really rich man, who knows and feels every day the
power which a full purse gives him, ever resort to
such imposition upon the world? Conscious of his
actual possession of wealth, and of the power and
influence which it can always command, despite
appearances, however humble, he regulates his household and his outward appearance to the world by
the maxims of prudent yet liberal economy, from the
observance of which possession of the most princely
fortune will not exempt any man who wishes to
avoid ultimate ruin.

The wealth of Great Britain, which constitutes
one half of her power,—the energy, intelligence, and
love of freedom of her people forming the other
half, is but an aggregation of the wealth of many
individual men; and what is applicable to the
individual wealth is equally so to the aggregate. If
either public or private wealth be meant to be preserved, it must be husbanded; and an empty parade
of what has existence only in appearance is not good
husbandry. It sounds very grandly. It fills both
the mouth, and the ear, and the imagination, to say

that, on the empire of the Queen of Great Britain,
the sun never sets; yet this, after the natural exultation of national vanity has been indulged, may be
but sound after all. Britain had no colonies when
Elizabeth reigned, and Britain had but few colonies,
and these few were in but a feeble condition, when
Cromwell sat in the monarch's seat; and yet the
voice of these monarchs fell not less loudly upon the
ears of the sovereigns of Europe than has the voice
of any British sovereign in the zenith of colonial
power.

If the powers of Europe are to be captivated by
sounds which can have little delight but for a British
ear, they may be influenced by hearing of the extent
of the British empire to give us credit for power,
because of the extent of the empire, and so confer
upon us that "influence" and that "power," which,
Lord Grey says, depend upon "opinion and moral
influence." But if the powers of Europe attend
more to substance than to sound, the probability is
that they may think that the very extent of the
British dominions is a source of weakness instead of
strength. With powers who take this just view,
our having "large colonial possessions in different
parts of the world" will weigh but little in the scale
which is to test our "power and influence," as compared with other countries,—France, for example,—
in which all the strength is concentered.

The unparalleled successes of our navy during the last war—a success which heaven vouchsafes but seldom to one nation—swept the navies of all other nations from the ocean, and left Britain queen of the deep. During that war we acquired many colonies by conquest, and during the peace which has since subsisted, we have formed many more,— and we have as yet maintained a free and unrestrained intercourse with these settlements, scattered as they are over the whole globe.

But, during that peace, several of the powers of Europe have been reforming their navies, and though none of them has yet succeeded in coming within a great distance of the British navy, either as to number or strength and efficiency, yet some of them are gradually doing so, and America bids fair, in the course of another fifty or one hundred years, to outstrip it. If America, or any of the powerful maritime states of Europe, were to go to war with us, every one must feel that our colonial possessions would be our weakest, and, therefore, most assailable point, scattered as they are at such prodigious distances from the seat of the imperial government, and entirely dependent as they are upon the imperial government for protection against foreign invasion. The Falkland Islands and the island of Hongkong might be attacked at one and the same time, by fleets sailing from opposite points of the compass;

yet "*nemo me impune lacesset*" is as much our motto, in regard to these comparatively insignificant possessions, as it is in regard to the capital itself, or any of our naval arsenals, and any attempt upon them must be as speedily avenged; but it would have to be avenged, not with the assistance of colonial blood or treasure, but with our own resources alone.

It may be said, if we emancipated our colonies and formed alliances with them, must we not defend them as strenuously when allies as we must have done while they continued colonists ? An insurance office, to use a familiar illustration, and to compare great things with small, will insure lives to any number and for any amount,—thousands of lives for millions of money. But no prudent office will take a large risk upon any *one* life; still less, though happy to insure millions of money upon thousands of lives, would such an office dream of insuring all the millions upon one life, lest, by the death of the individual, it might, in one moment, have to pay the whole money. In the multitude of its risks lie the safety and certainty of profit to an insurance office.

While our multitudinous colonies form integral parts of the empire, we put all upon one risk. If we had them but as allies, we should have each as a separate risk. Our treaty with one colony may be different from our treaty with another colony. One colony may be so strong as to justify us in requiring that our treaty with it should be *offensive* as well as defensive. Another may be so weak that our treaty must be defensive only. Another may be weak in men, but strong in wealth, and our treaty with it may stipulate for pecuniary or other contributions, in case of attack. With one colony we may treat that our engagements shall be offensive and defensive, in matters which concern us and the particular colony alone. With another we may stipulate for an offensive and defensive treaty which shall embrace other colonies. We might have the assistance of Van Diemen's Land, or of New South Wales, in protecting Singapore or Hongkong; or of New Zealand in protecting the Falkland Islands. In short, our treaties might be as various in their terms and in the obligations which they imposed on us, as are the countries and their inhabitants which now constitute our colonies.

Is this to reverse the fable of the bundle of twigs? By no means. The bundle could not be either bent or broken, although each individual twig could have been bent or broken, because all were tied closely together,—so closely that when one began to bend, the force of all the others was inevitably added to its own powers of resistance. But if, after the bundle had been tied, so many other twigs should be all laid round the bundle, separate from it and from each other, but all tied with one string to the bundle, such would more nearly resemble the British empire with its colonies. The colonies are tied together by the string of British origin, but they are all so scattered that they can contribute nothing to the support of each other, and might all be destroyed in detail.

CHAPTER XX.

EXAMINATION AS TO THE CAPACITY OF THE COLONIES FOR EMANCIPATION IN RESPECT TO THEIR POPULATION AND WEALTH.

SMITH, in the passage which has been already quoted, and which cannot be too often repeated, says, "To propose that Britain should voluntarily give up all authority over her colonies, and leave them to elect their own magistrates, to enact their own laws, and to make peace and war as they might think proper, would be to propose such a measure, as never was and never will be adopted by any nation in the world. The most visionary enthusiast would scarce be capable of proposing such a measure, with any hope at least of its ever being adopted. But if it were adopted, Great Britain would not only be immediately freed from the whole annual expense of the peace establishment of the colonies, but might settle with them such treaties of commerce as would effectually secure to her a free trade, more advantageous to the great body of the people, though less so to the merchants, than the monopoly which she at present enjoys.[a] By thus parting good friends,

---

[a] She has parted with the monopoly, vide supra, p. 78.

the natural affection of the colonies to the mother country, which our late dissensions have well nigh extinguished, would quickly revive. It might dispose them not only to respect for whole centuries together that treaty of commerce which they had concluded with us at parting, but to favor us in war as well as in trade, and, instead of turbulent and factious subjects, to become our faithful, affectionate, and generous allies, and the same sort of parental affection on one side, and filial respect on the other, might revive between Great Britain and her colonies, which used to subsist between those of ancient Greece and the mother city from which they descended."

There seems a prospect that Smith will prove to have been too severe upon our statesmen, when he thus prophesied that to emancipate our colonies was a measure, that " never was and never will be adopted," and which the most visionary enthusiast would scarce be capable of proposing," while at the same time he pointed out how very advantageous it would prove to Great Britain if carried out. Lord John Russell, in 1850, said, " I anticipate, indeed, with others that some of the colonies may so grow in population and wealth, that they may say our strength is sufficient to enable us to be independent of England. The link is now become onerous to us. The time is come when we think we can, in amity and alliance with England, maintain our independence."

What a source of congratulation and just pride would these expressions, uttered not by " a visionary enthusiast," but by a practical and illustrious statesman, have afforded to Smith, had he lived to hear them. Perhaps we ought to be satisfied with this profession by the minister of readiness to follow the course which Smith, only one hundred years ago, pointed out, had not Lord John Russell added, at the end of the hundred years, " I do not think that 'that time is yet approaching,"[a] and were there not those among us old enough to remember some such expressions as these of Lord John Russell, used by the statesmen of Smith's day, in regard to the British colonies, now forming the United States of America. The politicians of that day also did not think " the time " of the emancipation of the states " yet approaching," and they were right ; not only was it " not yet approaching," but it never did and never will approach. The sun was never to dawn of the day that would usher in emancipation of the North

[a] These words were uttered in 1850. In 1855, the *Melbourne Argus*, speaking of the delay of the government in sending a constitution to Victoria, says : "It will be well that they should recollect that even with their greatest speed, it is quite within the bounds of possibility, that the concession may be too late, and that, when the act for the granting of a new constitution to the colony of Victoria arrives, *the colony of Victoria may have ceased to exist!*"

American colonies, and see them parting from us
in amity, yet bound to us by a treaty of commerce,
which would make them our " faithful, affectionate,
and generous allies."

The glorious day of voluntary emancipation never
arose in time. It was superseded by the lowering,
sullen, angry day of " the declaration of independence," ushered in, as that was, by all the
demons of discord ; and yet, so justly had Smith
speculated upon the feelings which would have
actuated the North Americans had we emancipated
them and made them our allies, instead of our
enemies, that, after a war of many years, carried on
with all the exasperation with which a war between
relations usually is waged, and after a separation of
nearly sixty years, which of itself might be supposed
to have obliterated old relations in distinct nationality,
yet, after all this, when, in the years 1849 and 1850,
the political horizon of Europe showed as if the
crowned heads were about to make a crusade against
the freedom of mankind, in the person of Great
Britain, so as, in their short-sighted policy, to extinguish for ever the aspirations which had produced
the almost universal revolution of 1848, what was
the attitude assumed by the United States of
America ! They claimed their relationship with
us uninvited, and gave an unmistakable intimation
to the powers of Europe that a war of the kind

would have to be waged, not against Britain single-handed, but against Britain banded together with the whole power of the States.

So long as British history is read, so long will the United States cherish the remembrance of their descent, and be proud to vindicate it by rendering us every assistance, which one state can yield to another, unless, perhaps, when their own self-interest shall be opposed to ours; and they will do this, notwithstanding all the exasperation which our misrule of them produced, and so would all our other colonies do, if they were emancipated to-morrow.[a]

[a] Since the text was written, the feeling of the colonies towards the mother country has been tested, by affording them an opportunity of contributing to the "Patriotic Fund," raising for the relief of the widows of soldiers and sailors killed in our war with Russia. What will be the amount contributed by private individuals in Canada remains to be seen, but the legislature of that colony, which was once in rebellion, and has been all but emancipated, has voted £20,000, out of the colonial revenue, towards the fund; and, commenting on the suggestion of a contribution towards the expenses of the war itself, one of the influential journals of the colony says: "We see no reason for that as yet, but should the struggle be unhappily prolonged, as there is great reason to fear it will, the time may come when it may be our duty to contribute, not money only, but men also—not to give of our substance alone, but to shed our blood, as well; and this, we believe, should urgent necessity arise, will be cheerfully done."— Vide leading article in London *Times*, of 12th December, 1854. Since this note was written, that colony has furnished a regiment to the infantry of Great Britain for the suppression of the Indian mutinies.

But, "the time" for that is "not yet approaching!!" Not only is it not yet come,—not only is
it not near at hand, but it is "not yet approaching!"
Why? Because none of the colonies is so "grown
in population and wealth," as to be able to say "our
strength is sufficient to enable us to be independent
of England." The same minister who uttered these
words, tells us that, in 1850, the population of all
our remaining North American colonies was not less
than two millions, which was probably an under
estimate, since he shows, in the same passage, that
the population of Canada alone was, in 1848, no
less than 1,493,292, little short of 1,500,000.

If a million and a half of inhabitants, or if two
millions do not constitute a population sufficiently
numerous to be independent, what is the number
that will make it so? The population of Scotland at
the time of the union in 1707 did not come up to
either of these numbers, it was only 1,050,000; nay,
in the beginning of this century, in 1801, it had
only exceeded the smaller of these numbers, i.e.,
1,500,000, by 100,000,—it was then 1,599,000; and
it did not reach the higher of the numbers, or
2,000,000, till 1821, when it was 2,093,456; and
even so late as 1841, it had not much exceeded
2,500,000, being then 2,620,610. And yet, at the
earliest of all these periods, 1707, Scotland had been
for many centuries an independent nation.

In 1731, the population of all Ireland was only 2,010,221, and Ireland had at that time also been an independent nation for many centuries.

At the conquest, the population of England itself was only 1,500,000. In 1377, it was, as computed by Chalmers, only 2,350,000; and even in 1696, it had not then got beyond 5,500,000.

In 1801, the population of Denmark was only 1,527,061. In 1834, it was 2,033,265, and, in 1845, it had not reached more than 2,239,077. And no one requires to be told how ancient a monarchy Denmark is.

In 1820, the population of Sweden was only 2,584,690, and in 1839 it had reached only to 3,109,772.

In 1849, the population of Holland was only 3,206,804.

Surely, on a comparison of the population of these different countries, any hesitation about Canada being strong enough to be independent of Britain, so far at least as mere numbers are concerned, must seem unreasonable, and any delay, on that account, in making it independent, will appear almost extravagant if we take into consideration the rate at which the population of this colony has been progressing. For the fourteen years, ending in 1825, the increase in population was one hundred and five per cent. ! For the next six years, forty-eight per cent. ; for the next eleven years, one hundred and seven per cent. ; and for the next six years, forty-eight per cent. ;—giving an average annual increase for the thirty-seven years of eighty-one per cent. and a fraction. This is an advance in population such as even the United States cannot show. These states, at the time they declared themselves independent of Great Britain, had a population of about only 2,500,000. At 1790, this had reached nearly 4,000,000, and at no time between that year and the year 1840 did the decennial increase exceed thirty-seven and a half per cent. ; in the last period ending with 1840 it was little more than thirty-two and a half per cent.

If the United States, with a population under 3,000,000, and increasing only at the rate of thirty-seven and a half per cent. in ten years, were able to stand by themselves, — not only to be made independent *by* the mother country, but to make themselves independent in spite of the mother country, by force of arms, and to continue so in defiance of her most vigorous efforts to retain them within her dominion, surely the time for Canada being made independent by the mother country must be "approaching," when its population, already at 1,500,000, has been increasing sometimes at the rate of one hundred and seven per cent. in eleven years. And little else may be said of the Australian colonies, which, as yet though far behind Canada in population, their formation being comparatively but of yesterday, are advancing with such rapid strides, as to promise soon to overtake it.

If, then, there be *some of our colonies*, either already so grown *in population* as to have strength sufficient to be independent of us, or approaching to that growth, what is the state of the matter as to *wealth*, the other condition supposed to be necessarily precedent to independence?

It is acknowledged that one great test of the wealth of a country is the value of its exports, as they show what the country has got to spare of its productions, after satisfying the wants of its own inhabitants. Judged by this standard, what is the wealth of the two sets of colonies which have been mentioned, as compared with that of the United States at the time they achieved independence for themselves. The whole exports of the North American provinces did not, at that time, exceed £1,000,000. In 1845, the exports of our present North American colonies amounted to £1,929,605, within a trifle of £2,000,000, or double that of the United States at the time of the declaration of their independence, and in one year more, (1846,) they had risen to £3,201,992. If a surer test for the wealth of these colonies be wanted, it is to be found in the value of the property assessed for the purposes of local taxation. In 1828, the value of property thus assessed, in Upper Canada alone, was £2,256,874. In 1847, this value was £8,567,001, an increase, in twenty years, in the value of the property of the country of nearly four hundred per cent.

If we look to the Australian colonies, the result is still more startling. In 1828, with a population of 53,000, their exports amounted to the enormous sum of £180,000. In 1848, their population had increased to 350,000, and their exports to the almost incredible sum of £2,880,000,—nearly treble the exports of the United States at the declaration of independence, when their population counted 2,500,000, instead of 350,000. The value of Australian exports and of Australian fixed property, since 1848, when as yet Australian gold and copper mines had not been discovered, has probably reached figures which must appear to be fabulous, when compared with those of any other country of the same amount of population, even though that country should have existed for centuries, while these colonies had no existence even half a century ago.

CHAPTER XXI.

COMPARISON BETWEEN THE NATURE OF THE POPULATION OF THE
OLD SETTLED COUNTRIES OF EUROPE AND OF OUR COLONIES,
AND BETWEEN THE WEALTH OF THESE OLD SETTLED STATES
AND OF THE COLONIES, AS IT IS DIFFUSED THROUGHOUT THE
POPULATION, WITH A VIEW TO EXHIBIT THE CAPACITY OF THE
COLONIES FOR EMANCIPATION.

BUT, conceding that some of our colonies have
already so grown in amount of population and
wealth as to be able to be independent of us, it
may be said that that population is of a very
different kind, and in a very different condition
from the population of the minor independent states
of Europe. The observation would be a very just
one, but on investigation this difference will be
found to form an argument rather *in favor of* than
against emancipation of the colonies.

The history of all the states of Europe gives a
period at which their population consisted only of
three classes,—a king, nobles, and villeins, with
little, if any, intermediate class whatever, and in
which the villeins, infinitely the most numerous
class, were regarded as little better than machines,
contributing to the wealth and power of the king
and the nobles. Between the kings and their nobles

there has been a constant struggle for superiority, which in various states has had various results, from time to time, in proportion as the one or the other, the king or his nobles, have been able to draw to their side the assistance of the villeins, out of whom, in the lapse of ages, have sprung up the middle classes, now well understood to form the main strength of every state, as possessing the greatest amount of wealth, energy, and intelligence.

Nothing was further from the intention of the kings or of the nobles than to produce such a result; but it was the inevitable consequence of commerce and education. Commerce enriched the people, nobles as well as villeins, but while the wealth of the nobles increased in an arithmetical progression, and only in consequence of the increase of wealth in the villeins, which gave to the lands of the nobles and their produce a value they would not otherwise have possessed; the villein merchants accumulated their wealth in a geometrical progression, so to speak. In expenditure, the position of the two bodies was reversed; tilts, tournaments, crusades, and forays, exhausted the wealth of the nobles in a geometrical progression, while the careful husbandry and quiet life of the merchant spent his gains only in an arithmetical progression.

Commerce enriched the villeins and gave them the power which wealth in all conditions of society produces ; and printing gave them education, which taught them the value of that power and the means of wielding it, for the achievement of their liberties.

Out of the operation and co-operation of these different causes has resulted the existing condition of society, in the different states of Europe, which, though not identical in every one of them, exhibits in all of them four distinct classes,—king, nobles, middle class, and common people ; the two first enjoying all the externals of power, and, in some states, the reality also ; the middle class having, in fact, though not in appearance, the real power, without, except in a few states, such as Britain and France, possessing the means of wielding it ; and the common people, though the most numerous, being, as of old, the least considered, and, in most states, raised only a degree above what they were in the old feudal times. Even in our own glorious country, so celebrated for the freedom of its institutions, it is not many years since the condition of the common people began to share the consideration of our rulers ; the whole genius of our laws and institutions being directed to the protection of property, and disregarding almost entirely the means for preserving life and ensuring comforts to the common people.

If we are to wait until society in our colonies assumes the same forms, through the same means, as it has gained in the states of Europe, before our colonies can be considered capable of independence, we may adjourn the grant of independence till the Greek Kalends; and truly then may it be said that the time for their emancipation is not "yet approaching," nor will it ever approach.

The gradual formation of society in the European states, by the combined effects of birth, wealth, and intelligence, gradually operating upon a people which, at the outset, throughout all its classes, from the king down to the villein, was sunk in the grossest ignorance, can form no example, nor any criterion, for the formation of society in our colonies.

It may be stated, as a general proposition, that our later colonies, at least, have been peopled by a most active, energetic, and, for their station in the mother country, most intelligent portion of our countrymen. The very act of severing himself from all kindred, from all old associations of places and persons, from all old friendships and the chances which these afford of assistance in life, imply *a priori* in the emigrant a certain amount of energy and self-reliance, and the difficulties and hardships, which he has to encounter in countries newly settled, require from him the exercise of a high degree of both of these qualities.

It would be most erroneous to compare the settlers in our colonies with the great mass of the inhabitants either of England, Ireland, or Scotland, even a century ago, so far as regards general education and intelligence. The 1,050,000 which constituted the population of Scotland in 1707, and the 1,599,000, in 1801, included the lowest scum of the people in the large towns and in the rural districts,—a class who never leave their country as emigrants, who form probably by far the larger proportion of the population in every old country, and yet, who cannot be taken into account in estimating the progress of society, in times past at least, whatever change the growing philanthropy of the upper classes may produce in time to come, as their position hitherto has always been at zero in the scale of moral and political intelligence.

The same deduction must be made from the population of all the countries of Europe which have been mentioned,—Ireland, England, Denmark, Sweden, and Holland,—before their inhabitants could be compared with the inhabitants of our colonies; and after the deduction has been made, Canada will be found to be infinitely more populous at this day than Scotland was in the year 1821,.than Ireland was in 1731, than Denmark was in 1845, than Sweden was in 1839, or than Holland was in 1849; and almost as populous as England herself was in 1696, when all her glorious contests for freedom had been already achieved.

The comparison will be equally in favor of the colony of Canada, if we take its wealth into consideration, as compared with the wealth of the European states, which have been mentioned with a view to ascertain its fitness for independence, that is to say, if we consider, not aggregate wealth, nor yet the wealth of particular individuals, but how wealth is diffused throughout the community.

In the old-established kingdoms of Europe there has, of course, been a much larger accumulation of wealth than can possibly have occurred in a colony which has not been half a century in existence; but that wealth is principally in the hands of a few persons. The great body of the people have little, if any, property, and are entirely dependent upon their ten fingers for their daily bread. In the colony this is reversed. Every man must labor, no doubt, but almost every man has property of some sort or other, but no man has, or very few men, indeed, have property to any very great amount. Even the few who may have no property, and are dependent entirely on their labor, can sell that labor so dearly that they feel as independent as those that have already realized property; and, if they are sober and industrious, they are sure to place themselves shortly in that condition.

CHAPTER XXII.

SUGGESTIONS WHY EITHER THE COLONIES SHOULD BE AT ONCE
EMANCIPATED, OR A READINESS TO EMANCIPATE THEM, WHEN
REQUIRED, SHOULD BE AVOWED AND DECLARED BY STATUTE.

SOCIETY in the colonies, no doubt, has yet to go
through several phases before it assume its ultimate
form. But the material out of which that form is
to be moulded is entirely different from that out of
which the ancient states of Europe have been
fashioned. In Europe, a man is trammeled in his
mode of worship of the Deity, in his social habits,
and in his mode of dress. At every step, his
thoughts and his actions are controlled by the conventional rules and opinions of an old-established
society. In a colony, all these restraints are thrown
off. The emigrant from Great Britain is surprised
to discover how little he has hitherto been a free
agent. He begins to scan everything and estimate
it at its true, and not at its conventional worth. It
is possible he may not make a correct estimate; that
depends upon the qualities of his head and heart.
But, at all events, he is sensible that he has gained a
freedom of thought and of action, which he not only
did not enjoy in the old country, but which he was

not there aware he had been deprived of. He feels all the elasticity of a new existence, with all its impatience of restraint. Hence all the agitation and complaint which has disturbed the colonial office, and kept it in continual turmoil with one colony or another.

The government of a community, formed of such materials as our colonies, is not to be fashioned after the slow gradual course in which the European states have, in the lapse of centuries, been moulded into their present forms. It should be struck off at once from the anvil. It has been assumed that the colonists were not able to manage their own affairs, and this has been done for them by sending officers from the mother country. But the colonists have always considered the assumption to be as erroneous on principle, as they have, in almost every instance, as has been shown, complained of it, as grating and offensive in its results.

When men form themselves into a joint-stock company, for banking, mining, or manufacturing purposes, they fall naturally into the course of constructing a government for themselves. Common sense and every day's experience show them that to ensure order, peace, and prosperity, the power of management cannot be allowed to remain in the whole body; that to make it effective the many must deposit their power in the hands of a few. What is the formation of a new settlement, in an unexplored country, but an adventure of the same nature as a joint-stock company, though dissimilar in its details and results?

If fifty or one hundred men, tired of the struggle for an existence in an over-peopled country, resolve to put their fortunes to the hazard of striking out a course for themselves, and to explore the wilderness of a newly-discovered island or continent, there to make for themselves a new country and a nation, why should it be assumed that, with the country of their origin, they leave behind them their knowledge and experience of life. Our emigrants are not like the buccaneers of old. They are our better class of artizans, our decayed merchants, the younger sons of merchants and land-owners, and, not unfrequently, of the poorer nobility, retired officers of our army and navy, of disappointed members of the legal, medical, and clerical professions; of those, in short, who, with a will to work, have not, either from circumstances or from temperament, been able, in the struggle of life at home, to gain themselves a place, or have been jostled out of that in which they had been placed by the accident of birth or had reached by their own exertions.

Fifty or one hundred of such persons are as likely to take a correct view of their own interests, and to manage their own matters, as would two or four millions, and surely much better than could one man, (for a minister is, after all, but a man, with like infirmities of temper and intellect,) who is not of them, but living thousands of miles away from them. If they left home and arrived in the new settlement individually, without any previous association having been formed, they might not fall into order and system immediately; but the clashing of interests would soon, as in the case of everything else of the kind, point out to them the necessity for restraint and subordination, with a view to liberty as distinguished from licentiousness.

If the colonies had been allowed to construct themselves in this way, their institutions would have been formed according to the emerging wants of the community. The institutions might not have been perfect,—as what institution, whether imperial or colonial, is perfect?—but the imperfections would have been more palpable in their causes and effects to those who suffered from them than they could be to a minister, removed from all experience of their operation, and forced to trust to the representations of subordinates for information as to their causes and their effects.

If we had allowed our colonies to be self-formed, merely giving them, from time to time, such assistance as they asked, and not more, the probability is that they would have advanced to strength, both in population and in wealth, more speedily, and that they would have been much more peaceful and better affectioned towards us, than candor must confess they have been, or even perhaps are at the present day. At all events, if it were right that we should have kept them in a state of pupilage and subordination up to a certain period of their growth, that period seems to have passed, at least as to some of our colonies, or to be very near at hand.

The minister thinks it is not "yet approaching," but he "anticipates" that it will come some day. Unfortunately, while expressing this anticipation, he does not indicate what he would consider demonstrative of its approach ; neither does he indicate the mood in which he would view the approach, whether one of satisfaction or of disapprobation. Even if his words were to be construed, as probably they were intended to imply, that he would hail with satisfaction the arrival of the period at which the colonies shall have become sufficiently populous and wealthy to be independent of England, what record is there for the colonists to appeal to, when the time for their emancipation shall have arrived, according to every judgment, even that of the minister? What state of circumstances is described to which the colonists could, on its arrival, point as indicating the arrival of the period for their emancipation? None whatever. What, then, is to be the course of things? Are the colonies to continue depend...t until they shall agitate, substantively and expressly, for emancipation? From some of them whisperings of this have been already heard.

Surely, it would be much wiser to pass a declaratory act, as was done in the case of America, as to colonial taxation, by the 18 Geo. III, cap. 12, declaring the circumstances under which the mother country would be disposed to emancipate her colonies generally. The colonies could then, on arrival of the period, claim the right which had thus been conceded to them, and emancipation might then be accomplished amicably, and be accomplished by the arrangement of such a treaty of commerce as Smith has suggested.

But, if it would be difficult to define *à priori*, as probably it would be found to be, the particular circumstances on the occurrence of which the mother country would be disposed to concede emancipation, the more prudent course would be to pass, at once, an act declaring the readiness of the mother country to emancipate all such colonies as should desire emancipation, and to enter into treaties with them, as independent states, for the most amicable relations, political as well as commercial. Means could as easily be devised for gaining the opinion of the colonies upon the subject as have been devised for regulating their internal legislation, under the constitutions which have been given to them. In fact, the machinery contrived for that legislation would be admirably adapted for the purpose.

Emancipation would not, in this way, be given by the government,—it would be asked by each colony ; and we should thus not be open to a charge from the colonies that we had, in any case, abandoned them, nor to a suspicion from other nations of coming weakness and imperial dilapidation.

CHAPTER XXIII.

IF OUR COLONIES ARE NOT TO BE EMANCIPATED, SUGGESTIONS OF
IMPROVEMENT IN THE MODE OF RULING THEM, SO AS TO
PREVENT FUTURE HEART-BURNING AND DISCONTENT.

IF the colonies are to be retained ;—if, in the words
of Smith, we cannot "voluntarily give up all
authority over our colonies, and leave them to enact
their own laws, and to make peace and war, as they
might think proper;"—if we are still, as to all of
them, to give them governors of our selection ;—
if we are still, as to some of them, to allow them
to make laws for their internal government, but to
reserve to ourselves the right to regulate their
external relations; while as to others, we are to
retain the regulation of their internal, as well as of
their external relations ;—if giving up our colonies
voluntarily, though agreeable to our interest, should
be "too mortifying to our pride" to permit of our
making such a sacrifice,—or if the other motive for
repugnance to such a course, suggested by Smith,
shall prevail, if the sacrifice of the colonies is so
"contrary to the private interest of the governing
part of the nation, which would thereby be deprived
of the disposal of many places of trust and profit, of

many opportunities of acquiring wealth and distinction, which the possession of the most turbulent
and, to the great body of the people, the most
unprofitable province seldom fails to afford;"—if
these motives are so forcible that no government, of
whatever shade of politics, could be prevailed upon
to part with such sources of power and influence, at
all events let the colonies be governed on principles
more consonant to sound philosophy and human
reason than those on which our past colonial government has rested.

The governors of our colonies, with some few and
eminent exceptions, have generally been selected
from our naval and military officers. If a man has
been able to handle a fleet or an army with ability
in action, he has been rewarded with the governorship of a colony, apparently on the assumption that,
if he could govern men in a fleet, or in an army,
he must be able to govern men in a community,
though the duties are as dissimilar as can well be
conceived.

A man who, in the discharge of his naval or
military duties, with all the arbitrary power which
is necessarily placed in his hands, has been able to
control and manage men, who, on the other hand,
are compelled almost to abject submission to that
power, however arbitrarily or capriciously exercised,
contracts insensibly a peremptory, absolute manner,

both of thought and of expression. The consequence
is to produce obedience, even where there is no
power to enforce compliance, as there are few
persons in society energetic or independent enough
to oppose those in authority, even when they exceed
their powers. A military or naval governor, therefore, under ordinary circumstances, is able frequently,
from the mere force of manner, to conduct his
government quietly through the prescribed period
of six years; and, if the home government is not
disturbed by any collision between him and the
colonists,[a] he is supposed to have proved himself an
efficient and worthy governor, and on the first opportunity he is removed to some government, more
lucrative and important.

This is all very well and very natural, viewing the
matter from the direction in which the home government can alone see it. The pay of either service,
naval or military, is so small, however high the command may be, that it holds out no such pecuniary
prizes as are to be gained in the other professions.
It is natural enough, therefore, that the home government should wish to reward an eminent military or
naval officer by a civil appointment, for which, for
the purposes of the government, his habits *seem* to
qualify him. And if the officer discharge the duties

[a] Lord Bathurst's parting with a governor was, "Joy be with
you, and let us hear as little of you as possible."

of the appointment without exposing the Secretary
of State to trouble and annoyance, it is natural
enough that the Secretary should congratulate both
himself and the officer, and at the expiry of the
regulated period for all governorships, should reward
him with some better appointment.

But, viewing the matter from the direction in
which the colonists see it, it would be a mistake
to suppose that *in every such case* the governor
either had, or should have been considered to have,
given satisfaction *to the colonists.* He may have
been a martinet, and nothing more. The peculiar
circumstances of a colony,—the peculiarities of its
soil and climate, and of its geographical position,—
may require, on the part of its governor, the exercise
of liberal and enlightened views, both as to agriculture and commerce, before the capabilities of the
colony can be rendered effectual. The laws of a
colony, with a view to the mixed nature of its
population, and their peculiar manners and habits,
may require from its governor the display of qualities
of mind, obtained only by the study of philosophical
jurisprudence and legislation.

A naval or a military man *may* be qualified in
both of these respects; but if he be, it must be
accidentally, for neither the studies of his profession
nor its pursuits would necessarily qualify him in
either respect. And yet, should he be utterly

disqualified in both of these respects, the knowledge of his defects may never reach the Secretary of State, and in most cases it never does reach him. The relation of cause and effect between every erroneous act of government and its consequences is not so obvious that you can lay your finger upon the cause of any complaint and show it demonstrably. It is only where this is the case, and where the evil is crying and universal, that a colony becomes unruly and carries its complaints to the home government. But a colony may chafe and fret under an undoubted system of error, painfully conscious of the injury, yet ignorant of its cause. This may be discerned by a few of the inhabitants, and be represented to the governor, and yet their representations may be disregarded by a peremptory, self-opiniated, and ignorant governor, without this circumstance coming to the knowledge of the Secretary of State.

Nay, should the selection of the minister happily have fallen on a man, as well qualified for civil administration as his previous life had proved him to be for naval or military command, he may, nevertheless, be a man in every respect disqualified for being placed at the head of a community, without his defects in this respect being known to the Secretary of State, and without the possibility of their being represented to him.

The governor of a colony is the representative of

the crown, and is looked up to as such. From him the morals as well as the manners of the inhabitants must take their tone. His manners, while courteous and affable, should be lofty and dignified, and free from every levity; he should be above reproach, or even suspicion, as to integrity, not only of action, but of thought; he should be candid and ingenuous, ready to listen and to learn from every quarter, upright in all his dealings, and so free from the open or disguised indulgence of any vice, that the breath of slander should never taint his name.

A governor possessing all these requisites would be perfect,—he would have more of the angelic than the human character, no doubt, and a governor of such perfection may be unattainable. True; but what method is pursued of ascertaining that the intended governor of a colony has any *one* of these requisites, though the possession of some one or more of them must be necessary to ensure, not only the agricultural and commercial prosperity of the colony, but its advance in religion and morality. If any mode has been followed for informing the minister in these respects, before he appoints a man to be governor of a colony, it has been singularly unfortunate in its results.

If the governors of our colonies had been reason-ably well qualified for the discharge of all the high

functions of their very high office, we should not
have that chequered system of colonial policy, more
remarkable for its variety than its science or
uniformity of principle, nor should we have wit-
nessed that continual expression of dissatisfaction
and discontent by which our colonial rule has
become a by-word and a proverb of reproach.

When there is any substantive ground of complaint in a particular act of a governor, complaint
may be made, if the act is sufficiently grievous to
justify complaint, and, if it be not of that nature, it
is perhaps as well that it should be borne in silence.
But where there is no particular act to complain of,
where the whole tone and character of the government is in fault, without any one individual more
than another having right to complain, though the
fault may be glaringly obvious to those on the spot,
there is no channel through which the knowledge
of this can reach the Secretary of State. Error
continues till it is followed by disaster, and then
the fault is laid anywhere but on the right
shoulder. What an instance of the justice of this
observation is to be found in the Cape of Good
Hope any one may learn who has traveled
through the colony, and heard from the colonists
the follies and blunders of its governors, one
after the other, — each man considering himself
cleverer than his predecessor, and, without doubt

or hesitation, undoing what he had found already done, though it might have been done after much consideration and at great expense. It is to this circumstance that the mother country must give the credit of so many Kafir wars. The Kafirs are formidable foes, no doubt, more formidable, perhaps, than any other savages whatsoever; but the colonists believe that it is our own folly, or rather the folly and presumption of our governors, which has made them so. They say they did not bear that formidable character, nor deserve it, twenty years ago, and that they have acquired it only from ourselves. How many millions of money might have been saved to Great Britain, and how many hundreds of thousands to the poor colonists, if an able governor, at the beginning, had chalked out a consistent, philosophical system of intercourse with the natives, and of protection against their vicious propensities, such as was projected by that able and excellent man Governor D'Urban, for interposing between the colony and the Kafirs a country inhabited by the Kafirs, but over which, by the introduction of civilized institutions, their chiefs should have ceased to exert influence; and each governor that succeeded him had been enjoined to observe this, instead of each being allowed to indulge his own crude notions, and to attempt to build a reputation for himself on the destruction of that which he found to exist in his predecessors, not unfrequently in the teeth of instructions from the home government![a]

But even where there are substantive grounds of complaint, where the objection is not to the general policy of a governor, but to an individual act of his, it is a mistake to suppose that complaint is easy and redress certain. That is the exception : the rule is the reverse. Lord Grey says, " Every inhabitant of the colonies is entitled freely to address to the Secretary of State any complaint or remarks he may think proper on the measures of the local authorities, subject only to the rule that such letters shall be transmitted through the hands of the governor, (who is bound to forward them,) in order that he may, at the same time, send such explanations on the subject as appear to him to be called for;" and he infers that " it is hence impossible that the Secretary of State can be kept in ignorance of any errors or abuses committed by the local authorities."

The rule which requires that complaints against any colonial government must be transmitted through the governor of the particular colony seems undoubtedly a convenient one, in some respects, and yet it not unfrequently works most prejudicially to

[a] The text was written in the year 1854, prior to Sir George Grey's appointment as governor, and, consequently, prior to the opening of his frontier policy.

the complaining party. The intention seems to be that the bane shall be accompanied by its antidote, if there be one; that the minister shall not have to read the complaint, and then have to write to the colony for an answer, and wait for it before adjudicating on the complaint. It is obvious that much time and trouble is saved by requiring that complaints should be transmitted through the governor, and that he should accompany them with his own observations.

But, when it is inferred from this that " it is impossible that the Secretary of State can be kept in ignorance of any errors or abuses committed by the local authorities," a great deal more is inferred than is consistent with the fact—as must be obvious to any one who will reflect upon the subject.

These observations are now in some degree superfluous with regard to the North American and the Australian colonies and the Cape of Good Hope ; because, in these colonies, there is a parliament through which the subject can always make his complaints be heard, if they are worthy of being listened to. But there are very many of our colonies to which the boon of popular representation has not yet been conceded, and to which it seems improbable that it ever will be conceded. As to these, the rules of the service should, as far as possible, remedy the unfavorable position of the minister at home for obtaining correct

knowledge of what is passing in any colony, which
has been before adverted to, and should provide every
possible means for his obtaining correct information.
This would be so far achieved if the access of the
colonists to the minister were made, as nearly
as circumstances will admit, the same as the
access to the Home Secretary which the subject
at home enjoys, and the action of the necessary
intervention of the governor were made as open
as possible.

But the best official arrangements will never
altogether prevent error and abuse, while the community to be governed is at such a distance from
the imperial government as most of our colonies are
and must ever continue to be. As to the larger ones
—our North American, South African, Australian,
and New Zealand colonies,—what opportunities do
they not afford for founding new dynasties from the
collateral branches of our royal family, or the decayed
families of our ancient nobility!

If the two Canadas, New Brunswick, Newfoundland, and Nova Scotia were offered emancipation,
accompanied by an intimation of readiness to give
them, from either of the sources which have been
suggested, a sovereign, who should rule them under
a federal union of the five colonies, can there be
a doubt that they would readily accept the offer?—
if, moreover, part of such an arrangement should

be that a foundation for the nobility of this new dynasty should be taken from the decayed families or from the younger branches of the nobility of the mother country, to whom grants of reserved crown land might be given under certain conditions—entail being probably one of them,—in the mother country, many ancient families would be relieved from embarrassment, and in the new kingdom, there would thus be an old nobility, so to speak, to give tone and character to the new nobility to be gradually created by the ennobling of the colonists.[a]

If the same course were followed with Australia, South Africa, and New Zealand, and carried out in a grand and noble spirit, with the earnest desire to found great independent states, Great Britain would, in fact, be reproduced in three quarters of the globe; the parent stem would be freed from much useless wood, and these off-shoots, having life and vigor transfused into them, would rapidly gain strength to equal the parent tree in vigor.

With these kingdoms of her own creation, bound to her by every social tie which binds men or nations to each other, what a front of strength would Great Britain — backed as she and her daughter nations would undoubtedly be in such a struggle by the generous sympathies, if not by the active co-operation,

[a] The Governor of Maryland used to have power to grant patents of nobility.

of the United States of North America — present to the despotic sovereigns of the earth for the maintenance of freedom in thought, action, and utterance, should they attempt, as has been more than once threatened, and as will one day be attempted, to extinguish liberty in the ruins of Great Britain!

How worthy of the sovereign whom God, in His goodness and mercy, has given to reign over us would such a measure be, and how much in keeping with the management of her own proper family would be this management of the national family! What brilliancy would it add to the lustre of a reign, which has every promise of being famous in the annals of history for the virtues of the sovereign as a wife, a mother, and a queen! How would it extend to the furthest bounds of the earth those sentiments of enthusiastic affection, admiration, and respect with which the subjects of the three kingdoms regard our good and excellent queen! How glorious an occupation for the minister, who should be fortunate enough to have the elaboration of a measure which would make so many kings and regulate the happiness and prosperity of so many nations!